CHRIS HIDE

Enterprise Java for SAP

AUSTIN SINCOCK

apress™

Enterprise Java for SAP
Copyright © 2003 by Austin Sincock

Technical Reviewers: Rob Castenada, Scott Babbage

Editorial Board: Dan Appleman, Craig Berry, Gary Cornell, Tony Davis, Steven Rycroft, Julian Skinner, Martin Streicher, Jim Sumser, Karen Watterson, Gavin Wright, John Zukowski

Assistant Publisher: Grace Wong

Copy Editor: Rebecca Rider

Production Manager: Kari Brooks

Production Editor: Janet Vail

Composition, Proofreading, and Illustration: Kinetic Publishing Services, LLC

Indexer: Valerie Perry

Cover Designer: Kurt Krames

Manufacturing Manager: Tom Debolski

Library of Congress Cataloging-in-Publication Data

Sincock, Austin, 1974–
   Enterprise Java for SAP / Austin Sincock.
      p. cm.
   ISBN 1-59059-098-8 (hardcover : alk. paper)
   1. Java (Computer program language)   2. SAP R/3.   I. Title.
   QA76.73.J38S56 2003
   005.13'3—dc21
                                          2003013230

All rights reserved. No part of this work may be reproduced or transmitted in any form or by any means, electronic or mechanical, including photocopying, recording, or by any information storage or retrieval system, without the prior written permission of the copyright owner and the publisher.

Printed and bound in the United States of America 12345678910

Trademarked names may appear in this book. Rather than use a trademark symbol with every occurrence of a trademarked name, we use the names only in an editorial fashion and to the benefit of the trademark owner, with no intention of infringement of the trademark.

Distributed to the book trade in the United States by Springer-Verlag New York, Inc., 175 Fifth Avenue, New York, NY, 10010 and outside the United States by Springer-Verlag GmbH & Co. KG, Tiergartenstr. 17, 69112 Heidelberg, Germany.

In the United States: phone 1-800-SPRINGER, email orders@springer-ny.com, or visit http://www.springer-ny.com. Outside the United States: fax +49 6221 345229, email orders@springer.de, or visit http://www.springer.de.

For information on translations, please contact Apress directly at 2560 Ninth Street, Suite 219, Berkeley, CA 94710. Phone 510-549-5930, fax 510-549-5939, email info@apress.com, or visit http://www.apress.com.

The information in this book is distributed on an "as is" basis, without warranty. Although every precaution has been taken in the preparation of this work, neither the author(s) nor Apress shall have any liability to any person or entity with respect to any loss or damage caused or alleged to be caused directly or indirectly by the information contained in this work.

The source code for this book is available to readers at http://www.apress.com in the Downloads section.

*This book is dedicated to my wife Kelli, for her eternal love and compassion;
to Greg, Sharon, and Shanon, for always believing in me;
and to Kayla and Simone, for always bringing a smile to my soul.*

Contents at a Glance

About the Author .... *ix*
About the Technical Reviewers .... *x*
Acknowledgments .... *xi*
Introduction .... *xiii*

Chapter 1	Extending SAP: Past and Present Technologies *1*	
Chapter 2	Exploring the Java Platform *17*	
Chapter 3	Understanding Object-Oriented Design and Development *35*	
Chapter 4	JCo 101: Programming with SAP's Java Connector *49*	
Chapter 5	Building a Desktop Interface to SAP *91*	
Chapter 6	Extending SAP to the Web *133*	
Chapter 7	Developing Web Applications with Struts *173*	
Chapter 8	Crossing the Chasm: Bridging SAP and an External Database *233*	
Chapter 9	Advanced Java Programming in SAP *271*	
Appendix	Alternate RFC Development in SAP *297*	
Index	.... *309*	

Contents

About the Author .... *ix*
About the Technical Reviewers .... *x*
Acknowledgments .... *xi*
Introduction .... *xiii*

Chapter 1 Extending SAP: Past and Present Technologies *1*

SAP and Centralized ERP *2*
A Brief History of SAP and the Internet *7*
Alternative Development for SAP *12*

Chapter 2 Exploring the Java Platform *17*

The Enterprise Java Platform *18*
Java Essentials for SAP *24*
Deploying Applications with Java *27*
Summary *34*

Chapter 3 Understanding Object-Oriented Design and Development *35*

Getting Object Oriented *36*
Implementing Object-Oriented Designs *40*
Building Object Systems with Design Patterns *43*
Summary *47*

Chapter 4 JCo 101: Programming with SAP's Java Connector *49*

Working with the Java Development Environment *50*
Connecting to SAP Using JCo *57*
Building a Simple Application with JCo *60*
Summary *88*

Chapter 5 Building a Desktop Interface to SAP 91

Using Configuration Files 92
Providing Object-Level Access 99
Developing a Graphical User Interface 112
Summary 131

Chapter 6 Extending SAP to the Web 133

Looking at the Application Server 134
Installing Tomcat 135
Building a Sample Application 138
Sharing JCo System Resources 164
Summary 172

Chapter 7 Developing Web Applications with Struts ... 173

The Model-View-Control Design Pattern 174
Using the Struts Framework 181
Deploying an Initial Application with Struts 189
More Struts Development 218
Summary 231

Chapter 8 Crossing the Chasm: Bridging SAP and an External Database 233

Java Database Connectivity 234
Deploying the Hypersonic SQL Database 240
Building Database Tables 244
Bringing It Together with Struts 260
Summary 269

Chapter 9 Advanced Java Programming in SAP 271

Introducing JCo Connection Pools 272
Calling Java Objects from Within SAP 279
Building Custom Java Tab Libraries 290
Summary 296

Appendix Alternate RFC Development in SAP 297

Mapping BAPIs to Custom RFCs 297
Updating the InterfaceCaller Class 303

Index 297

About the Author

AUSTIN SINCOCK is a technical author, SAP/Java integration specialist, and generally nice guy. He has been a strong proponent for the development and use of Enterprise Java to provide access to SAP R/3 systems for more than five years. This focus has resulted in several technical lectures, numerous tips and articles, and a small club of devoted but slightly deranged fans in the northernmost reaches of Norway. Austin has managed product application suites and technical projects in SAP environments since 1996 and looks forward to a career of global notoriety followed by a gradual but inevitable decline into anonymity.

If you would like more information about him or just a friendly email pal, Austin can be reached at austin@opensourceguru.com or on his Web site at http://www.opensourceguru.com.

About the Technical Reviewers

ROB CASTANEDA is Principal Architect at CustomWare Asia Pacific, where he provides architecture consulting and training in EJB/J2EE/XML-based applications and integration servers to clients throughout Asia and America. Rob's multinational background, combined with his strong real-world business experience, enables him to see through the specifications to create realistic solutions to major business problems. He has also contributed to and technically edited various leading EJB and J2EE books.

SCOTT BABBAGE is an eBusiness consultant at CustomWare Asia Pacific. He provides services to various multinational clients based upon standard Java/J2EE and integration technologies using a variety of ERP systems such as SAP and JDEdwards.

Acknowledgments

ALTHOUGH THE ACT OF WRITING IS accomplished by an individual, the will and drive to do so is usually shared by many wonderful people. I would like to acknowledge the following people for their contributions, both direct and indirect, to the creation of this book:

Kelli Sincock, for letting me delay the flooring installation (among other details of home remodeling) in favor of writing this book.

Monica Berndt, who was a major motivator in my writing and lecturing efforts on building Java applications for SAP.

Lucas McGregor, for his excellent Java technical support and general encouragement.

Gamma Enterprise Technologies and Matthew Minkovsky, for offering me the opportunity to build technology initiatives focusing on SAP and Java.

Mojo Jojo, the black, furry one, for his relentless devotion to my mouse cursor and constant attempts to rewrite this book via pawprint.

Nigel Sincock, for his blind faith in the housing and training of a wayward American in the art of SAP development.

John Zukowski and everyone at Apress, for the chance to offer my experience with SAP and Java to a global audience.

Introduction

AFTER MANY YEARS AND SEVERAL technological near misses, SAP has positioned Enterprise Java to become a key development technology and to play an important role in mission-critical Internet integration. SAP views Enterprise Java as a strong platform that can be used to deploy robust, scalable applications that provide integration with SAP and non-SAP systems. Through a comprehensive set of tutorials and code reviews, this book introduces the latest Java technologies and the techniques you need to start building robust, scalable applications today.

Who Should Read This Book

The fact that you cracked open a book entitled *Enterprise Java for SAP* means that you are one of the many developers looking to explore the world of Java development for SAP. So far, for many of you, this exploration has been a frustrating and even fruitless search for any tidbit of information on programming for SAP in Java. If this description sounds familiar, then you may find *Enterprise Java for SAP* a required read.

This book is specifically targeted at developers who are fluent in SAP's programming language, ABAP, and are looking to learn the Java language. Although targeted at the less experienced Java developer, this book is a great resource for more experienced programmers who need to build applications with SAP's Java connector (JCo).

What This Book Covers

In addition to spending a lot of time with JCo, this book also offers insight into the open source tools, available for free on the Internet, that are not normally useful in an SAP environment. It shows you how to apply the best practices embodied in these tools and how to use them to kick start your Java development effort. The only prerequisite you need to process this information is ready access to an SAP system that can be used as a sandbox or for development.

Chapters 1–3 of *Enterprise Java for SAP* describe the fundamental principles of object-oriented and Java development and allow you to transition smoothly from the more procedural view of SAP development.

Chapter 4 introduces SAP's JCo, including a step-by-step review of what it takes to connect to an SAP system from a Java application. The JCo connector is one of SAP's core components in its larger Enterprise Java development platform. Learning the ins and outs of programming with JCo will give you greater insight into future SAP technologies.

Introduction

Chapter 5 shows you how to build a desktop client application for SAP using a Java user interface toolkit. Based on the Java Swing toolkit, this application can be used to support requirements for a custom application that must reside on the user's desktop.

Chapter 6 takes you through the steps for deploying a Java application server and details a basic SAP login application from a Web browser. The Java application server acts as the foundation on which you can build and deploy Enterprise Java components tailored for access to your SAP system.

Chapter 7 demonstrates Struts, an open source framework that you can use to build highly maintainable Web applications for SAP. Struts is an effective means to minimize your Java development effort and create components that can be easily reused in future development efforts.

Chapter 8 teaches you how to deploy and configure an open source database system, called Hypersonic SQL (hsql). In addition, it shows you how to build a material catalog that retrieves information from both SAP and the Hypersonic database.

Chapter 9 walks you through some advanced Java programming techniques specifically tailored to SAP's JCo. These topics include server development, connection pooling, and custom Java tags.

The appendix covers the development of custom Remote Function Call (RFC) interfaces and how to access these interfaces through the JCo connector. This appendix is helpful if your SAP system does not implement the RFC interfaces required by the tutorials in Chapters 4–8.

Conventions Used in This Book

This book uses special font and formatting conventions in order to clarify and highlight key programming concepts and techniques. The following section describes these conventions and reviews how they are applied throughout the book:

> `Code Statements`: In addition to explicit code blocks, code snippets are often found within the conceptual or descriptive text of the book. This code appears in a differentiated font so that it better stands out from the surrounding text.
>
> `Modified Code`: Code that has been modified within a larger block of code is put in bold. This helps you determine what has changed and how those changes relate to the text description.

Introduction

<ENVIRONMENT VARIABLE>: An environment variable is either an explicit setting within your operating system or a value that you should replace with something else. If the former, you need to create or modify the value set to the variable used by your operating system. If the latter, it is a relative value that you must set based on your existing environment. For example, because I can't predict the organization of your file system, I use a variable instead.

Start ➤ Run: The ➤ symbol indicates an action that must be taken within the user interface of your operating system. Typically, this interaction occurs using the mouse or a keyboard shortcut. Start ➤ Run means click the Start menu button in Microsoft Windows and select Run from the pop-up menu.

URLs: URLs offer pointers to important sources of information that you can find outside of this book. These links are printed in a different font so that they are easily differentiated from the conceptual or application code text.

This book also uses special formatting to deal with information that indirectly relates to the main subject of a section. The following styles indicate the different types of information available through each.

NOTE *Notes highlight important details about the development or interesting tidbits about a given subject. I use notes to give you a heads-up on any tricks I learned throughout the years or any gotchas that you might run into.*

TIP *Tips are quick indicators of additional information that can be found on the Web or in print publications. My tips also offer alternative techniques for development that you might want to incorporate within your application. I have tried to focus on the Web for providing additional content and I highly recommend that you follow the links listed in these tips and elsewhere.*

CAUTION *Regardless of how well thought out a system or language is, there is always something that can go wrong. I use caution texts to make sure you are not caught off-guard by unexpected errors, system complications, and so on.*

Where to Go From Here

Although *Enterprise Java for SAP* is not an exhaustive study of Java development for SAP, it definitely gets you going in the right direction. SAP has some very new and exciting technologies coming out that rely very heavily on Java. Current technologies, such as SAP Portal, offer advanced Java development tools that let you build highly interactive Web and portal applications. On the horizon, SAP technologies like Web DynPro enable an even tighter coupling between SAP applications and Java programming. In fact, SAP's Web DynPro is positioned as the newest evolution in business application development for SAP, and it is very much reliant on Enterprise Java and JCo.

When you have finished this book, you will have a complete, working Java-based Web application for SAP. More importantly, however, you will be armed with some of the latest object-oriented programming techniques and prepared for a future where Enterprise Java is as integral to SAP development as ABAP.

CHAPTER 1

Extending SAP: Past and Present Technologies

WELCOME TO THE WORLD of Java development for SAP. This book takes a step-by-step look at the various techniques and functions of building Enterprise Java applications that tap into an SAP application server. Rather than an exhaustive review of any single Java technology, the goal of the book is to provide a strong overview of the most popular Enterprise Java features and functionalities.

The following chapters guide you through the development of several related Java and Enterprise Java applications. Each tutorial roughly builds on the one before it, culminating in a mini database application that works concurrently with an SAP system. This book was written under the philosophy of "learn by doing," so a great deal of the text is devoted to hands-on application development. In addition, because Java is an object-oriented language, much of the focus is on building reusable applications and components. That way, your future efforts are at least benefited, if not reduced, by previous development.

This chapter looks at the following:

- A brief history of SAP and the Internet

- Alternate development technologies to Enterprise Java

- A quick review of synchronous, external interfaces

Beginning with a historical perspective on SAP's evolution, this chapter provides insight into the rationales and principles behind building applications for the enterprise.

SAP and Centralized ERP

In its more than 25 years of existence, SAP has gone through a number of changes in both technology and attitude. One of the earliest commercial iterations of SAP, release R/2, consisted of a mainframe server supported by numerous green screens or dumb terminals. Inheriting from the mainframe architectures made popular in the 1960s, SAP R/2 represented a major advance in business application functionality. These early systems provided manufacturers with a clear and consistent picture of enterprise processes that had been previously obscured by a heterogeneous collection of paper and computer-based systems. Indeed, it was precisely this heterogeneity of tools that drove SAP's early successes. By consolidating similar, functional aspects of manufacturing into a single, holistic model, companies gained unprecedented insight into existing business practices. This view served to both validate and disqualify prevalent models and modes of functionality within the manufacturing world.

From Mainframes to Servers

The success of such a singular, unilateral understanding of the enterprise allowed SAP to create and propagate powerful new mechanisms for the manufacturing industry. This unprecedented view allowed companies to make phenomenal gains in productivity and the ability to explore cutting-edge practices in automation and efficiency. Based on the new insights provided by systems like SAP R/2, new theories of manufacturing, such as Materials Requirements Planning (MRP), were designed and implemented. All of these factors formed a basis for the evolution of SAP's highly centralized philosophy of business application development.

The late 1980s saw the rise of client/server architectures within the commercial market. Transitioning from centralized mainframe systems to relatively lightweight servers and top-heavy desktop clients enabled companies to reduce backend hardware costs. Moreover, the client/server architecture finally allowed companies to host cost-effective application and database servers in-house. Previously, these systems had to be hosted by a third party or deployed internally at great financial expense.

Realizing this trend in technology was inevitable, SAP revamped much of its internal system functionality and added new business applications to the front end. The practical upshot of this effort was the SAP iteration called release R/3. The R/3 release represented a major turning point for the company. Building on the less expensive client/server architecture, smaller companies could now implement SAP R/3. Although the price of SAP R/2 restricted its customer base to Fortune 1000-style companies, sales of the R/3 product release soared around the world.

This new client/server release offloaded a great deal of the front-end application processing to the client desktop. Release R/3 saw the introduction of the illustrious SAP Graphical User Interface (SAP GUI). Still around today, the SAP GUI provides visual communication between the R/3 application server and the client desktop. As a visual metaphor for the R/3 business applications, SAP GUI far outstripped the limited capabilities of the R/2 green screen terminals. For more than a decade, SAP GUI has provided a useful, although restricted, screen mechanism that interacts with SAP's business applications. Figure 1-1 depicts a traditional R/3 screen, as seen through the SAP GUI.

However, times have changed and technology has changed more quickly. Users are accustomed to more refined, flexible desktop interfaces. The advent of the World Wide Web showed company employees that the visual interface was highly mutable and even customizable on an individual basis. The strong user interface designs and controls that came out of Apple and Microsoft continued to make computers easier and simpler to use. SAP was faced with growing dissent surrounding the SAP GUI interface. The complaints levied against the graphical interface pertained to its lack of flexible screen flow and a drab look and feel.

Chapter 1

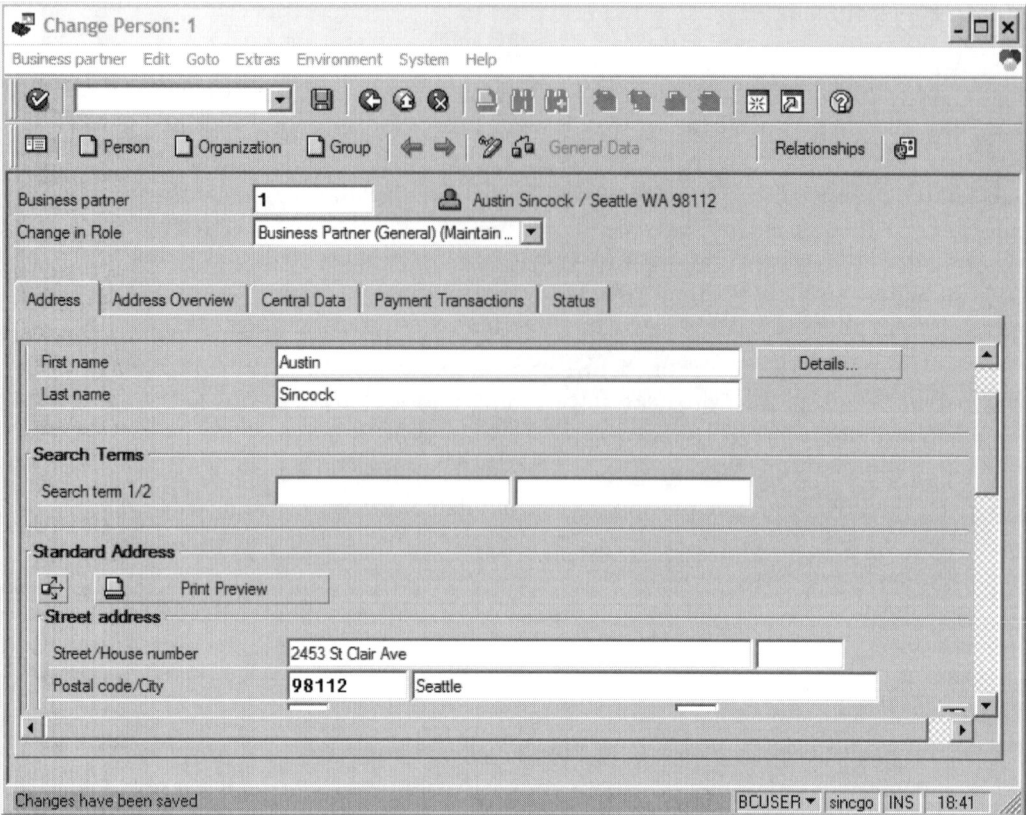

Figure 1-1. Business Partner functionality in the R/3 GUI

In response, the company began exploring alternate technologies associated with user interface (UI) design and implementation. The SAP GUI XT toolkit was one such example, however insufficient, that provided a more flexible mechanism that could be used to deploy key business applications. Ultimately, the drive to supply a customizable, user-friendly front end culminated in the World Wide Web. Based on current Internet standards, such as HTML, XML, and Web Services, SAP is moving toward a more integrated technical model that has the kind of functionality that can be readily delivered through a Web browser or an external system.

Talking to the SAP Black Box

Regardless of the concern over graphical user interfaces, the major obstacle faced by SAP in the past several years evolved directly from the successful transition from mainframe to client/server architecture. That the philosophy of centralized business applications had proven so profitable meant that the R/3 release had become an effective black box to the outside world. The logic of an all-encompassing

Enterprise Resource Planning (ERP) system used to manage every aspect of the enterprise dictated a very closed, proprietary business application infrastructure.

Partly for practical reasons and partly because of marketing necessity, SAP launched its massively popular R/3 system with very few connections to the outside world. With its advanced financials, manufacturing, and sales modules, SAP was seen as a true one-size-fits-all ERP system. Companies looking to deploy SAP often modified internal business practices to match those prescribed by the R/3 system. Older database systems became "legacy" and were totally discarded in favor of this newer, holistic approach.

This mentality led SAP to believe that the R/3 system could support every aspect of even the largest corporations. Where a given subset of functionality did not exist, companies had the option to build new applications using SAP's proprietary development language, Advanced Business Application Programming (ABAP). Certain industry-specific modules soon became available, such as those for the oil and pharmaceutical concerns. These industry solutions, or ISOs, relied almost exclusively on the R/3 infrastructure for application deployment and support. Unfortunately, the "best practices" lessons learned in the 1960s and 70s were lost in the rush to add more and more business functionality to the SAP R/3 monolith.

Although ABAP is a very strong fourth-generation language (4GL), much of its limitation lies in the fact that it relies totally on an R/3 application server. Likewise, it enforces a fairly rigid set of user interface design and development practices, allowing little variation or influence from newer theories and technology. Applications developed within the SAP aegis must rely on a relatively small set of external interfaces and protocols in order to communicate with non-SAP systems. Of course, this centrist view of the enterprise environment allowed many companies to apply more productive business practices than they could using several disparate systems.

However, time and experience have proven that a single, all-encompassing ERP system cannot guarantee support for all current and future business needs. The surge in middleware sales seen in the mid- to late 1990s provides ample evidence of companies looking to tie together dissimilar systems for increased functionality. From BEA's Tuxedo to IBM's MQSeries, middleware suites have been implemented to support transparent integration of systems across the enterprise. Again, a couple of major complaints were levied against SAP: first, it lacked readily accessible external interfaces, and second, companies faced many challenges integrating SAP into non-SAP systems.

The typical avenues for such integration dealt mainly with batch data processing and limited remote procedure call (RPC) interfaces. Batch processing, similar to that available in Electronic Data Interchange (EDI), meant that business transactions could not take place in real time. Transactional documents sent into the SAP system were queued and executed at specific times each business day. Response documents had to be handled after the fact, with the requesting system waiting anywhere from a day to a week for a transaction status.

The SAP RPC functionality was even more limited. Where a large cross section of standard business documents was available for batch and EDI processing, the RPC interfaces revolved around system-level interaction. These RPCs, called Remote Function Calls (RFCs) by SAP, allowed an external system to make nonbusiness-specific function calls into the SAP system. RFCs functioned in real time, giving them a slight but insignificant advantage over batch processing. Unfortunately, neither of these external transaction mechanisms was sufficient for dealing with the growing need of many companies to provide seamless user access to multiple backend systems.

In response to these concerns, SAP introduced the Business Application Programming Interface (BAPI) in their 3.1 version of the R/3 release. BAPIs were built as business transactions running on top of the existing RFC layer. BAPI was designed to process key business applications in real time using data from external systems. Likewise, the BAPI specification provided a response document in real time, opening the door to techniques such as a two-phase commit between different systems.

Although the BAPIs went a long way toward defining a real-time business interface strategy for SAP, initial efforts surrounding BAPI development were somewhat limited. R/3 version 3.1 was released with relatively few BAPIs, and those focused on only the most commonly used business applications. Since that time, SAP's BAPI catalog has grown immensely, and it currently maintains a strong selection of interfaces for almost every major R/3 functional module. This commitment to BAPIs ensures that an application developer has an ever-wider range of applications to use via an external system. Moreover, applications built on BAPIs today will be supported by future releases of SAP.

CAUTION   *SAP sometimes offers newer BAPIs for the same business transaction within a successive release of R/3. In doing so, SAP recommends that the previous BAPI version be considered deprecated and that applications using that BAPI be migrated to the newest version. SAP typically continues to support the older BAPI for two or three subsequent versions, so you do not need to adopt new BAPIs immediately.*

SAP finally realized that a strictly centrist philosophy of enterprise application development would likely hinder future sales and began exploring some different technologies they could use to open up the R/3 system. As the millennium drew to a close, the Internet loomed larger and larger on SAP's horizon as a required networking and communication technology. To better understand SAP's ultimate position on external enabling technologies, it helps to review several of the attempts SAP made to enable R/3 functionality across the Internet.

A Brief History of SAP and the Internet

Building connectivity to the Internet has meant different things at different times to SAP. Their first attempts implied a very similar mentality to the centrist view of enterprise applications prevalent since SAP's inception. However, through fits and starts, SAP developed or licensed several successful Internet-based technologies, some of which are still currently used.

Here is a short timeline of these technologies:

Internet Transaction Server (ITS): Developed by Ixos; introduced around 1998

Business Connector (BC): Licensed from webMethods; introduced around 1999

Customer Relationship Management (CRM)/Internet Sales: Built by SAP; introduced around 2000

Web Application Server (Web AS): Built by SAP; introduced around 2001

The ability to reach users via a Web-based application has allowed companies to quickly introduce new functionality, both inside and outside of the corporate firewall. As a thin client architecture, the Web provides an ideal avenue for business reporting and lightweight functional needs. Recognizing this need, SAP has made valiant efforts to support their customers in harnessing the power of the Web, via both Internet and intranet development. The following sections review each of these applications or tool kits and place each within the bigger picture of Internet development for SAP.

Internet Transaction Server

The Internet Transaction Server (ITS) was designed to work as a standalone Web application server. ITS operates by relying on the existing screen and workflow of the R/3 application server's business transaction system. ITS uses a procedure, commonly known as "screen scraping," to allow a developer to expose any transaction that has a screen-based representation within the SAP GUI. This close tie to the R/3 system makes it very simple for developers to create Web transactions that largely mirror existing SAP business applications. Unfortunately, ITS was not designed to scale to the traffic levels typical of the Internet. One of its greatest drawbacks is this required link to a continuously open SAP session.

When a user logs into an R/3 application server, she is given an open user session across the network. This session must be constantly maintained so that the application server can effectively communicate back to the SAP GUI client. Once this session terminates, the user loses her connection to the R/3 system and must log on again. ITS also relies on the use of a continuous R/3 session in order to maintain communication with a Web client or browser. This dependency raises two very strong concerns over whether ITS is sufficient enough to bridge the gap between SAP and the Internet.

The first issue is the fact that World Wide Web application servers use a stateless interface to communicate with the Web browser. A stateless interface is so called because the Web server does not maintain the status of a Web browser from one request to the next. Effectively, this means that the Web server does not "remember" a given Web user between calls among the various Web pages handled by that server. The strongest advantage of a stateless interface is that it allows for a higher level of simultaneous traffic. In the case of a Web server, these higher loads of Web browser traffic are possible because the server does not maintain a continuously open connection to each client.

On the other hand, the SAP GUI front end is a stateful client. As explained earlier, this means that from the time a user logs on to the R/3 system using SAP GUI to the time he logs out, the SAP application server must maintain an open connection or session with the client. This stateful interface is required so that the SAP application server can constantly "know" where a given user is within a given transaction. The highly screen-based, transactional nature of SAP's business applications makes them inherently reliant on a session connection to acquire and send data to the underlying R/3 function modules and database tables.

The second concern raised over ITS is that an undue load can be placed on the R/3 application server because of these continuously maintained session instances. ITS's dependency on SAP's transactional screen flow means that, like SAP GUI, it must also provide a stateful interface to each client. Even when that client is inherently stateless—a Web browser, for instance—ITS must use SAP's session connection to allow an end user to "walk through" an R/3 business application.

On the front end, an ITS server is able to maintain communication with a Web browser using several different client-side Internet technologies. Perhaps the simplest and most common is that of writing small text files to the client machine through the Web browser. These text files, known as *cookies,* are a popular mechanism for saving small amounts of data to the client machine without intervention from the end user. By writing cookies through the Web browser, the ITS server is able to "remember" and differentiate between various clients across the network.

Despite this use of cookies, ITS still maintains an open connection or session to the SAP application server in order to ensure that screen-by-screen transactions are processed correctly. The most obvious limitation of this system lies in the finite number of sessions available on the R/3 application server. Having to share these sessions between internal users, corporate users, and external users via ITS, the R/3 application server can quickly become bogged down and virtually unusable. However, this type of implementation is suitable for an intranet or local area network, where only key SAP transactions need be exposed to a limited, known number of users. The value of ITS lies in its ability to offer a fairly common solution to the complaint that SAP GUI transactions are nonintuitive or lack user-friendliness. Likewise, should a company not wish to deploy SAP GUI to every desktop, ITS can Web-enable SAP transactions on an "as-needed" basis. ITS is not recommended for applications that might have a high or variable number of users, or an application that needs to be deployed across the Internet.

Business Connector (BC)

With the growing popularity of XML as a document standard for business transactions, SAP decided to license an XML translation tool from a company called webMethods. Rebranding the tool as the SAP Business Connector, the company began distributing it as part of the R/3 installation environment. Although customer licensing of the Business Connector has changed over time, the essential functional value to the R/3 system remains the same.

The continued and widespread use of Electronic Data Interchange (EDI) by enterprise-scale companies demonstrates the necessity of transmitting business documents via a system-to-system connection. However, the cost of implementing EDI and the yearly fees charged by Value Added Networks (VANs) has made this type of EDI difficult to deploy for all but the largest of SAP customers. SAP introduced the Business Connector in order to provide EDI over the Internet via standard XML documents. However, the Business Connector can also be used to enable internal and Web-based applications to communicate with an R/3 system.

Unlike ITS, the SAP Business Connector relies almost exclusively on the aforementioned BAPI and RFC interfaces. The Business Connector can also handle SAP Intermediary Documents (IDocs), which are part of the R/3 batch processing mechanism. However, the focus of this chapter is on the real-time interfaces offered by SAP to enable external system access; IDocs are outside of this scope. The Business Connector provides a graphical interface that developers use to browse and select from the various RFCs and BAPIs maintained by the R/3 application server. Each interface can be singly translated into an XML document, depending on the type of schema or document model the developer chooses. However, the power of SAP's Business Connector resides in its ability to chain multiple RFC and BAPI calls into one seamless transaction.

The Business Connector's translation and mapping tools allow developers to map an incoming XML document to a variable number of SAP RFCs and BAPIs. By creating a pipeline for inbound XML requests, the SAP Business Connector tool kit is used to facilitate complex system-to-system interaction. The XML document layer provides a high level of interoperability between different systems based on a standard document type. SAP's Business Connector is well suited for business document interchange over the Internet.

Essentially, the Business Connector deploys a listener on a specific network port. This port can either be a published protocol (HTTP, FTP, SMTP, and so on) or a higher-range generic port. Once deployed, the Business Connector is designed to wait for and accept incoming XML documents from an authorized source. In effect, the Business Connector acts as a server or daemon, brokering requests and responses to and from the R/3 application server. Certain business transactions require data from both the inbound XML document and a previous response from the R/3 application server. Pipelines within the Business Connector can be programmed, using Java, to handle this type of complex interaction.

An XML document that comprises a single transaction (for example, Sales order create) may require several calls to different R/3 interfaces to be processed. SAP's Business Connector allows a user to map specific pieces of data from an incoming XML document to fields within an R/3 interface. Once an application has initiated a call to SAP, the Business Connector can map data from both the XML document and the data returned from SAP into a second call to an R/3 interface, and then repeat the process with data returned from the second call. Based on the results from these calls to SAP, the Business Connector translates response data from the R/3 system into outbound XML documents. These XML documents are finally transmitted over the network to the call's originator. A high level of complexity surrounds data mapping and translation to and from the R/3 system. The Business Connector provides a strong tool kit and development environment to successfully accomplish this type of system-to-system communication.

Ultimately, the Business Connector was not designed to provide a Web application development environment for SAP. With its depth of features and challenging tool set, this effective connector comes with the cost of a fairly high learning curve. Developers who specialize in system-to-system integration would do well to learn SAP's Business Connector, as would companies requiring that level of sophistication. In addition, the Business Connector is an excellent alternative to traditional EDI because it allows secure, refined communication over a broad network medium, such as the Internet.

However, for general Java and Web application development, the Business Connector is overkill. The pipeline feature, which makes complex, end-to-end transaction automation possible, requires a great deal of expertise and is not easily utilized by a wide range of programmers. When coupled with its challenging visual interface, using SAP's Business Connector to create sustainable Web applications is problematic, at best. Check out http://www.sapgenie.com/mysap/bus_connector.htm for a good overview of the Business Connector and links to some helpful resources.

SAP CRM/Internet Sales

SAP offers their Customer Relationship Management (CRM) system as either a standalone instance of the R/3 system or as part of an integrated solution tied into an existing backend R/3. Part of this new CRM offering is a Web application called Internet Sales. Internet Sales bears a marked resemblance to the Online Store application that is built on top of the ITS. In essence, Internet Sales allows customers to manage the purchase ordering process over the Web. So why is Internet Sales included in an analysis of Internet-based development tools for SAP? Unlike previous offerings such as ITS, which relied on an open session with SAP and business application screen flow, Internet Sales uses only RFC and BAPI interfaces combined with a stateless connection to the R/3 system.

Internet Sales represents a major commitment by SAP to the continued use of BAPIs as the prescribed real-time interface for accessing SAP. In the case of CRM R/3, SAP provides additional RFC and BAPI interfaces to handle the enhanced functionality of CRM. These interfaces are used heavily by Internet Sales to offer Internet customers a truly scalable, high-performance Web application.

Unfortunately, Internet Sales is currently only available to SAP customers who have purchased the CRM application suite. These customers have two options for implementing CRM. In the first instance, a customer must migrate all existing sales functionality from the backend R/3 to the CRM R/3 instance. This effectively restricts the use of current R/3 Sales and Distribution functionality to that provided by the CRM system. Customers may opt to keep this functionality within the existing R/3 system and manually map fields in CRM back to this application server. Data can then be linked up based on a prescribed synchronization schedule. That way, developers can utilize the full power of the newest RFCs and BAPIs, while the R/3 administrators maintain data in the back R/3 system. You can find more information on CRM and Internet Sales on SAP's Website at http://www.sap.com/solutions/crm/internetsales/.

Internet Sales is important from a developer's perspective in that it represents one potential avenue for delivering future SAP applications. Should SAP choose this route, many more external applications similar to Internet Sales will be built in Java. Likewise, this application relies very heavily on the Java Connector to communicate back to the RFC and BAPI interfaces. As a model, Internet Sales demonstrates the capabilities that SAP has already perceived in Enterprise Java development and makes a strong case for continued software efforts in this arena.

Web Application Server (WebAS)

Nearly concurrent with the release of CRM, SAP announced their new Web Application Server (WebAS). The WebAS was designed to replace the existing

R/3 application server with a more Internet-centric technology. Unlike the R/3 application server, the WebAS can also function as a standalone Web application server. This server can be used to deploy Web applications as well as provide traditional access to SAP through the SAP GUI. Developers can build and deploy Java applications that directly tie in to the BAPI and RFC interfaces of the R/3 system. Likewise, SAP developers can embed ABAP programming directives within HTML pages to create dynamic Web applications. Check out http://www.sap.com/solutions/netweaver/brochures/ for an overview of SAP technology offerings including the WebAS.

As you proceed, remember that all of the Java application development you learn in this book is directly applicable to the WebAS. In addition, the tutorials in subsequent chapters can be readily deployed within this server, with only very minor modifications.

Alternative Development for SAP

The previous section looked at several different application suites and tool kits that were designed to provide access to an SAP system over a network. Each of these technologies is proprietary and requires a certain amount of financial investment to purchase and deploy. However, SAP does provide several readily available connector technologies that you can use to build external applications. These connectors are generally found on the SAP installation media, so check with your BASIS administrator for access to them.

CORBA and the Java RFC Server

The Common Object Request Broker Architecture (CORBA) was developed as an open standard for implementing distributed applications across a network. A *distributed application* is one that allows different physical computers on the network to share common functions. *Distributed computing* means that a developer can build applications that cross the boundaries of programming language, operating system, and even hardware.

The Object Management Group (OMG) designed CORBA as a vendor-independent framework and architecture for applications that need to interoperate across different hardware and software lines. You can get more information on the OMG as well as a list of specifications and processes at http://www.omg.org. Essentially, the CORBA specification defines how certain types of objects interact with one another over the network. An object encapsulates a given set of functionalities, which can be used within multiple applications or instances. Each instance represents a unique version of the associated CORBA object because the object is being shared by different applications. The developer defines a published interface for the CORBA object, which allows other developers to pass data to and from this object. This interface is created through a high-level language called the Interface Definition Language (IDL).

The IDL interface can be thought of as the public contract offered by the CORBA server to anyone who wants to use that object. An application or client that requires access to a CORBA object must go through the published IDL interface. IDL is also required to send data back to the requesting user of that object.

One of the most powerful aspects of CORBA is the fact that the IDL interface definition is completely independent of an underlying programming language. This means that an IDL interface can be used in almost any development environment, by almost any language. The OMG has created standardized mappings between IDL and the most popular programming languages, including Java, COBOL, Python, C++, and so on. The ability to separate the interface (IDL) from the implementation (software language) is the very heart of CORBA development. By allowing the developer to hide complex code behind published IDL interfaces, cross-platform application development can take place both safely and securely.

In CORBA, network communication takes place over a specific protocol called the Internet Interoperability Protocol (IIOP). IIOP allows applications across the network to use objects deployed within an Object Request Broker (ORB). An ORB deals with incoming and outgoing interaction with an object's IDL interface. Based on generated stubs and skeletons, the ORB translates incoming IDL calls into the fundamental object programming language. These stubs and skeletons act as proxies for the actual client and server. Without going into too much detail, the stub takes the call from a client application and sends it to the ORB. The ORB uses a generated IDL skeleton to pass that call on to the actual code-level implementation of the object. The process reverses when the CORBA object sends its response back to the originating application.

Based on this notion of published object interfaces, SAP developed the Java RFC Server to allow external applications to access R/3 functionality. The Java RFC Server shipped with the SAP Automation toolkit 4.5A. It included application libraries designed to work with a CORBA-compliant ORB. RFC and BAPI interfaces within the R/3 application server formed the basis for CORBA objects within this framework.

In essence, the underlying logic of the skeleton stub was the external BAPI or RFC interface. Based on the IDL interface and the generated proxy stubs, the Java RFC Server translated calls from a Java application into a C language application programming interface (API). This C API was provided through SAP's RFC software development kit (SDK), which is a standard set of libraries used to access RFC and BAPI interfaces. SAP used CORBA because there were no native

Java libraries that could be used to access these interfaces. The CORBA specification made the most sense because it allowed a seamless translation between the Java and C programming languages. Likewise, SAP was able to reuse the existing C libraries provided through the RFC SDK.

Riddled with bugs and memory leaks, SAP's Java RFC Server struggled to meet any of the stability or scalability requirements for offering a strong connectivity platform. Although CORBA itself is a great way to deploy high-performance, distributed applications, the Java RFC Server was limited to a single ORB implementation, provided by Orbix. By limiting this connector to one commercial vendor, SAP effectively doomed any form of widespread, production implementation. This restriction, more than anything else, caused SAP's implementation of a CORBA connector to be scraped eventually. If your company relies on CORBA for distributed applications, check out Actional's Control Broker at http://www.actional.com. Control Broker provides a strong implementation for CORBA connectivity for SAP, and it can be used with more than just the Java programming language.

If you are interested in getting more information about CORBA and how it has been implemented in Java, search http://www.devx.com for a great article on the subject.

Microsoft's COM/DCOM Bridge

COM, or the Component Object Model, was developed by Microsoft to allow program components to intercommunicate within an operating system. Most operating systems rely on some type of binary executable to run software applications. These application executables are largely unable to interact with one another at a component level. Instead, they are forced to use prescribed, intersystem communication mechanisms such as sockets, TCP/IP, memory-mapped input/output (I/O), and so on. On the other hand, Microsoft COM components can directly interact with one another without being limited to interfaces provided by the operating system.

Components developed as COM objects use the operating system as a central repository. The operating system deals with the responsibility of creating new objects, deleting unused objects, and handling the communications between them. One of the greatest strengths of the COM specification is that objects are not tied to a single application; this means that COM objects can be used by almost any other COM-based component in the operating system. This modularity creates a high level of reusability for the discrete functionalities housed in a COM object. However, COM does not provide strong distributing networking capabilities. Generally speaking, the operating system does not provide sufficient transactional support when dealing with applications that require cross-network communication.

NOTE *In distributed computing, a transaction refers to the complete, round-trip processing of data among all required systems. This means that any data marshalling, system requests, and response messaging must be handled before the transaction is considered terminated. A transaction might consist of a commit to a series of databases in a certain sequence. Should one of the commits in this series fail, the transaction must roll back every other successful database commit. In this way, the transaction is assured of either finishing properly or terminating cleanly and pulling out unwanted database commits.*

Current operating systems are not designed to handle the specific requirements for implementing this cross-network transactional support. An application server must be loaded on top of the operating system to provide these additional capabilities. To handle transactional, COM-style objects, Microsoft introduced the Microsoft Transaction Server (MTS). The MTS deploys and monitors COM objects to ensure that applications have access to the encapsulated functionality when they need it.

However, the Microsoft Transaction Server extends the COM model to allow applications across the network to access components housed within the MTS server. COM components that need to be accessible to the network must be developed under a slightly different specification. The Distributed Component Object Model, or DCOM, enables COM-based components to communicate directly over the network in a secure and reliable environment. Similar to what happens in CORBA, DCOM components can run across many different types of network transports, including popular Internet protocols such as HTTP and TCP/IP. DCOM components provide a published interface for other components and applications to access hidden, underlying functionality. In order to build and deploy transaction-based applications, DCOM components must run within an MTS application server.

SAP introduced their DCOM Component Connector as part of their Business Framework application suite. The Business Framework suite is available on standard SAP R/3 installation media. SAP's DCOM Connector allows developers to expose and connect to RFC and BAPI interfaces as COM components within the DCOM framework. By using the DCOM Connector, you can quickly introduce R/3 connectivity into your Microsoft-based development efforts.

Developers can create business logic around discrete SAP DCOM components using standard ActiveX tools and languages such as Visual Basic. Likewise, the DCOM Connector provides some required features for implementing mission-critical transactions. These features include a two-phase commit to allow rollbacks from unsuccessful transactions and connection pooling to enable sharing of database connections for a large number of users.

Unfortunately, DCOM components are largely limited to the Microsoft operating system. The MTS is only fully supported on one of the various Microsoft platforms. Moreover, the uncertainty surrounding the .NET infrastructure has cast some doubt on the future of existing technologies such as DCOM. With its limited support across different operating systems and the lack of a "best-of-breed" application server, SAP's DCOM Component Connector is useful on a fairly limited scale. If your development organization is strongly Microsoft-centric, then the DCOM connector may be the right choice for external SAP applications. However, SAP's Java Connector offers all of the power of DCOM with none of the inherent operating system and platform limitations.

For an exhaustive comparison of COM, CORBA, and Java, check out the article titled "A Detailed Comparison of CORBA, DCOM and Java/RMI" by Gopalan Suresh Raj at `http://my.execpc.com/~gopalan/misc/compare.html`. This article takes an in-depth look at these technologies and provides specific code examples for each.

CHAPTER 2

Exploring the Java Platform

THE FIRST CHAPTER IN THIS BOOK provided a quick rundown of the various technologies used by SAP to provide customers with infrastructure connectivity. After several hits and misses, including the as yet unknown fate for Microsoft's .NET Framework, SAP seems to have settled on Enterprise Java as the platform of choice for middleware integration. Does this mean that you shouldn't pursue one of the other avenues outlined in the previous chapter? Absolutely not. The path you follow for developing infrastructure and Web-aware applications should be based on your company's overall platform and network implementation.

If you have an entire development staff devoted to building Visual Basic and COM applications, then the SAP COM/DCOM bridge is the perfect choice. If your company needs to deploy a light version of several key SAP transactions strictly within the intranet, SAP's Internet Transaction Server (ITS) provides all the tools you need. However, if your company is looking to provide scalable, robust applications and middleware components that must have around-the-clock availability and deal with heavy amounts of network traffic, the Java 2 Platform, Enterprise Edition (J2EE) is exactly what the doctor ordered.

This chapter looks at the following:

- A history of Enterprise Java

- Integrating Java as middleware for SAP

- Deploying Java applications from the desktop to the Web

To start off, let's delve into the background of Enterprise Java and a history of the Java programming language.

The Enterprise Java Platform

In order to understand what Enterprise Java development means for SAP, you must first look at the Java platform as a whole. Once you have grasped the big picture view of Java, seeing how individual pieces fall into place throughout the course of this book is a lot easier. The following section briefly charts the evolution of the Java specification, from lowly applet viewer to the industry-wide powerhouse of today.

Networking a Programming Language

The rationale behind the original release of the Java specification was to provide the first truly "network-aware" programming language. This language was to be platform independent, simple to install and configure, and very network centric.

Out of these lofty ideals and high expectations came a new type of application, the Java applet, which was destined to become the bane of Web browsers and developers, alike.

The Java language, originally code named "Oak," was designed for embedded hardware programming. The first prototype consisted of a handheld touchscreen that you could use to control various pieces of home entertainment equipment. In order to better pursue the consumer electronics market, the tiny development team was spun off from Sun as a company called FirstPerson. Beginning with fairly meager resources, the FirstPerson team tried to find buyers for the Oak-based handheld through digital cable and movie-on-demand companies, as part of a set-top box offering. This ill-fated venture eventually derailed, but it inadvertently launched one of the greatest evolutions in network programming that the technology industry has ever seen—the Java development platform.

Executives at Sun realized that the power of FirstPerson's handheld lay not in the hardware implementation, but in the potential for a true cross-platform development language. Based on the notion of "Write Once, Run Anywhere" computing, the Java language was first demonstrated as part of a custom Web browser developed by Sun in 1994. At that point, the Internet and Web browsing had finally started to catch on with the introduction of NCSA's Mosaic (NCSA is the National Center for Supercomputing Applications), which showed the combined power of text and graphics across a global network.

Fortunately, Java survived the dissolution of FirstPerson and was reabsorbed into Sun as part of the "Liveoak" project. Looking to find a place for Java, a few ex-FirstPerson developers rushed to create a Mosaic clone, which they called WebRunner. Unlike Mosaic, this browser provided an integrated virtual machine in which Java code could be executed and new types of content could be delivered over the Internet. In 1995, WebRunner was demonstrated to a group of largely disinterested technology professionals, who initially mistook the product for another HTML-style Internet language. However, WebRunner amazed the audience by displaying animation, allowing users to interact with images, and providing truly dynamic content through a seemingly standard Web browser. With this demonstration, WebRunner raised the bar for content and services across the Internet and set the stage for the Java applet. Check out *A Brief History of the Green Project* at http://java.sun.com/people/jag/green/index.html for a first-person history of Oak, and *Java History 101: Once Upon an Oak* http://www.devx.com/Java/Article/10686/1954 to see the differences between this language and what eventually became Java.

By the time Java had been integrated with Netscape Navigator, developers had been downloading and building applets at a phenomenal pace. Java applets were truly centralized applications that could be downloaded on demand, used on an as-needed basis, and then discarded as necessary. This, at least, was the promise. In reality, applets were little more than another way for individuals and companies to dress up and add relatively useless functionality to Websites. Java applets certainly have their place in commercial development, with several large-scale groupware and collaboration firms relying heavily on applet functionality as part of their revenue models.

For the most part, unfortunately, applets proved to be buggy, bandwidth hogs, were unusable to the public as a whole, and found only relatively small niches within the corporate community. Bear in mind, Java applets performed exactly as advertised—they allowed new applications to be delivered and installed over the Internet to any platform that supported a Java Virtual Machine (JVM). But the drawbacks were twofold: mixed Java implementations on different Web browsers that often resulted in applets that behaved erratically, and developers who could now deliver buggy applications to users on a global scale. Both factors served to detract from the initial buzz generated by Java applets, and both ultimately caused most users to feel betrayed by the hype and most pundits to deride what truly was an amazing development in network programming.

The Evolution and Philosophy Behind Java

As Sun evolved the Java platform, it also enhanced the marketing position surrounding this technology. Sun had been a giant proponent of network computing for many years and saw Java's place as the first link in a chain that would ultimately fulfill the promise of portable computing.

Anathema to Java's philosophy is the idea that a language should be limited to a given operating system, computer platform, or even physical hardware device. Even in applet form, Java was meant to bridge the gaps instituted through years of proprietary application development, whether that entailed using a closed operating system or a physically embedded chip language. In a way, Java applets were really meant to be a metaphor to help people ultimately envision the possibilities with Java. No one should have expected the Web browser to be the final interface for interaction over the network and certainly not over the Internet. However, this seems to be exactly what happened, and global implementation of animated cursors and multimedia displays delivered through Java did not meet expectations.

Despite this opposition, Sun firmly stood by its claim that computing in the future would extend far beyond the individual machine. After the initial hype behind Java died down, Sun continued evolving a truly platform independent language that would be highly mature by the time the rest of the industry caught up with them.

Such persistence has finally paid off; the Java platform is ubiquitous, not only across the corporate enterprise but in everyday aspects of which you might not even be aware. One reason for Java's pervasiveness is the fact that Sun provides three unique flavors of the Java platform, each tailored to the medium in which it operates.

Java 2 Platform, Standard Edition (J2SE): Promotes client-side and desktop development of applications designed for consumer and corporate use. J2SE provides application libraries, which encourage quick, responsive programming techniques, while maintaining a high level of application security. This type of development is well suited to enterprise applications that need to be centrally organized and rich in functionality so that network and desktop maintenance is reduced without sacrificing quality and end user satisfaction.

Java 2 Platform, Enterprise Edition (J2EE): Provides components on which to build modular pieces of business logic that can be combined to create large-scale transactional applications. The J2EE specification also supplies a foundation for the Java application server, which automates many of the low-level details behind developing mission-critical applications. As a result of this automation, the enterprise developer is better able to focus on the tasks at hand, namely implementing business logic specific to a company's needs and responding to changes in a very timely fashion. These transactional components, called Enterprise JavaBeans (EJB), are reusable, easily maintained, and can be readily combined with other J2EE components to support a variety of interfaces, both human and machine.

Java 2, Micro Edition (J2ME): Gives developers an incredibly small Java Virtual Machine (JVM) and a set of application libraries designed to support consumer and corporate embedded devices. These devices range from set-top boxes to personal digital assistants (PDAs) to cellular phones, with J2ME providing a development platform to transparently develop and deploy new applications for each of them. Your own cellular phone likely has the J2ME built into it, which means that it is capable of downloading new Java-based applications directly into the phone's memory. Whereas the J2EE specification delivers true distributed computing within the traditional client/server landscape, the J2ME fulfills the promise of pervasive computing that reaches far beyond the traditional office space.

Fitting Java into the SAP Picture

As Java continues to evolve in each of these areas, the demand for skilled programmers to support the growing need for such applications will increase exponentially. In fact, consumer demand for more intelligent entertainment products is constantly on the rise, and even Java-based desktop applications have seen an upsurge in recent years.

However, most of the immediate demand for Java developers is coming from the enterprise level. Corporations have realized that large scale, proprietary software implementations are costly and often ineffective, and they are beginning to migrate toward more flexible, future-proofed applications and frameworks. On the flipside, enterprise organizations have also realized that all-in-one application solutions are not the panacea they were once thought to be. Without the ability to easily grow and add new functionality to these centralized, monolithic solutions, companies have had to face proprietary development languages, leagues of project consultants, and specialized training for their employees, all just to support typical company growth.

With Enterprise Java, developers can tap into the power of these all-inclusive software products, while still maintaining the freedom of a truly open development platform. Using Java, developers can readily build middleware components that provide reliable, transactional integrity between different enterprise systems, such as SAP and Oracle.

The Enterprise Java platform provides three key ingredients to successful middleware integration.

Flexibility: Through platform independence, Java development can be deployed across a variety of operating systems and hardware configurations. This allows a developer to build applications on her platform of choice and deploy them to almost any system within the enterprise. Likewise, Enterprise Java provides a consistent application platform throughout the company. This consistency reduces much of the network administration overhead required to deal with different language runtime environments.

Scalability: Enterprise Java application servers can be deployed on almost any hardware/operating system configuration. An initial deployment of application servers might consist of several low- to medium-scale computers. As network traffic and server load increases, these application servers are easily migrated to more powerful machines. Moreover, additional Java application servers can be added to provide clustered and load-balancing support. Essentially, applications written in Java and deployed in an application server can scale up to meet increasing demands from end users.

Exploring the Java Platform

Standards-based: The J2EE specifications describe a set of standards that allow developers to implement across a common set of technology components. This means that no one company owns the rights to Enterprise Java; rather the ability to modify and add functionality is based on the Java Community Process (JCP). The JCP is a consortium of companies and individuals across the globe that design and authorize new entries for the Java specification. Java is not a closed, proprietary architecture. This means that any developer can review all of the fundamental Java source code and that a single company cannot arbitrarily dictate the future of this programming platform. This ensures that a company choosing to standardize on the Java platform will not be left hanging based on the success or failure of a single vendor. Furthermore, the number of companies who support and offer Java applications, application servers, and related tools is on the rise. Should a given server vendor go under or become unsuitable for future needs, there are many more to choose from. The essential point is that an investment in Java is future-proof and can be relied on for technology needs, both now and ten years down the road.

SAP has recognized that Enterprise Java is a protected investment for their customers and is now an active participant in the Java Community Process. SAP sits on a number of different committees working to design Java Specification Requests (JSR) for future functionality.

> **NOTE** *JSRs provide the centralized mechanism for defining and authorizing new and modified Java functionality. Maintained by the JCP, JSRs deal with both proposed and final Java specifications. Reviewing current JSRs provides a strong overview of Java's immediate future. Additional information is available at* http://www.jcp.org.

SAP actively participates in the committee to define a Java portal specification, extensions to deal with electronic business using eXtensible Markup Language (ebXML), and new functionality for the next release of the J2SE. This dedication indicates SAP's belief that Enterprise Java should form the basis around corporate-wide middleware integration strategies. Likewise, SAP's participation helps guarantee that future Java specifications will be aware of the unique needs in developing applications for Enterprise Resource Planning (ERP) systems and customers.

In addition to SAP, the JCP boasts committee staffs from such notable companies as IBM, Hewlett-Packard, Oracle, and Nokia. Backed by these industry leaders, Java will continue to grow and mature, both now and well into the future.

Java Essentials for SAP

If you haven't guessed already, Java encompasses a great deal of functionality across many different venues of software development. This vastness might seem overwhelming at first, but Java's rich feature-set means that it can be used to build almost any type of application. Java represents the distillation of several decades of object-oriented programming (OOP) and language development. However, the rationale behind building an object-based language might not seem very clear. The following section details a quick history of object-oriented languages and their importance when it comes to developing applications for SAP.

Object-Oriented Basics

Object-oriented programming represents the next step in abstracted development languages. Early programming languages dealt directly with the computer hardware, writing commands at the machine layer at a mere step up from binary. Indeed, languages such as Assembly are still used today in applications that require direct communication with the hardware platform.

Over time, new programming languages were invented to create a broader level of developer accessibility. Programmers were no longer required to have intimate knowledge of the hardware specifications in order to build applications. These languages were designed with more human-readable syntax in order to be easily learned and deciphered by less specialized developers. Early examples include Fortran and Basic, whose sole purpose was to translate a legible programming language structure into machine-level commands. Although languages such as these created a greater legion of application developers, their structure still followed that of the computer world and not the real one.

Building Up to Objects

Procedural languages, like COBOL, follow a very specific execution structure. Numbered lines of code are always executed in succession, requiring the programmer to think in a very linear fashion when building applications. Moreover, when you develop using a procedural language, you often have to produce thousands of code lines, creating a nightmare for anyone who tries to debug or modify the application. For a historical perspective on this type of development effort, check out Fredrick P. Brooks's timeless look at corporate programming, *The Mythical Man-Month: Essays on Software Engineering* (Addison-Wesley, 1995).

The introduction of subroutines brought some relief to software development by allowing programmers to break up an application into logical chunks of code. Subroutines could then be called through the main program structure and executed as if part of the numbered line sequence. This technique definitely served to better organize development efforts and even create a more defined division of labor among programmers. However, subroutines did little to emulate real-world style syntax because of their continued reliance on inline execution.

As an SAP developer, you are likely familiar with subroutines as function modules. The R/3 system houses and relies on thousands of function modules to encapsulate its incredibly complex business logic. With the exception of ABAP Objects, the ABAP/4 programming language is not much different from its highly procedural predecessors. ABAP applications execute commands inline, calling function modules to provide additional functionality. In fact, a major component of the SAP Workbench is the Function Builder, which is fundamentally an advanced tool set for building subroutines.

The next evolution in development languages came with the introduction of object-oriented programming. Developed in the late 1960s by the Norwegian Computing Center, Simula was one of the first object-oriented programming languages. Simula comprised many of the object-oriented techniques still found in today's modern languages. It introduced the idea of discrete pieces of code as objects that were capable of inheriting functionality from superclasses. One of the most widely used languages today, C++, borrows directly from key concepts first pioneered in the Simula language.

Introducing Real-World Programming

The interest in object-oriented development stems from two simple principles. The first is that programming languages can be used to provide a high degree of abstraction from the hardware layer of the computer. This layer of abstraction means that developers are insulated from low-level details that might impede or even corrupt the development process. Abstraction is a key concept in most programming languages, but object-oriented development takes it a step further.

As mentioned earlier, procedural languages force the developer to think like a computer, developing code inline so that it can be executed accordingly. The second major principle behind object-oriented programming is that the developer should be able to model code based directly on real-world analogs. Essentially, this refers to the language's ability to encapsulate a discrete piece of functionality as an object and provide predefined mechanisms to act on that object. Chapter 3 drives deeper into this concept and explores the idea of object-oriented development and its analogies in the real world. For an excellent primer on object-oriented concepts, check out *The Object-Oriented Thought Process* by Matt Weisfeld and Bill McCarty (Sams, 2000).

Java represents one of the most advanced object-oriented programming languages available today. Following on the heels of C++, Java borrows much of that language's better traits, while solving many of the frustrations felt by C++ developers. Java provides better memory management and hides some of the nagging details that most developers don't need to deal with, such as garbage collection and pointers.

> **NOTE** Garbage collection in Java is simply a fancy way of saying that Java cleans up after itself. Throughout the course of an application's execution, instances of data are stored in the memory space of the computer. This memory space is finite and can be overfilled, causing the application to terminate. When they were using C++, developers had to be aware of what data was using up which memory or heap space. That data would need to be manually purged by the application to prevent memory leaks. Java provides a built-in mechanism for determining what data in memory is no longer relevant (referenced) by the program and automatically frees up that memory.

Overviewing Java Programming Techniques

In order to start building Java applications for SAP, you need to understand key programming techniques. This section details some good object-oriented practices and shows you how these concepts have been integrated into the subject of this book.

Design and Development in an Object-Oriented Environment

The world of object-oriented development is fairly complex; to work with it, you must make sure the development effort is well organized and have insight into historically verified design techniques. Chapter 3 deals with object-oriented programming concepts specific to the Java language. It also introduces the concept of design patterns as a way to develop applications based on tested methodologies.

Chapter 4 deals with basic Java syntax and introduces the first Java application for the SAP tutorial. It also provides a first glimpse at the real benefits behind object-oriented programming through an executable Java application. Once finished with this chapter, you will have basic Java syntax covered and should understand SAP's Java connector.

Chapter 7 introduces the Java implementation of a specific design pattern. This pattern allows you to draw on the experience of many previous object-oriented developers when building graphical user interfaces.

Throughout the book, you will deal with more and more advanced Java programming techniques. However, the ultimate goal is to develop real-world applications for SAP and not to provide an exhaustive Java reference. For a more in-depth look at general Java development for the Web, check out *J2EE Frontend Technologies: A Programmer's Guide to Servlets, JavaServer Pages, and Enterprise JavaBeans,* by Lennart Jorelid (Apress, 2001).

Exploring Key Internet and Web Technologies

Many organizations are looking to expand access to the SAP R/3 system via the Internet and World Wide Web. Key to this expansion is a crossover of understanding between SAP and these Internet technologies.

Chapter 6 demonstrates the installation and use of a Java application server. It also discusses the combined use of HTML and Java to provide dynamic content within a standard Web browser. This chapter culminates with a tutorial application that gives a user access to discrete SAP functionality via JavaServer Pages (JSP) for dynamic content and SAP's Java Connector (JCo).

Chapter 7 elaborates the use of Web-based applications for SAP. It introduces an open source Java toolkit called Struts that simplifies application development for the Web.

Integrating Databases

Most enterprise organizations run on multiple backend database systems. Although it is very likely for a company to standardize on SAP's business applications, additional database systems are often required to support homegrown or niche functionality. Whatever the case, you can use Java to tie these disparate systems together.

Chapter 8 demonstrates how to install and use the Hypersonic SQL database system (hsqldb) to store data external to SAP. Here, you learn some basic SQL syntax and employ a standard Java Database Connectivity (JDBC) connector to provide interaction with this database system. The main tutorial in this chapter deals with integrating a call to both the hsql database and SAP through a Web front end. In doing so, the end user need never be aware of the storage location for a given piece of information. This type of transparency shows the power of middleware integration across the enterprise and gives you a good starting point for additional external integration development.

Deploying Applications with Java

Before getting into the particulars of Java development, let's take a quick look at the different techniques for deploying Java applications.

Java can be deployed on a myriad of platforms, from a cellular phone to the end user's desktop to mission-critical application servers. Although the Java programming language is platform independent, its application deployment mechanisms are not.

In order to run a Java application, the platform of choice must first have access to a JVM. The JVM is a runtime interpreter that takes precompiled Java code and executes it as a native application. Once again, the idea of abstraction is key here because the JVM effectively abstracts the programming logic almost completely away from the hardware platform. However, the JVM is dependent on the hardware/operating system configuration, which means that it contains native operating system interfaces specific to that platform.

This may seem like a limitation, but the industry-wide support garnered by Java virtually guarantees a JVM implementation on each of the major platforms. This support has even been expanded to most PDAs and many popular model cellular phones.

Types of Java Deployment

With access to so many different avenues for Java development, a programmer can build applications to fit almost any need. The first step to that development is to determine what type of deployment configuration best suits the application's needs. Sun has provided three major flavors of Java, each tailored to the specific requirements of a general platform. Using these flavors as a guide, here are the three deployment mechanisms available to Java developers:

> **Handheld deployment:** This type of application deployment deals with small form factor and lightweight memory footprint devices such as PDAs and cellular phones. Aside from the obvious memory considerations, you must format the output to these devices to accommodate reduced viewing areas. Application deployment typically consists of a synchronization mechanism, where the user must physically connect to and update the Java application. The application resides entirely within the device, utilizing outside resources such as cellular connectivity to retrieve dynamic data. You may find handheld deployment useful in situations that require the robustness of a Java application running on an extremely portable device. One example is that of a warehouse manager who uses a handheld device running a custom Java application to scan and monitor inventory. The device can then synchronize with the central enterprise database system via a wireless connection or from a physical docking station.

> **Desktop deployment:** Similar to handheld deployment, the Java application resides wholly within the local computer. Developers use this type of deployment for software applications that have little need for network connectivity. Examples include document publishing and configuration tools. When you deploy to the desktop, you must update each machine individually, if the application changes. Likewise, desktop applications rely less heavily on network connectivity for dynamic data. Of course, you could use a desktop Java application to communicate across the network, but Java provides an easier deployment mechanism for this purpose. You can use desktop deployment to give users more complex Java applications that don't necessarily require a connection to the network.

Server-side deployment: The advent of global communication across the Internet demonstrated the power of server-side deployment. In order to deliver dynamic content that requires little or no desktop configuration, Java provides an application server specification and server-side component libraries. Using either a commercial or open-source application server, developers can quickly build and deploy applications to any end user on the network with an installed Web browser. Though this type of deployment allows for a high degree of dynamic content within the application, you must have a network connection to use it at all. For an excellent review of the most popular application servers, check out `http://www.butlergroup.com/reports/appserv/` and `http://www.serverside.com`.

In later chapters in this book, I deal with desktop and server-side application deployment, but I do not cover handheld development. For more information on programming for devices with small memory footprints, check out *Wireless Java: Developing with J2ME,* by Jonathan Knudsen (Apress, 2003).

Deploying Java Applications over the Web

Whether you choose desktop or server-side deployment depends on your application's requirements and whether you have access to network connectivity. A major drawback to server-side development using a Web front end involves the graphical limitations of HTML. Web pages are usually restricted to form-based text input and provide very basic visual formatting for display to the end user. By developing a desktop application in Java, you can provide access to the full range of graphical application components, from tabbed application windows to iconic visual hints and sound.

Likewise, desktop applications do not require a connection to the network, unless the software functionality specifically calls for one. Desktop applications built in Java are usually designed to run standalone, operating on files and directories strictly within the local machine. On the other hand, desktop clients such as SAP's Java GUI rely on a network connection to the R/3 application server. This type of application provides little functionality through the desktop deployment, other than visual formatting and a network communication layer. Similarly, someone from a desktop or technical support group is required to make updates or modifications to this application.

A slight twist to the desktop versus server-side deployment debate centers on the use of Java applets to provide strong visual formatting with dynamic configuration and update capabilities. Applets also rely on server-side deployment, but they allow the user to benefit from more refined graphical application components. However, applet development can be a little tricky, and it requires a greater technical investment. On the flipside, some applications require the more advanced user interface available through the Java applet component libraries. The applet feature set is strong enough that, with enough time and effort, it can deliver full scale, desktop-style applications directly to the end-user's Web browser. Unless the visual elements or application functionality require the use of an applet, you should go with strict HTML-based server-side Java.

This book provides no applet tutorials. However, when you understand SAP's Java Connector and basic Java development techniques, building a Java applet won't be much more of a stretch.

The Web browser interface provides a generally consistent client for deploying applications. I qualify that statement with "generally" because certain incompatibilities between the various Web browsers still exist. Typically, this is not an issue because a developer can build Web applications with at least a basic browser version requirement. A Web browser interface offers the singular advantage of almost universal deployment within most desktop computers. This means that you do not need to perform much in the way of effective client-side administration, and you can reduce some desktop support overhead. Different browsers offer different features, and one of the most popular could not be described as a lightweight client. For the most part, however, users are likely to have a browser previously installed, and your Web applications can be designed to support the widest possible variety.

The Enterprise Java specification outlines a simple mechanism for integrating Java syntax with HTML scripting tags. JSP pages combine the power of dynamic Java with the flexibility of a lightweight HTML client. Because Java code can be added directly to new or existing Web pages, your company can easily reuse current resources, such as Web designers and developers. JSP pages also have the benefit of being compiled at runtime. Rather than stopping and restarting an application server to add new functionality, you can modify and transport JSP pages within a live system.

Additionally, the JSP pages specification allows you to hide complex Java code within HTML-style tag libraries. These tags look and feel very similar to standard HTML tags, and anyone with a working knowledge of HTML scripting can readily used them. Tag libraries allow the developer to move beyond the restrictions of HTML while still exploiting the widespread acceptance of this standard. These distinctions also help to successfully divide the development effort, with Java programmers delivering business logic and Web designers handling the formatting and display responsibilities. Refer to Chapter 9 for a brief tutorial on Java tag library development.

In the end, many companies find that, despite its limitations, HTML formatting suffices for end-user deployment across a network. Java tag libraries can effectively supplement some of these inherent restrictions and add the benefit of dynamic Java code to static Web pages. HTML is a relatively straightforward scripting language for developing client interfaces, and it requires little overhead from the application server. Finally, most desktop computers already come with a Web browser that provides an immediate application interface with little reliance on support from a network administrator. Because most users are likely familiar with Web browser controls, this interface consistency reduces training and induces a faster overall acceptance process.

Looking at the Java Application Server

Server-side deployment centralizes application components within the Java application server. This allows a system administrator greater control over application resources and provides monitoring and transactional services to ensure that the application is always available. This type of deployment is ideal for either intra-company or Internet-wide functionality; it adds new servers to scale as network traffic increases.

Mission-critical applications must have round-the-clock availability. Because administrators can deploy and host applications within a centralized server, they can implement key features to guarantee this level of support. These features include the following:

Clustering: You can link a group of application servers together in a cluster. The cluster assigns a set of primary and secondary servers that constantly monitor the availability of deployed applications. Should one or more servers become disabled, another server in the cluster seamlessly steps in to take up the load. To the end user, this hand-off is transparent, appearing as if the application were being served by a single physical machine. Clustering is required for any application expected to function 24 hours a day, 365 days a year.

Load balancing: Similar to clustering, a group of servers share the total load of application traffic existing at a given moment in time. As the name implies, simultaneous network traffic is balanced among a set of application servers. Should one server become overloaded with user traffic, it can offload the excess to another application server in the group. When an application server must deal with a high or variable amount of traffic, load balancing is essential. When these user requests are not evenly balanced, servers exposed to the Internet usually grind to a screeching halt.

Transaction monitoring: As mentioned in the previous chapter, an enterprise transaction often consists of a complex series of calls to various databases and business applications. When used as middleware, the Java application server can report on the use of various, deployed transactions. Transaction monitoring also ensures safe and secure use of the resources allotted to the application server and any transactions that it houses. Such resources include database connections, business logic components, and temporary data storage.

Application servers are used for a number of different purposes throughout the enterprise. You are already familiar with one of these uses in the form of the R/3 application server. The R/3 application server provides transactional access to an underlying database through SAP's business applications. This application server also provides a runtime environment for ABAP applications and function modules. Historically, application servers hosted applications written in a single, specific programming language. SAP developed ABAP as a proprietary 4GL language to build complex and refined business applications. Unlike other languages, ABAP is tied intrinsically to the R/3 server and cannot readily be executed outside of this environment. This design allows ABAP to be highly optimized and integrated into the SAP platform. Likewise, SAP tightly controls any modifications made to the language syntax and its functions so that developers are guaranteed a smooth transition from one language version to the next.

Similarly, you can only run certain types of Java applications from within a Java application server. In a sense, these application servers act as an operating system in which specific programs can be executed. Just as software written for a Linux system will not run in Windows, non-Java applications cannot be run within a Java application server. The Enterprise Java specification provides components that are designed to take advantage of a Java application server. These components include EJBs, Java Servlets, JSP pages, and so on. Later chapters in this book focus heavily on Java Servlets and JSP.

Components hosted within an application server can be bundled into larger applications. Like the COM objects discussed earlier, Java objects deployed by the application server provide published interfaces. These interfaces not only allow Java objects to interact with one another, but they also act as mechanisms for communication with the outside world. Typically, this type of object-based, middleware implementation is handled through the use of EJBs. Although not handled in this book, EJBs are used to house complex units of technical or functional logic, while offering relatively simple, external interface routines. EJBs, CORBA stubs and skeletons, and DCOM components serve very similar purposes in the larger scheme of distributed computing. Through various methods, these technologies allow applications to communicate at a very modular, component-based level, even across a network as broad as the Internet.

However, the new trend in application servers is to make them so that they provide support for applications written in multiple programming languages to be deployed within the same framework. SAP has promised that the new Web Application Server will support both Java- and ABAP-based components. On the flip side, companies such as Microsoft see the future of distributed computing as a generic interface for every business object, therefore interoperability will be allowed regardless of the language on which these objects were built. The final chapter of this book describes, in greater detail, some of these new principles and how they have currently been implemented.

Microsoft .NET

The .NET platform is largely Microsoft's response to the J2EE platform. Unlike J2EE, it is designed as an integration point for different backend systems around a single operating platform. .NET's programming framework is comprised of a new OO language called C# (sharp) and a somewhat revamped Visual Basic. It operates on top of a command language runtime (CLR) that can natively execute applications developed in these languages. The CLR also provides services such as security, debugging, and memory management so that developers are able to focus on higher-level application programming.

The .NET Framework relies on a combination of XML and HTTP for network communication. These technologies have been bundled into the Simple Object Access Protocol, or SOAP. SOAP is a lightweight messaging protocol used to encapsulate Web Service request and responses messages. Any application capable of consuming and producing SOAP messages over the network can interoperate via these Web Services. Rather than relying on a common programming language for portability, .NET uses these XML-based SOAP messages to tie different applications together, regardless of the underlying hardware/software platform.

.NET can be hosted and utilized by a number of different Microsoft products, including Windows 2000 Server, Exchange Server 2000, and the Windows XP operating system. The framework also specifies a common authentication service to provide centralized access to key datastores. Known as .NET Passport, an example of this service's implementation can be found in the .NET Passport login provided at http://www.msn.com.

For more information on the .NET platform, check out http://www.microsoft.com/net/.

Needless to say, an application server is an essential aspect of development when you are building external applications for SAP. The number of commercial Java application servers increases every year, allowing your company to choose a price/feature combination suitable to your existing and future needs. Likewise, there are numerous open source implementations of the J2EE application server, which are ideal for initial and prototype development work. The Tomcat application server used in this book is Sun's reference implementation for the Java Servlet and JavaServer Pages specifications. This means that Tomcat complies very precisely with those aspects of the J2EE specifications, as originally set forth by Sun.

Summary

The Enterprise Java specification outlines a series of standards and protocols that a vendor must implement in an application server in order to be considered J2EE compliant. This guarantees that Enterprise Java applications can be built and deployed in different application servers, regardless of the vendor or provider. However, commercially available application servers provide additional value through services such as load balancing, clustering, and failover. These services are not outlined in the J2EE specification and can mean the difference between a successful and disastrous deployment of a production Java application. You should carefully evaluate the available Java application servers, ensuring that you make your decision according to the specific needs of your company.

Though these servers may change and evolve over time, the fundamental principles remain the same. Application servers provide optimized hosting and refined management of business transactions. Centralized application deployment requires less resource allocation and overhead from system administrators and desktop support personnel. The Enterprise Java specification outlines a scalable and secure middleware platform to ensure transactional integrity for mission-critical applications. Vendors such as BEA and IBM offer best-of-breed commercial servers whose features include support for clustering, load balancing, and monitoring. With the current uncertainty around newer middleware platforms, Enterprise Java offers the most proven, reliable infrastructure for building and connecting applications to SAP.

CHAPTER 3

Understanding Object-Oriented Design and Development

THE FIRST TWO CHAPTERS IN THIS BOOK provided some history and context for developing Java-based SAP applications. Hopefully, you are now ready to dive into some object-oriented development. This chapter introduces the basics of object-oriented development and prepares you for the Java tutorials of the following chapters.

The chapter looks at the following:

- Basic object-oriented programming concepts

- Designing object-oriented applications

- Utilizing proven solutions with design patterns

The goal of this chapter is to familiarize you with the foundations of object-oriented programming. I will reiterate and expand on many of the terms and ideas discussed in the following sections throughout the remaining chapters. Don't worry if some of the concepts don't make sense at first. As you begin building Java applications for SAP, object-oriented development and design fundamentals become quite a bit clearer.

Getting Object Oriented

Object-oriented programming represents the latest round of abstraction in the world of computer language development. As with almost every advance in programming, object-oriented development is designed to model the human perception of reality more closely. This is a reality of items and actions, where single units can act alone or in concert to affect the surrounding world. Object-oriented development is an attempt to emulate these reality-based constructs so that computer programming can take on a stronger cast of real life.

A number of different metaphors have been used to help conceptualize object-oriented design and development. Although the idea of relying on a metaphor to explain a language modeled on reality seems ironic, it provides the necessary bridge between concept and application.

Using Metaphors to Understand Object-Oriented Development

One of the most common metaphors involves viewing the code object as a black box. The outside world cannot see the programmatic logic housed in this box, and they can only act on it through prescribed methods. Essentially, the black box is a discretely organized unit of unknown complexity that one or more developers provide to other users for a specific function. The user does not need to understand how the black box works, only how she should access its functions and understand its responses.

The black box metaphor provides you with a fairly limited understanding of object-oriented development, but it does allow for some basic insights. A more detailed metaphor likens this development to a bicycle analog. The code object in this example represents a real-world bike. This bike is a physical object, with known abilities and attributes. Object-oriented development would first describe this bike as a generic bike object, containing the basic functions and properties of a bicycle. These functions include pedals to supply power, handlebars for steering, and brakes for stopping. Of course, the generic bicycle might contain more than just those three, but this example keeps the bike relatively simple.

Working with Object Methods

Each of these functions represents an action that can be taken by a user on the bike. By acting on the pedal function, the user is relying on the pedals as a predefined mechanism for supplying power to the bike. This pedal action is one method the developer creates to operate the bicycle object. If the bike represents a discrete unit of object code, or an object, then the actions used to operate the bike are the object's methods.

In object-oriented development, methods are the mechanisms the developer prescribes as a way of acting on the logic within the object. Similar to the black box metaphor, this logic is hidden from the user. This user does not need to understand how the actual object works, only that it contains these methods as appropriate mechanisms for operating the internal logic.

However, the bicycle metaphor is more accurate in the sense that the developer can give the user a look at key features of the object without requiring the user to understand everything about the programmatic functionality. Notice that the generic bicycle created earlier did not deal with gears and ratios and cables. The only person who needs to understand how these components work is the developer responsible for their design and implementation. The limits to which the user must understand these components are the actions described by the developer for their appropriate use. For instance, the pedals work the front gear, which uses the bike chain to work the rear gear, and so on, until the user obtains the desired result of this action—forward motion. However, these components can have a certain level of visibility on the bike so that the user has visual confirmation of the bike's function. In the same way, object-oriented development allows the developer to provide internal documentation of key aspects and features of an object.

The Java platform specifically implements such an internal documentation feature, called Java documentation, or Javadoc for short. *Javadoc* is a mechanism by which the developer adds explanations of object features, attributes, and methods using a specialized comment formatting. Using the Javadoc generator, the developer can retrieve notation formatted using these comments, which is automatically saved as Web pages. In this way, developers can leave meaningful comments behind, not only for future developers, but also for actual users of the commented objects. Should an object such as the generic bicycle not function properly, the user has recourse to documentation that helps them better understand how to use that object. For more information on Javadoc formatting and stylistic conventions, check out *How to Write Doc Comments for the Javadoc Tool* at `http://java.sun.com/j2se/javadoc/writingdoccomments/index.html`.

Creating Instances from Object

The generic bicycle object describes a set of baseline features that every bicycle must have in order to operate. As mentioned earlier, pedals, handlebars, and brakes make up the core feature set of this bike object. These actions are represented by methods within the bike object and allow the user to operate the object without really understanding how the object works. However, the power of object-oriented development is found in the fact that not only can objects such as the bike be used and reused, but that such objects can form a foundation for new objects.

At this point, the generic bike is pretty boring, providing little more than a general blueprint for an operating bicycle. The bike developer has two choices for making this object more customizable. The first is to describe a series of bike attributes that deal with the basic properties of a bicycle, outside of the actions required to operate it. Such attributes might include a paint scheme, tire size, and number of gears. By incorporating attributes into an object, the developer allows the user to customize key properties to better suit how he plans to use this object. In Java, this is known as *creating an instance* of an object.

In Java, an instance is simply the representation of a given object within the structure of the overall application. Once that instance is created, the user, in this case the application, can access all of the functionality provided by that object. In many cases, an object's developer provides initial attributes for that object, some required and some not, so that when the instance is created, the object functions appropriately. Some required attributes of the bike object are number of gears, hand versus pedal brakes, and tire size. The paint scheme is an optional attribute, with a default value of unpainted.

In order to use the bike object, the application, or user, must set those required values when an instance of that object is created. Creating an instance, otherwise known as *instantiation*, means that the object representation contains the attribute values either set by the application or added as default by the developer. If properly instantiated, the bike object instance is defined with a set number of gears, a given tire size, and the choice of either hand or pedal brakes.

Optionally, the application may have set a color scheme or may leave the bike unpainted. This type of development is analogous to a factory model, in which a single, narrowly defined style of bicycle is produced according to a restricted set of customizable options. Much object-oriented development consists of using these types of objects within a development effort to logically encapsulate different types of functionality. Whether using standard Java objects or objects built by another developer, the object-oriented programmer relies heavily on the use of reusable objects as the building blocks for an application. By using only those methods and attributes the developer prescribes, the instance of an object is ensured to function according to its design.

Expanding Objects Through Inheritance

The second option for developing this bike object relies on the user for the actual bicycle implementation. In the previous example, the generic bike object contains only three methods for operating the bicycle, with no possibility of adding more. What if the user needs to be able to shift gears? Currently, there is no gearshift method in the bike object, so users of this object are always forced to operate in a single gear. Granted, the original bicycle was designed to only allow a single gear, and it functions exactly according to those design specifications. However, this rigid definition of a bicycle ultimately serves to restrict the properties and actions of a bike object instance.

A more flexible approach provides a working bicycle blueprint with basic actions such as those described earlier and allows modular components and actions to be tacked on to the bicycle as a totally new object. This concept is known as *inheritance*, meaning that the user develops a new bike object (not an instance) that inherits key features from the initial bicycle object and adds appropriate methods and attributes to supply additional functionality. This new bicycle object is a subclass of the bicycle object superclass.

The concept of inheritance is integral to Java development, but it is not a major focus of this book. In actuality, every Java object inherits from a single Java superclass, called `Object`. This inheritance occurs transparently to the developer so that no development effort is required to use this class. The Java `Object` superclass provides all of the methods you will need to allow a given instance of the object to function within the Java Virtual Machine (JVM). This superclass deals with garbage collection routines, object initialization, and so on, and it even contains methods that can be directly used by the Java objects that inherit from it. In effect, the `Object` class describes what an object is within the Java programming language's object-oriented framework.

The bicycle superclass, called `Bicycle`, describes the basic functionality of a bicycle, so that any class inheriting from it already has key aspects predefined. As an example of reusable development, the developer could create an entire fleet of unique objects, each inheriting from the `Bicycle` object, but representing a slight variation on the bicycle theme. All would have two wheels, pedals, and handlebars, but one might have shock absorbers and a method for off-road riding. Another might need two seats and an extra set of handlebars and pedals to act as a tandem bike.

Inheritance allows the developer to create a common, reusable framework for a generic set of application functionality. Again, the idea of object-oriented development as an abstraction of the real world is reinforced through the common hierarchical categorization of attributes into more and more discrete units of functionality. Just as we use biological taxonomy to organize the natural world into kingdom, phylum, class, and so on, we use inheritance to organize the programmatic world of object-oriented development. The human mind seems better equipped to create and maintain these types of organizational systems based on a tightly hierarchical, descendent schema.

However, unlike the science of biological taxonomy, Java allows objects to inherit from multiple superclasses, which often leads to close scrutiny of the Javadoc documentation. Inheritance in Java is confusing for anyone newly initiated into the world of object-oriented development. Rather than getting bogged down into specific issues around inheritance, simply bear the concept in mind as you begin developing Java objects. As you build more refined Java applications, you will begin to see where certain features can be abstracted into reusable superclasses that can then be utilized by anyone else who needs those features in the development effort.

To summarize: objects in Java are discrete units of programming logic. Methods are prescribed actions that allow the user to act on that object. An object must be instantiated as an instance in order to use that object's functionality within an application. When an object is instantiated, the developer may require certain attributes to be set so that the instance functions properly. An object that inherits from another object contains all of the methods of the original object, or superclass, as well as any additional methods the new objects developer adds.

Implementing Object-Oriented Designs

As with any other style of programming language, object-oriented development is much more than concept and syntax. The previous section introduced the basics of object-oriented programming. Subsequent chapters deal with Java syntax and various programming techniques. Unfortunately, simply understanding the language and its implementation is not enough. In order to create sustainable applications, the developer must first understand and execute strong object-oriented designs.

Designing an object-oriented framework is a painstaking process that can only be learned through time and experience. The power and flexibility of languages like Java can quickly lead to highly complex and even redundant applications if good design practices are not in place. Fortunately, newly initiated Java developers can rely on many proven "best-practice" designs as illustrated in the next section. At this point, it is more important to understand the rationale behind object-oriented design than to launch right into Java development.

Dividing Labor Between Developers

Good object-oriented design (OOD) means that different developers at varying times can effectively work on the same application or framework. Techniques such as inheritance and polymorphism allow one developer to encapsulate business or functional logic that can be used by many future programmers. Moreover, not every developer on a given project or across the company has all of the requisite knowledge to build an application.

Especially when dealing with SAP, technical developers tend to specialize in a few different areas. A developer might have worked with the production planning staff for so long that he understands the functional side of SAP almost as well as the technical. Another developer may have specific warehouse management experience from having written hundreds of reports and applications for the system. When the company requests a new application bundling data requirements from both modules, relying on a procedural language like ABAP can cause the lines of responsibility between developers to become blurry. Both developers would likely require access to the same ABAP application or function module, with bruised toes and delayed deadlines being the obvious result.

Strong OOD practices implement a design that requires different functional Java objects to be developed based on a specific SAP business area. Each developer is responsible for a specific object or set of objects that encapsulate the business logic of a given SAP module. Once those functional objects are developed, they could be integrated easily into the overall application framework, providing discrete business logic to other objects in the system. This division of labor is one key aspect and benefit of object-oriented design.

Planning for the Future

Good OOD should always prepare for the future. Whether you are a consultant or an employee, you will often be tempted to build for next week, rather than next year. Schedules and deadlines always loom too quickly on the horizon and force your development efforts into a fast-track mode. Sometimes the applications produced by these efforts are exactly suited to their purpose: a throwaway SAP report you need to determine a specific year-end financial closing, or a quick and dirty legacy data load you need to finish an SAP upgrade. However, most middle-tier and front-end development is expected to withstand the test of time, whether that time span is measured in years or decades.

Consultants leave. Employees change positions, change groups, or even change jobs. Inevitably, the responsibility for an application, Java or otherwise, needs to change hands. Without strong OOD practices in place, that application probably gets rewritten by its new owner or left behind as new development efforts take place.

Object-oriented development encourages the definition of well-documented object methods that future developers can effectively utilize. Although second-guessing an application's future is next to impossible, developers can build objects that are reusable across multiple software iterations. This means you need to create components that deal with specific functional areas or responsibilities, rather than attempting to encompass all aspects of an application or framework.

When you follow good object-oriented design practices, you need to create well-documented methods that can be readily used by future developers. By building methods and objects for as wide an application audience as possible, the developer implements strong design practices to ensure that his work is not wasted or thrown away. Likewise, as software requirements change, these objects can be relied on to properly support the original business logic specifications without calling for modification.

By this point, it should be evident that Java objects are capable of maintaining incredibly complex programmatic logic. Furthermore, the complexities of these objects remain hidden behind straightforward methods and interfaces. Whether you are providing the database connection for a middleware implementation or a sophisticated business object designed to support Web-based reporting, object methods offer simple interfaces through which you can access complex code.

Low-level details of the object are buried behind public methods that describe exactly how the developer wants the object to be used. In this way, a developer can communicate key concepts about the usage of an object without having to work directly with the future application programmer. Through good OOD, the division of labor is further clarified, both across the immediate development effort and future efforts. The current development is ensured to have a more lasting effect and longevity against changing requirements, people, and even companies.

Discovering Object Dependencies

The final aspect of object-oriented design that is pertinent to this book is that of object dependencies. Each of the tutorials found in the following chapters builds on the examples of the prior chapter. Objects developed in one chapter are refined and reused in the next. Over the course of the book, the objects in your

Java development become very reliant on each other. This reliance is one form of object dependency and should be well defined throughout the design of the application. OOD allows developers to effectively control these software dependencies, describing their relationships from the outset rather than allowing them to grow over the length of the development effort.

A great deal of effort should be made to reduce object dependencies whenever possible. An object dependency occurs when one object maintains intimate knowledge of another object, to the extent that one object should change, the other would also require modification. Good object-oriented design strongly discourages the creation of too many of these intimate dependencies. Of course, there are times when objects must be tightly integrated with each other, making object dependencies inevitable.

Not every dependency is a bad thing. As you will see with development in this book, certain objects must have a strong guarantee that another object will perform in a certain way. In order to gain this level of surety, the first object must understand key details in regard to the object it's using. However, you must take these dependencies into account when you create the initial object design of your system. The next section in this chapter details some proven patterns designed to account for and reduce dependencies within a system solution. Moreover, you can effectively manage object dependencies through commercially available design tools. Microsoft's Visio provides sets of visual components based on common modeling languages to build diagrammatic representations of a software or hardware system.

In fact, object design is important enough to warrant its own unique modeling languages, in addition to these tool sets. Currently, the most popular of these modeling languages is the Universal Modeling Language, UML. UML provides a set of diagrams and methodologies for detailing the design specifications of a software system. Tools such as Rational XDE support UML modeling of object components and even provide automatic code generation based on these designs. To learn more about UML and to find links to various tutorial resources check out http://www.uml.org.

However, before attempting to create new system designs overwhelms you, let's take a look at some tried-and-true design solutions called design patterns.

Building Object Systems with Design Patterns

The history of object-oriented development dates back to the early 1970s. Out of this legacy, many different languages and techniques have evolved to bring programming to the masses. As a function of this massive, multidecade development effort, literally millions of lines of object-oriented code have been written. Over time, these applications began to embody repeated ideas and solutions for similar problems. Of course, the functionality implemented for each application was different and based on the specific problem at hand, but a common trend was beginning to develop among many object-oriented applications.

Based on the notion of recurring solutions to similar problems, a design pattern codifies the relationships between the various programming objects within a system. These objects are not language specific, but they can be implemented with almost any object-oriented language. The essence of a design pattern is that a particular problem has been commonly seen as having a recognized solution, and this solution can be abstracted not only from its functional implementation, but also from the programming language.

The Dressmaker's Pattern

At first glance, this definition of a design pattern may appear too rigid to provide any real value. The number of solution systems that can be developed from these recurring problems would seem to be rather limited. Indeed, the cardinal text on the subject, *Design Patterns: Elements of Reusable Object-Oriented Software* by Erich Gamma, et al. (Addison-Wesley, 1995), contains fewer than 30 design patterns. So what possible value can these have in your development effort?

Consider the analogy of a factory turning out high-fashion women's clothing. The hiring manager has rounded up 50 of the best dressmakers in the world in order to turn out the finest quality garments. To get the effort going, the floor manager holds up a fully tailored prototype dress and tells the dressmakers to copy this dress exactly. Even though these are the finest dressmakers in the world, each would ultimately create a dress that is slightly different from the next. Rather than simply showing them a dress, the floor manager should have created a dressmaker's pattern and distributed it to each of his staff. With the pattern, each dressmaker can create an exact duplicate of the original by simply cutting and sewing the appropriate lines. Regardless of the material used, color of thread, or decorative accents, each dress would conform to the specifications of the original pattern.

A design pattern in object-oriented development is similar to the dressmaker's pattern. Just as the dressmaker's pattern is not the dress, the design pattern is not a language-specific implementation of the solution system. The design pattern is meant to foreshadow the eventual look of the solution by describing how objects interact with one another to solve a recognized problem.

Applying Historically Proven Solutions

The power of the design pattern stems from the fact that it is developed on the shoulders of experts. Design patterns have been tested throughout many different language implementations and functional applications so that they represent widely recognized solutions to common problems. Their use also makes it simpler for different developers to maintain the same application. The design pattern provides a common architectural language through which developers from different object-oriented programming backgrounds can communicate. Likewise, by using a specific design pattern, you can more easily recognize the function of an application or system.

This chapter closes with two descriptive examples of commonly used design patterns. Developers often use the Singleton pattern to control specific access to an object instance to ensure performance or a shared context throughout the JVM. The Façade pattern hides overly complex object methods or object subsystems signatures behind a simplified set of interfaces.

Controlling Object Access with the Singleton Pattern

As implied by the name, the Singleton pattern lets you create one and only one instance of a given object. Recall the earlier discussion of creating object instances before an object can be used within a JVM. Normally, an application can create as many instances of a given object as it wants to, ultimately running the risk of overloading the system memory with extraneous Java instances. Despite the fact that the JVM provides strong garbage collection routines, an object's developer may want to ensure that at any given moment, only a single instance of that object resides in memory. This is useful when an object houses shared system resources or provides a common database connection.

> **CAUTION** *Database connections are best implemented through a connection pool and if they are not based on the Singleton design pattern. However, the Singleton offers a very simple mechanism for ensuring that one and only one connection to the database exists at any time, and so it serves a purpose in this example.*

As a design pattern, Singleton is a very simplistic mechanism. The Singleton pattern requires that the object maintain control of its own instance, rather than relying on the JVM to do so. The actual implementation is up to the developer and the programming language she chooses to use. In Java, a Singleton object intercepts any request to create a new instance of itself, and then it checks to see whether an instance has already been created. If an instance of the Singleton object exists, the object simply returns that instance back to the requesting application. From the perspective of the application attempting to create a new instance of this object, it sees the instance returned by the Singleton as exactly what it requested. This way, the developer ensures that only one instance of the object exists within the JVM and any application requesting a new instance transparently shares a single instance with any other application executing within the virtual machine.

The UML diagram in Figure 3-1 shows one possible configuration for a Singleton object.

```
┌─────────────────────────┐
│        Singleton        │
├─────────────────────────┤         ┌──────────────────┐
│ -instance:Singleton     │- - - - -│     Return       │
├─────────────────────────┤         │ unique instance  │
│ +Singleton()            │         └──────────────────┘
│ +getInstance():instance │◀─┐
└─────────────────────────┘  │
             │               │
             └───────────────┘
```

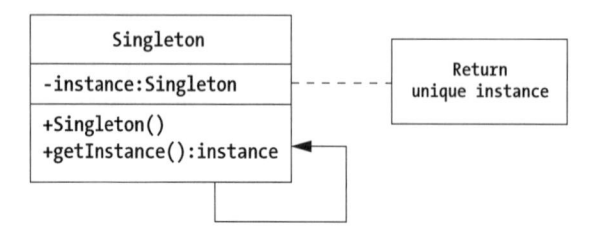

Figure 3-1. UML diagram of a Singleton object

Notice that the Singleton object contains a method called `getInstance()`. This method returns a unique instance of the Singleton object, which has been previously instantiated. If no instance exists, this method creates a single instance and returns it to the calling class.

Hiding Complex Object Interfaces with the Façade Pattern

The Singleton represents one of the simplest design patterns. A slightly more complex pattern is that of the Façade. The developer uses this pattern to hide complex object or system interfaces behind a single, easy-to-use interface. The Façade allows the developer to hide subsystem infrastructure in order to reduce the number of objects that clients are forced to deal with. So when would this pattern get used?

The Façade pattern is appropriate if your object framework consists of a complicated series of components that can be logically grouped into one of more subsystems. Client objects that need to access functionality in these subsystems would be required to understand the methods and attributes of each individual object. Rather than forcing these clients to do so, the Façade pattern lets you provide a single, common interface. By exposing a set of simpler methods to the client, this interface, or façade, effectively hides the object details of components in your system.

The UML diagram in Figure 3-2 demonstrates a client calling a single Façade object interface. The Façade object goes on to create instances of more complex objects in the appropriate order. That interface then returns the respective data sets derived from the `ComplexObj1` and `ComplexObj2` objects.

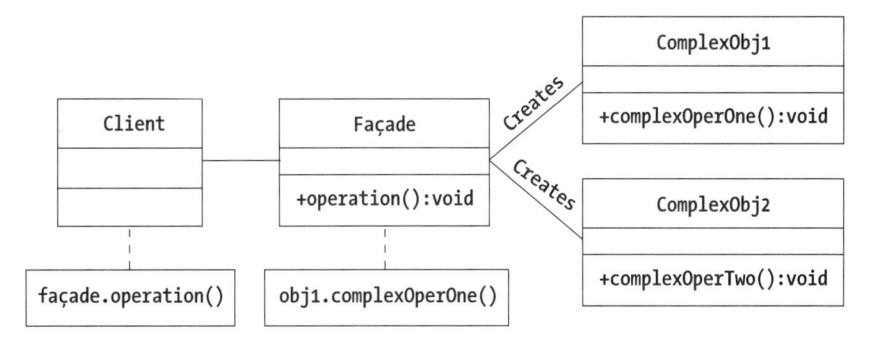

```
                                      ComplexObj1
                              ┌─────────────────────────┐
          ┌──Creates──────────│ +complexOperOne():void  │
┌─────────┐   ┌─────────────┐ │                         │
│ Client  │───│   Façade    │ └─────────────────────────┘
│         │   ├─────────────┤
│         │   │+operation():│──Creates──┐
└─────────┘   │    void     │           │  ComplexObj2
    │         └─────────────┘           │┌─────────────────────────┐
    │              │                    └│ +complexOperTwo():void  │
┌─────────────┐ ┌──────────────────┐     │                         │
│façade.      │ │obj1.complexOper  │     └─────────────────────────┘
│ operation() │ │    One()         │
└─────────────┘ └──────────────────┘
```

Figure 3-2. UML diagram of the Façade pattern

Although the Façade pattern might seem somewhat advanced at this point, it does demonstrate the remarkable power of design patterns. Throughout the course of a development effort, complex subsystem or object infrastructures can be quite common. This pattern codifies a proven solution for simplifying access to these components. By reducing the complexity faced by a client object, the Façade pattern makes future modification and use of its underlying object framework much simpler. Furthermore, the coupling of client and subsystem is weakened, thereby reducing object dependencies from one to the other. Finally, the Façade pattern does not restrict the use of underlying subsystem components. Should a client object need direct access to those objects, it can readily do so without violating the nature of the pattern.

There are many more design patterns available with more being introduced each year. Some patterns have gained wider recognition, while others are the product of niche software development. Regardless of their origin, researching and applying design patterns to your object-oriented architecture can greatly reduce the development effort, while ensuring a design based on proven solutions. By conducting a quick search on the Web, you can turn up a number of well-documented design patterns, many of which provide Java-based code examples of their use.

Summary

Developing complex systems requires tools that reduce the complexity of development. The foundation of object-oriented design is to abstract the intricacies of machine language programming into a more human-legible context. This chapter provided a quick history on the evolution of OO in order to prepare you for future Java development. However, Java is likely not the only object-oriented language you will use in your future career, or have used in the past.

To use a final metaphor, let me just say that you should consider object-oriented development as your toolbox and Java as one tool among many potential tools. Design patterns facilitate development with these OO tools because they are formalized solution systems that can be used with any object-oriented language. By relying on proven solution development, you build integrity and reliability into your applications. By implementing design patterns in your code, you gain valuable insight into the world of object-oriented programming and are not forced to learn OO development in a vacuum. Throughout the course of this book, you will see and utilize OO design and patterns to create object systems that meet real-world needs.

CHAPTER 4

JCo 101: Programming with SAP's Java Connector

Now that you have looked at key Java programming concepts, it's time to move into some meat-and-potatoes development. The initial chapters in this book explained the conceptual basis for building SAP applications in Java. By now, you should be fairly comfortable with the rationale behind the SAP/Java convergence and be ready to jump into the fray of tutorial applications.

This chapter introduces the fundamentals surrounding SAP's appropriately named Java Connector (JCo) and works through the steps you need to follow to set up a productive development environment.

Having said that, this chapter does not represent an exhaustive look at all JCo particulars. Rather, it focuses on specific concepts and development techniques that allow you to kick start your programming efforts. I am a great fan of hands-on development, especially when it is surrounded by minimal, although insightful, interference from conceptual programming discussions. If you have some experience with Java development, you may want to quickly review this section so that you can better understand JCo, and then you can get right into the tutorials.

This chapter looks at the following:

- Installing your Java development environment

- Installing the SAP Java Connector

- Detailing how to connect to SAP with JCo

- Building an application to connect to SAP

Working with the Java Development Environment

Unlike SAP, Java does not provide a conveniently preconfigured development environment similar to the features found in SAP's development platform, the ABAP Workbench. You can develop all of the examples in this book using a standard text editor, such as Microsoft Notepad or the various UNIX flavors of vi. Of course, most full-scale development efforts rely on some sort of integrated development environment (IDE).

IDEs are commonly designed around a specific programming language such as Visual Basic or Visual C++. You can use a number of different IDEs to develop Java applications, like Borland's JBuilder, Eclipse, and Sun's ONE Studio. In fact, SAP has moved strongly toward Eclipse as its Java IDE of choice. Eclipse is an open source product, and you can download it from http://www.eclipse.org.

Here are several distinct advantages of using such a development tool:

Project-based development: Although much of the development in this book relies on a small number of related Java objects, most projects span multiple Java libraries and classes. You are very likely to be working with classes specifically developed for your project team in order to ensure proper division of labor across team members. A project allows you to see all of the related and supporting Java objects within your development and easily navigate among these components.

Automatic library support: No one can be expected to remember all of the methods and attributes associated with the sundry Java objects used in a typical development effort. Many Java IDEs support the ability to automatically read a given class file's methods, properties, and attributes, and display those to a developer as they write code. Usually, these come in the form of a pop-up window, from which the correct property can be selected. This not only reduces the time it takes to write out method names and attributes, but it also allows the developer to focus more on the code and less on having to look up every individual method or parameter.

Syntax highlighting and format: Java, like any other programming language, can often become confusing to read as more code lines are added to an application. One key feature of a good IDE is that you can use color to highlight language-specific syntax such as variables, parameters, comments, and methods. Likewise, such IDEs let you automatically format your code based on the language specification, which gives greater readability not only to you, but to anyone who may need to modify the code in the future.

However, this book does not focus on development through an IDE. As with any other new subject, you will learn Java programming best by starting from first principles. Because these environments obscure much of the low-level development effort, IDEs tend to be somewhat frustrating for developers who are trying to learn the Java language. After you complete the sample applications in this book, you will have a strong understanding of basic Java development practices and be very comfortable with building code by hand.

Chapter 4

The initial Java development environment consists of several key pieces:

- Java Software Development Kit (JSDK)
- SAP's Java Connector (JCo)
- A text editor
- System variables
- Command-line interface (DOS-style command prompt)

The next section details how to install and configure the development environment.

Installing the Java Development Kit

Start by downloading the JSDK from Sun's official Java Website. Go to http://java.sun.com and navigate to the Java 2 Platform, Standard Edition (J2SE) download page.

The tutorials in this book were built using JSDK1.4. This version of the development kit has proven to be a very stable and robust release for developing enterprise applications. Of course, any development you do in JSDK1.4 is immediately forward compatible with the later releases of the JSDK.

I highly recommend that you stay current with the later releases of the development kit, if only so that you become familiar with the extended functionality provided in each. As mentioned earlier, the Enterprise and Standard Java 2 specifications are constantly evolving. Each successive release of these specifications provides a greater range and depth of Java application libraries that you can use in your development.

> **NOTE** *For the sake of brevity, this book focuses on development that uses the Microsoft Windows operating system. Each operating system, including those in the Windows and UNIX families, has slightly different methods for configuration and development. However, as long as you basically understand the operating system you are using, you should be able to accomplish the requirements outlined in this book on any platform.*

Once you have downloaded the development kit, you need to install it into a base location and define key system variables. Throughout the remainder of this chapter, the convention <JAVA_ROOT> is used to indicate the Java installation directory. When it installs the JSDK, the wizard provides you with a default location that, for the sake of simplified navigation, you should change to something like C:\JDK1.4. Another approach is to centralize all development tools under a common root directory, such as C:\dev. In this case, <JAVA_ROOT> would refer to C:\dev\jdk1.4.

The simplest way to define system variables under MS Windows is to use the autoexec.bat file, regardless of operating system version. When you set system variables in the autoexec.bat file, the variables are always set when the system boots up. A throwback to the old days of DOS, the PATH statement allows command execution of any application in the path string, regardless of current directory location. In order to compile and execute Java code from the command line, you must add the JSDK executable directory to the existing PATH statement in autoexec.bat.

First, locate and open autoexec.bat. You can find this file in the root drive of the operating system—typically C:\. Open this file using MS Notepad or the equivalent and locate the line that reads PATH=. This should be followed by several different directory locations, such as C:\Windows;C:\Windows\system. If the PATH statement does not appear here, then simply add the line PATH= to the last line of the file.

Now, append or prefix the directory <JAVA_ROOT>\bin to the end of the PATH statement. If there are preexisting directories in the PATH line, be sure to separate the first directory and the new Java directory with a semicolon. The PATH statement should now look something like this:

PATH= C:\JDK1.4\bin;C:\Windows;C:\Windows\system;

Loading the Java Connector

To complete the next step—downloading the JCo zip file from SAP's Online Service Website—go to http://service.sap.com/connectors and log on using your Online Service System (OSS) identifier and password. Select the SAP Java Connector and download the latest JCo 2.0 version. Once the download is complete, unzip the JCo files into a directory such as C:\JCO2, then navigate to this directory with a file browser. This directory contains two dynamic link libraries (DLLs) and a single Java Archive (JAR) file along with several subdirectories.

The DLL files must be copied into the system directory located underneath the Windows install directory. If you are running Windows NT or Windows 2000, that directory is likely C:\WINNT\System32 or C:\Windows\System32. When you copy these libraries into the system path, any Java application you write using JCo will be able to access these libraries.

> **NOTE** So why does the Java connector require DLL (non-Java) libraries? SAP originally created libraries in the C programming language to allow developers to make direct RFC calls to the R/3 system. SAP's JCo wraps those C libraries in Java to provide platform-native access into the R/3 system. When you use Java and C in this way, you are using a Java Native Interface (JNI). This simply means that the underlying connector structure is still based on the C programming language and that code must be ported in order to support different platforms or operating systems.

The next step is to make sure that the development environment installed in the previous section can use the `sapjco.jar` file. The JSDK provides a simple mechanism you can use to deploy optional-package classes (formerly known as standard extensions) that are automatically loaded by the Java Virtual Machine (JVM) when an application is compiled or executed. Optional packages are encapsulated in JAR files so that almost every one can be made an optional package.

> **NOTE** The file extension `*.jar` indicates that the file contains one or more compressed Java libraries or class files. The class file represents an individual Java object that can be executed within the JVM. You can use a standard unzip utility such as PowerArchiver or WinZip to open and view the contents of a JAR file, but you do not need to extract any of these files from the archive. Similar in nature to Microsoft's DLLs, the JAR format can be used to compress and deploy Java applications across multiple platforms.

The `sapjco.jar` file is located in the top-level directory to which the JCo zip file was extracted. Copy this file into the `<JAVA_ROOT>/jre/lib/ext` directory.

Along with the system files and JARs, the JCo zip contains extended documentation you should review—including tutorials, examples, and the Javadoc documentation. You can find this information on your local machine at `<JCO_INSTALL>\docs\jco\intro.html`.

So that's it! Your fully fledged development environment is up and running. The final step is to reboot your computer so that the changes you made to the `autoexec.bat` file will take effect.

Testing the Development Environment

When you initially deploy a Java development environment, you are apt to run into unforeseen glitches. However, once the environment is up and running, it is fairly simple to support and maintain. This maintenance includes adding new classes to the optional packages directory, compiling Java code, and copiously debugging when some newly compiled code doesn't run.

However, when you are trying to compile code, nothing is more frustrating than being told this at the outset:

`java.lang.NoClassDefFoundError:`

This is inevitably followed by a long string of forward slashes, acronyms, and abbreviations that are often vague and usually incomprehensible. The way to diagnose a development environment is to build a very basic Java application and attempt to run it.

If we think of SAP as a high-end German luxury automobile, whose maintenance and care can only be managed by specialists, Java would be like an American muscle car, just begging to be experimented on by teenagers and weekend warriors. Indeed, Java demands that you get down and dirty with the development effort, ensuring that a great deal of metaphorical keyboard grease has lodged itself under your fingernails before you have finished. Unlike SAP, which provides a fairly robust programming environment, the standard JSDK offers little in the way of development support. Certainly it provides all of the fundamental command line tools in addition to some helper applications and documented tutorials, it does not have many extended debugging tools, and has almost no visual components.

All of this says that Java development, while at times frustrating, is truly a fun and satisfying experience once most of the little niggling details have been worked out. So with that said, it's time to build the most famous tutorial application ever written, the dreaded `HelloWorld`! This exercise gives you a chance to not only test the development setup, but also learn how to use a text editor when you are developing Java applications.

If you haven't already done so, create a development directory somewhere on the file system, preferably something easy to remember like `C:\dev`. A good deal of code will be created, compiled, and run from this directory, so don't bury it too deeply in a labyrinth of multisyllabic path names and inadvertent `space` characters.

Go to Start Menu ➤ Run and enter `notepad.exe` in the `Open:` dialog. Once you have Notepad opened, select File ➤ Save As, and type in the file name `HelloWorld.java`. Save this into your development directory, that is, `C:\dev`. Check the file browser window to ensure that the file ends with the `.java` extension because Windows has a nasty habit of tacking on unsuitable file extensions just when you least expect it.

Are you ready to get into some code? Then enter the following into the text editor:

```java
/*
 * This Implements an Incredibly boring application
 * that Austin made me write.
 */
public class HelloWorld {
    public static void main(String[] args) {
        System.out.println("Hello, World!");
    }
}
```

Congratulations, you have just re-created the most mundane application in the known programming world! But will it work?

To find out, first bring up a command prompt. Go to Start Menu ➤ Run and enter `command.exe` in the `Open:` dialog. After you hit the `Enter` key, you should find yourself staring at a blank, black window, highly reminiscent of that DOS prompt you had hoped to leave behind over a decade ago.

Change into the development directory you created earlier and type in **javac**. After you hit the `Enter` key, the screen displays a list of command line options associated with the `javac.exe` tool. If you don't see the aforementioned list, and you get back something closer to `Command not found`, double-check the `PATH` statement in your `autoexec.bat` file. Ensure that both the base Java directory and the executable directory are included (i.e., `C:\JDK1.4\bin`). Otherwise, you are ready to compile the `HelloWorld` application.

NOTE *There are two essential command line tools for Java:* `java.exe` *and* `javac.exe`. `javac.exe` *lets you compile the application code into Java bytecode. Bytecode is the binary class library that can then be executed within a JVM.* `java.exe` *is the JVM runtime in which compiled bytecode is executed. Both tools have a number of command line options, including the ability to set your* `CLASSPATH` *at runtime, set system properties, and send text input that can be used by variables in the application.*

To compile the `HelloWorld` example, type **javac HelloWorld.java** at the command line and hit the `Enter` key. The application compiles and control returns to the command prompt. If you list the files in that directory now, you should see a new file called `HelloWorld.class`.

Finally, you are ready to execute the `HelloWorld` application. At the command line, type **java HelloWorld** and hit Enter. The screen displays the following printed line in the command console:

```
Hello, World!
```

This exercise might seem like somewhat of a cliché, but by compiling and executing the `HelloWorld` application, you have validated the installation of the JSDK and ensured that the Java development tools are available from any directory within the file system. It's time to dig into the main course—developing with SAP's Java Connector.

Connecting to SAP Using JCo

At this point, you have written your first official Java application (at least in the course of this book) and are probably itching to get started on some SAP development. In order to better understand the programming techniques you will be using, you need to walk through the high-level steps that successfully connecting to SAP using JCo requires.

Now that you have grasped the concepts surrounding SAP's JCo, actually using its application libraries will make a lot more sense.

Calling SAP R/3

The SAP JCo application libraries encapsulate a fairly complex set of connection components that enable two-way communication with the R/3 system. Because JCo relies on SAP's transactional methodology, it must be careful when translating from Java code to SAP functionality in order to guarantee data integrity. In order to do so, JCo requires that the following steps be taken, beginning with the Java representation of the Business Application Programming Interface (BAPI) and Remote Function Call (RFC) data structures.

> **CAUTION** *While reviewing the steps outlined in the following sections, keep in mind that JCo should never directly modify the SAP database, nor should it be used to call underlying R/3 function modules that do not have a BAPI or RFC interface. The JCo libraries represent a "best practice" approach to outside communication with the R/3 system based on the use of authorized RFCs and BAPIs. If using JCo seems frustrating, realize that you are keeping well within the boundaries of SAP's prescribed use of the system and are unlikely to jeopardize your company's license agreements with SAP.*

Step 1: Initialize the RFC Connection

Before it makes calls to the BAPI/RFC interface layer, the application must first be authenticated and authorized to use the SAP system. This means that you need to have an SAP user profile and password created for you in the target R/3 client. The initialization phase requires that the JCo application pass the hostname, client number, user ID, password, language key, and system number to SAP and allow it to authorize your use of the system. Once the application has initialized this connection, it can use and reuse that connection throughout the course of the program execution.

Step 2: Create a JCo Repository

An RFC or a BAPI call is made up of a series of related parameters, structures, and tables. These can either be coded manually, or the application can initialize a JCo repository based on the existing SAP interface catalog. This application needs to create a single repository for each R/3 system to which it needs to connect. Throughout the course of the tutorials in this book, only one R/3 client connection is necessary, but know that JCo is extensible enough to allow applications to cross-communicate between R/3 systems. The SAP connection created in the first step is used here to retrieve a repository from SAP.

Step 3: Retrieve a Specific Function from the Repository

In this step, the application retrieves metadata for a specific RFC or BAPI interface. Metadata does not represent actual data; rather it is the definition of data containers, whether that be field types, structures, or relationships. JCo makes it very easy to retrieve this metadata from an SAP functional interface such as an RFC or BAPI. Once an application has that metadata, it can readily populate the fields, structures, and tables to make a successful remote call to the R/3 system. Figure 4-1 shows a table and structure, along with their underlying fields, from the BAPI_MATERIAL_GETLIST interface.

JCo 101: Programming with SAP's Java Connector

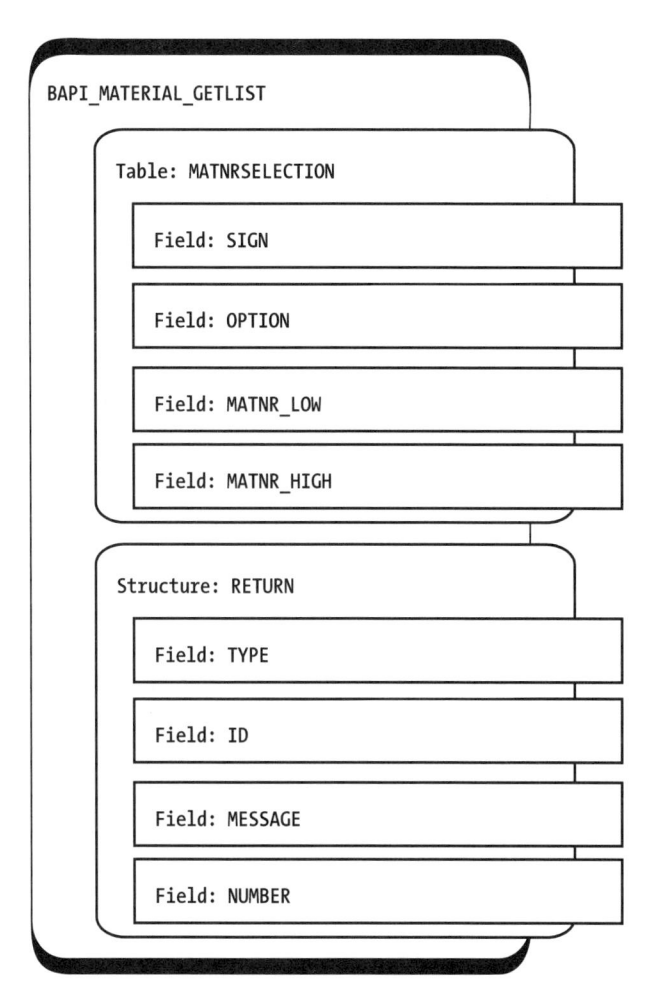

```
BAPI_MATERIAL_GETLIST
    Table: MATNRSELECTION
        Field: SIGN
        Field: OPTION
        Field: MATNR_LOW
        Field: MATNR_HIGH
    Structure: RETURN
        Field: TYPE
        Field: ID
        Field: MESSAGE
        Field: NUMBER
```

Figure 4-1. Structures and fields of a BAPI metadata interface

This may seem like a roundabout way to get to SAP, but consider the number of Web page forms you are asked to fill out every day. Although each form may have similar fields, rarely are they organized in exactly the same manner. If you attempt to fill out this form in the precise orientation of a previous form, the result is inevitably an error. Your brain automatically collates the unique metadata for a given form and then mentally fills in the fields with the appropriate data. In the same way, an application must explicitly retrieve the metadata from SAP for a given RFC or BAPI so that it can reference and populate those fields with the appropriate data. Likewise, this metadata describes the outbound fields and structures so that the application can understand responses from the R/3 system.

Step 4: Populate the Metadata Structures

The application now has a working interface model that it needs to make a successful RFC or BAPI call. This model can consist of single parameters, individual structures, or tables of related data, and often all three. In order to make sense of all this, JCo provides convenient Java objects to represent each component. However, it's your job to ensure that the data gets put into the right spots. To populate these structures, you must take information from whatever input has been defined (command line, Web form, and so on) and put that data into the correct fields of the application's SAP metadata structure.

This can be one of the more difficult concepts to visualize because you are limited to a text-based view of the data and related structures during development. Don't worry; the subject of populating these structures is reviewed exhaustively later in this chapter.

Step 5: Execute the Call to SAP

This step is fairly straightforward, but to take it, you will use all of the components mentioned in the previous steps. After executing a call to SAP, the application gets a return from the R/3 system containing any new transactional information (sales order confirmations, purchase orders, and so on) or master data (material descriptions, customer numbers, and so on).

Step 6: Read the SAP Return Structure

Once a call has been executed, the application is left with return records from SAP. These records can be used for several different purposes, including determining whether the call was made successfully, as well as retrieving any pertinent data sent from the R/3 system. Finally, the application decides what data needs to be displayed back to the end user, formats it as such, and terminates its execution.

With that said, it's time to begin to develop your first SAP application built with Java.

Building a Simple Application with JCo

This initial application is fairly straightforward because it is largely a continuation of the `HelloWorld` code that you developed earlier. It is a continuation because your first SAP program is also run from a command line, and its code is very similar in structure to `HelloWorld`.

> **TIP** You can find the code for this chapter in the Downloads section of the Apress Website (http://www.apress.com).

Using Basic Java Code Syntax

There are a number of different types of objects that you can build and utilize, and each has its place in the wide world of Java application development. You are going to start with that lowly, yet indispensable, Java executable class, which can readily be run from the command line with nothing more than a JVM on hand.

```
import com.sap.mw.jco.*;

public class MaterialList {
    public static void main(String[] args) {
        System.out.println("This class looks up materials.");
    }
}
```

This very simple piece of code forms the basis for the entire initial development effort. Similar to the HelloWorld application, if you were to copy, compile, and run this code, you would end up with a message in your command console that read:

```
This class looks up materials.
```

However, note that an import statement is included as the first line in the application class. This line allows your Java application to have complete access to the JCo application libraries and to treat these libraries as if they were entirely part of your development. In this case, you tell the application to make available any class libraries located in the com/sap/mw/jco/ directory of the sapjco.jar file.

Now, check out the following statement:

```
public class MaterialList
```

This line indicates the name of your Java class (MaterialList), and it is the filename used to compile and execute the application.

Finally, take a look at this statement:

```
public static void main(String[] args)
```

This line indicates that the class can be run from a command line and that it will retrieve any command line variables as part of the args array. The term main actually refers to a Java method in your application, and the parameter required to use it is an array of String objects. Java classes that contain a main method are assumed by the JVM to be executable, and the JVM automatically attempts to run any logic it finds within the main method block.

For more information on specific Java syntax, visit Sun's Java Website (http://developer.java.sun.com/developer/onlineTraining), which has excellent reference and tutorial materials.

Developing with JCo

In Java, every block of code must be contained with curly brackets; {...}. This tells the compiler where to differentiate between various methods and the Java class itself. Notice that the following code snippet contains two sets of these brackets, one within the other. The outer brackets encompass the entire class, with the exception of import statements and comment lines.

> **NOTE** *The following JCo development assumes that your company has implemented both SAP Materials Management (MM) and Sales and Distribution (SD) modules. If this is not the case, Appendix B details the creation of custom tables, structures, and RFC interfaces that replace the BAPI function calls used throughout the book. For example, rather than using* BAPI_MATERIAL_GETLIST, *you use a custom RFC called* Z_RFC_MATERIAL_GETLIST. *Because these interfaces are implemented with the same parameter, structure, and table names as their BAPI counterparts, you simply need to replace the function name with the appropriate custom RFC.*

```
import com.sap.mw.jco.*;

public class MaterialList {
    public static void main(String[] args) {
        System.out.println("This class looks up materials.");
        // You will adding code here to build your first SAP Java object
    }
}
```

Inside the class brackets, you will find methods, variables, and programming logic. Any programming logic added here will be run once and only once when the class is loaded. This is in contrast to the main method, which is called each time the class is executed after it loads.

> **NOTE** Single-line comments are prefixed with a // and comment blocks by /* (open) and */ (close). Java also provides special syntax for Javadoc comments. These comments are designed to be used in generated documentation to detail the use of a given class library. Javadoc comment blocks start with /** and end with */. These comments are used in generated documentation to explain the use of a given class library, method, and so on.

The end of this chapter provides a more in-depth look at using class level variables and programming. For now, all of the upcoming code should be added to the main method block of your Java class.

Defining Java Variables

To define Java variables, you must first define a series of unique variables that the application will use. Java requires that you define and initialize each variable before you use it in the body of the code. In other words, you can define variables anywhere within your code as long as you do so before you attempt to use said variables. But for the sake of readability, these variables should be defined at the beginning of the application's main method.

```java
public static void main(String[] args) {
// These are standard Java String variables
    final String SAP_CLIENT ="100";
    final String USER_ID ="username";
    final String PASSWORD = "password";
    final String LANGUAGE = "E";
    final String HOST_NAME = "hostname";
    final String SYSTEM_NUMBER = "00";
    String matSearch;

// These are JCo specific variables
    JCO.Client aConnection;
    IRepository aRepository;
```

Broadly speaking, you have defined two different types of variables in this example. The first set, initialized as String variables, are standard text strings. String is actually a Java object that the standard Java 2 development libraries provide. Java might seem a little confusing in that a variable can be defined as a data type (int, byte, boolean, and so on) or as a Java object (String, BufferedReader, and so on). By convention, the first letter of a data type is lowercase, and the first letter of an object is uppercase. So, from the previous example, String is a Java object rather than a data type. For now don't worry too much about the distinction.

The second variable type defined here is specific to the JCo API. The last two variables, JCO.Client and Irepository, are both part of the sapjco.jar file that was installed earlier. These variables are used to access the JCo connector, and, through the Java wrapper, the underlying C libraries previously mentioned.

Lastly, note that the first six variables have been prefixed with the word final. This is the Java equivalent of defining a constant variable, one that cannot be changed by any other operation in the application. In this case, the SAP system variables have been defined as constant, as have the username and password required by the R/3 system for authentication. When this code is added to your development, be sure to replace the text strings between the double quotes ("...") with data specific to your R/3 system. If you have any questions regarding what those variables should be defined as, contact your BASIS administrator for the required information.

Other variables are defined throughout the body of the application, but there is a rationale behind keeping those specific variables at the top of the code.

Connecting to SAP

You will recall the previous somewhat lengthy discussion on how JCo connects to SAP conceptually. It's time to take a look at how simple it actually is to implement such a connection within the application.

```
try {
    aConnection = JCO.createClient(SAP_CLIENT,
                                   USER_ID,
                                   PASSWORD,
                                   LANGUAGE,
                                   HOST_NAME,
                                   SYSTEM_NUMBER);
    aConnection.connect();
```

In the variable declarations, aConnection has already been defined as an instance of the JCO.Client class. This class maintains the information you need to authenticate a user in the SAP system and provide a connection to the Java application. In this code, the aConnection variable is initialized as the Java instance returned by a call to the `JCO.createClient()` method. This simply means that the application has passed certain parameters, in the form of the previously defined R/3 system variables, to a method that exists as part of the JCO library class.

Having initialized aConnection, the application can now access that object's connect() method. The connect() method attempts to authenticate this instance against the R/3 system using the parameters passed to JCO.createClient().

The try { statement at the beginning of this code snippet indicates that an exception may be thrown somewhere within the following code block. An exception is Java's methodology for handling expected errors in a nice clean way that doesn't automatically terminate the entire application.

In this case, if the application were physically unable to reach an SAP R/3 system across the network, an exception would be thrown that indicated the problem. Due to the vagaries of network connectivity, this is definitely an error that should be caught by the application. Java's exception handling allows the class to retrieve and legibly display this error to the application's user. A try { block must always be followed by:

```
}
catch (JCO.Exception ex) {
    System.out.println("Call to SAP has failed.");
    ex.printStackTrace();
}
```

As documented in the SAP JCo API, JCO.Client.connect() throws an instance of JCO.Exception when an exception occurs. This exception can provide messaging back to the user as to the nature of the problem, or it can be used as a debugging tool by the developer. Either way, the exception must be handled in the application otherwise the class cannot be compiled correctly and can never be executed.

> **NOTE** *The* ex.printStackTrace() *statement provides a convenient mechanism for writing the entire exception body to a command line. Although not a good technique for indicating a problem to the end user, the* printStackTrace() *method can be an invaluable tool throughout the application debugging process.*

aConnection is now authorized to access the RFC/BAPI layer in the SAP system. The next section details how to use this instance in order to retrieve a JCo repository object.

Initializing the SAP Repository

Ironically, the conceptual complexity represented by a JCo repository is not reflected in its programmatic implementation. The following single statement is the total sum of work required to retrieve a JCO.Repository from SAP:

```
aRepository = new JCO.Repository("SAPRep", aConnection);
```

The application has initialized the aRepository variable, which is a new instance of the JCO.Repository class. When it initialized the aConnection object, the application called a method on another Java class and used the return from that method to populate an object. This time, you create an instance of the JCO.Repository class by relying on its default constructor. A class's default constructor refers to a basic set of parameters (or no parameters at all) that are used to directly instantiate an instance of that same class. In doing so, you replicate that Java class and make it available for use within an application.

Here, you used the default constructor of JCO.Repository, passing two required parameters, to give your application a fully implemented instance of the SAP metadata repository. The first parameter is a simple text string, indicated by the use of double quotes ("..."). This text string defines the name of your repository and is an arbitrary identifier that can be used later in the application.

More importantly, the second parameter passed to the default constructor is the same aConnection object that your application had earlier initialized and authenticated against the SAP system. You are using the aConnection object to tell SAP that you are an authorized user of the system and that you have the rights required to retrieve the metadata repository.

Your application is now ready to use this repository to retrieve the metadata required for a specific RFC or BAPI call to SAP.

Retrieving the RFC Metadata Interface

The metadata structure is the format in which you must put the inbound data before SAP can understand it. To better understand this interface, open the R/3 Function Builder in SAP, choose a BAPI, such as BAPI_MATERIAL_GETLIST, and display the various parameters, structures, and tables that are available for getting data in and out of SAP. The combination of these components within the BAPI constitutes the metadata interface. In order to successfully call this BAPI, your application must add the inbound data to the appropriate fields, just as in the example of filling out forms through a Web browser.

As in the case with repositories, the explanation tends to be more cumbersome than the code. So here is the code:

```
IFunctionTemplate functionTemplate =
    aRepository.getFunctionTemplate("BAPI_MATERIAL_GETLIST");

JCO.Function function = new JCO.Function(functionTemplate);
```

The first line uses the repository that was initialized in the previous code snippet to retrieve a function template object (IFunctionTemplate) for an R/3 BAPI called BAPI_MATERIAL_GETLIST.

Once you have that function template, your application can create a JCO.Function object that gives it the ability to communicate with SAP using that specific BAPI. The second line of code uses the default constructor of JCO.Function to instantiate an instance of the JCO.Function class, called function.

Before moving into the heart of this application, take a look at the code you have written up to this point:

```
import com.sap.mw.jco.*;
public class MaterialList {
    public static void main(String[] args) {

    final String SAP_CLIENT ="100";
    String USER_ID ="username";
    String PASSWORD = "password";
    String LANGUAGE = "E";
    String HOST_NAME = "hostname";
    String SYSTEM_NUMBER = "00";
    String matSearch;
    JCO.Client aConnection;
    IRepository aRepository;

    System.out.println("This class looks up materials.");
    try {
        aConnection = JCO.createClient(SAP_CLIENT,
                                        USER_ID,
                                        PASSWORD,
                                        LANGUAGE,
                                        HOST_NAME,
                                        SYSTEM_NUMBER);
        aConnection.connect();
        aRepository = new JCO.Repository("SAPRep", aConnection);

        IFunctionTemplate functionTemplate =
            aRepository.getFunctionTemplate("BAPI_MATERIAL_GETLIST");
```

```
            JCO.Function function = new JCO.Function(functionTemplate);
// We will be adding more code here shortly
        }
    catch (Exception ex) {
        System.out.println("Call to SAP has failed.");
        }
      }
}
```

Feel free to copy this code into your text editor, replace the SAP system variables, and compile the application. If you have added the appropriate JAR files to the optional packages directory, including the JCo libraries, the application should compile without a problem. Now run the application from the command line and you should again get the message:

```
This class looks up materials.
```

That nothing else happened is a very good sign because it indicates that you successfully connected to SAP and retrieved the metadata interface for BAPI_MATERIAL_GETLIST. Moving right along, it's time to actually use that connection for something meaningful.

Adding Data to the SAP Function Call

At this point, the situation becomes a little trickier. The challenge in formatting and sending structured data under the restrictions of a two-dimensional code syntax can be confusing, at best. That is not to say that Java or object-oriented development is two-dimensional or even that such a term is appropriate to describe a programming language. Rather, the way you construct that code is two-dimensional; you are limited to entering text into an editor with no strong visual reference to guide you. Perhaps the future of computing will give you the ability to realize three-dimensional development, physically building such data structures in a virtual environment. Until then, you are forced to labor under these limitations with a decent, although limited, two-dimensional metaphor for modeling fairly complex field, structure, and table relationships.

The BAPI that has been chosen illustrates the use of populating a table with data as a mechanism to call SAP. The BAPI, BAPI_MATERIAL_GETLIST, contains several different tables that can be used to retrieve information for a highly select number of materials. In order to get a useful response back from SAP, your application needs to populate a single table—MATNRSELECTION.

Again, if you look at BAPI_MATERIAL_GETLIST in SAP's Function Builder, you find a table called MATNRSELECTION. This table allows you to specify a sign, an option, and a full or partial material number in order to get back a list of matching materials.

Even though you already know the table name, you must first retrieve a list of tables from the function object, and then specify the table you want to use in your application.

```
JCO.ParameterList tabParams = function.getTableParameterList();
JCO.Table materials = tabParams.getTable("MATNRSELECTION");
```

The first line creates a new instance of the object JCO.ParameterList with the variable name tabParams. In order to instantiate this object, the application uses the function instance that was created earlier using the function template for BAPI_MATERIAL_GETLIST. The method that is called on the function object is getTableParameterList(), which does not require your application to send any parameters, hence the empty open/close parentheses. This method gives the application a representation of all the tables available to it through the BAPI interface for BAPI_MATERIAL_GETLIST.

Next, create an object representation of the specific table you need to populate in order to call the BAPI. You have already used SAP's Function Builder to determine that the application must populate the table MATNRSELECTION in order to get the appropriate data from the R/3 system. Now, you instantiate a JCO.Table object named materials by calling the getTable() method on the tabParams object created in the previous line. In this case, getTable() requires that your application pass the name of the R/3 table to represent, so you send it the MATNRSELECTION table name.

What you end up with is a Java object representation of all the fields available in the MATNRSELECTION table as well as Java methods for appending, inserting, and deleting rows from this table. The power of object-oriented development is that you don't need to manually code any of these methods; the JCo application libraries provide these for you automatically.

You are almost ready to populate the SAP table with your own data, but first a small digression. The following code may seem a little out of place when you are right in the middle of calling SAP, but let's take a look at it.

```
if (args.length == 0)
    matSearch = "*";
else
    matSearch = args[0];
```

69

If you recall earlier, this application is designed to take a search value entered on the command line and use it to retrieve specific materials records from SAP. If you revisit the `public static void main(String[] args)`, you see that `args` is a variable specified as an array of `String` objects. That you have developed a Java class executable from the command line means that your `main` method must specify an array of `String` objects as a required parameter. Any values entered after the class file name in the command line Java execution are automatically entered in this array of `String` objects as an element. So that if the command line statement looks like this:

```
java MaterialList1 value1 value2 value3 value4
```

you will be able to use `value1`, `value2`, and so on as data within the application, made available through the `args` array.

The previous code snippet demonstrates your application's ability to loop through the `args` array and use whatever entry is found in the first element as the material search variable. The `if... else` block is necessary to ensure that you don't attempt to retrieve data from an empty array. If you do not enter any values on the command line, the array will be empty when the application executes, and the JVM will throw an exception and terminate if it tries to access the first element of the empty array. The `if... else` block allows you to specify a default value of * if the array is empty (meaning the length of the array equals 0) or to use the first element as your search value if the array has been populated from the command line.

This simply allows the application to have a little more flexibility. For the most part, executing the application without any values on the command line should not be a problem. However, if your R/3 system contains a massive number of material records, I highly recommend that you limit your searches during development and testing. Otherwise, you might end up with a very angry BASIS administrator breathing down your neck for wasting valuable resources on the SAP application server.

So, you finally get to add data to the `MATNRSELECTION` table using pure Java code. Exciting, isn't it? Well, this is what it takes:

```
materials.appendRow();
materials.setRow(0);
materials.setValue("I", "SIGN");
materials.setValue("CP", "OPTION");
materials.setValue(matSearch, "MATNR_LOW");
```

You start by using the `appendRow()` method on the `materials` object to add a new row to your table. Next, using the `setRow()` method, you set the row pointer to make sure you are populating the correct row in the table. Of course, because you only have one row, this is an extraneous step, but good development practices always start in the prototype. Now, you get to use the setValue() method three times to populate the required fields in the current row. setValue() requires two String parameters in the form of ("field value", "field name"). This may seem a little backward, so don't be surprised if you get the following runtime error message.

```
Field XXX not a member of BAPIMATRAM
```

If you do, double-check the order of parameters you used when you were calling the setValue() method for the appropriate field in the error message.

The SIGN field can be one of two values: I for inclusive or E for exclusive. The distinction is that, dependent on your search options, I returns every record matching those options, and E returns those records that do not match those options.

The OPTION field allows you to specify various matching parameters, which are based on standard R/3 search options when you are using SAP GUI. These include GE for "greater than or equal to," LE for "less than or equal to," and so on. This application uses CP for "contains pattern": this tells SAP to match any material identifier against the value you send it. This allows the application to use the asterisk, *, as a valid search criteria so that you can retrieve all material records in the R/3 system if you need to.

The final field in this example specifies the low number range of materials you would like to search against. The MATNR_LOW field refers to the unique material number assigned to every record in the R/3 material master. SAP allows you to add both a low and a high range, as in the standard SAP GUI search functionality, in order to better limit a given search. However, for the sake of simplicity, this application uses only the low range in order to perform the search against the entire set of material master records in the R/3 database.

You have finally arrived at the moment of truth! Let's make that call to SAP.

```
aConnection.execute(function);
```

Do you remember the aConnection object that we used earlier to authenticate the user profile in SAP? Here it is again, only this time the application is using a method called execute() and passing in the function object that has now been populated with the required table and field data. Figure 4-2 illustrates the nested structures and fields of a BAPI interface represented by the JCo API.

Chapter 4

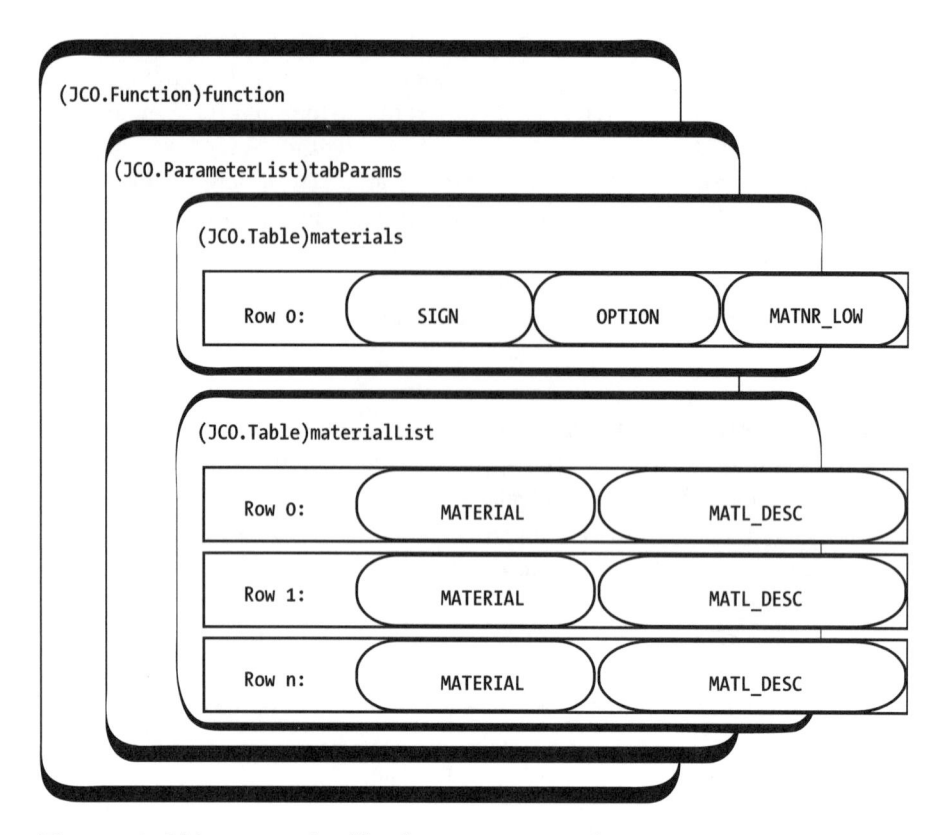

Figure 4-2. Objects contained by the `JCO.Function` *class*

Barring any unforeseen complications, it's time to take a look at the material records, if any, that SAP has returned to the application. Just as you used a series of objects and method calls to represent the inbound R/3 table in the application, you must do the same here to represent the outbound table and field data.

```
JCO.ParameterList resultParams = function.getExportParameterList();
JCO.Table materialList =
    function.getTableParameterList().getTable("MATNRLIST");
```

Bear in mind, after calling the `execute()` method, the `function` object gets automatically updated via JCo with any and all return information from the BAPI interface. Again, JCo provides the methods your application needs to pull data out of the `function` object and displays it back to the end user.

The first line in this code snippet instantiates an instance of the `JCO.ParameterList` class, which has been called `resultParams`, using the `getExportParameterList()` method in the `function` object. This gives your application access to all of the outbound return structures from the `BAPI_MATERIAL_GETLIST` interface. You will use this object to ensure a successful call to SAP, pull out specified tables, and retrieve any valid material data. For now, let's just get at the material data, rather than worry about any system messages SAP might have sent back.

Using a series of inline method calls, you can retrieve an object representation of the MATNRLIST table. How do you know that you need the MATNRLIST table? Again, by going back to the Function Builder in SAP, you can verify that this is the correct table for displaying the list of materials that matched the search criteria. Notice that Java allows your application to chain method calls together, using the results of one method to feed the parameters of the next.

Here, you first use the getTableParameterList() method in the function object to retrieve a JCO.ParameterList object. However, rather than explicitly instantiating another Java variable as a ParameterList class, the application calls the getTable() method on the implied ParameterList object, passing in MATNRLIST as its sole parameter. This may seem a little confusing at first, but it does make for more legible code in the long run.

> **CAUTION** *Take care when chaining method calls because Java places no real limitation on the number you can nest in a single line. If you use them incorrectly, you can end up with some nightmarishly long lines that are virtually impossible to decipher!*

The materialList table object is populated and ready for some action. The next step is to loop through the rows in that table and display the field data in each row. Unfortunately, this is a little trickier than it sounds, so bear with me.

```
if (materialList.getNumRows() > 0) {
    do {
        System.out.println("<<<**--------Basic Material Record--------**>>>");
        for (JCO.FieldIterator fI = materialList.fields();
            fI.hasMoreElements();)
        {
            JCO.Field tabField = fI.nextField();
            System.out.println(tabField.getName() +
                            (":\t") +
                            tabField.getString());
        }
        System.out.println("\n");
    }
    while(materialList.nextRow() == true);
}
else {
    System.out.println("Sorry, couldn't find any materials");
}
```

You start off with an `if...else` block, whose basic function is to figure out whether or not SAP has returned any rows of data within the MATNRLIST table.

```
if (materialList.getNumRows() > 0) {
    ....
}
else {
      System.out.println("Sorry, couldn't find any materials");
}
```

To check whether SAP has returned any data, your application simply calls the `getNumRows()` method of the `materialList` object and ensures that the result is greater than zero. If `getNumRows()` returns a result less than or equal to zero, the else block displays the message "Sorry, couldn't find any materials" and the application terminates.

The next block is a `do...while` loop, whose function is to execute a continuous loop until the result from `materialList.nextRow()` does not equal true.

```
do {
    ....
}
   while(materialList.nextRow() == true);
```

The `nextRow()` method has two functions within this application. Whenever the `nextRow()` method is called, the row number in the `materialList` table object is automatically incremented. The application's first pass in your do loop uses the row found at position zero within the table. The while statement tells the application to increment the row position and continues executing the loop.

This brings you to the second function of the `nextRow()` method—the one that makes sure the application is still within the boundaries of the table. The JVM would throw an exception if your code attempted to access a nonexistent row within the `materialList` table. Therefore, because the `nextRow()` method returns a Boolean value of TRUE or FALSE depending on the existence of the incremented row, you simply check that the return is TRUE and allow the loop to continue. When the application hits the end of the table, the `nextRow()` method returns a value of FALSE, and the application seamlessly exits from the `do...while` loop.

Nested within the `do...while` loop, you find another type of control block available in Java—the for loop.

```
for (JCO.FieldIterator fI = materialList.fields();
     fI.hasMoreElements();)
{
    ....
}
```

JCo 101: Programming with SAP's Java Connector

A for loop allows your application to initialize a variable, describe the termination condition, and increment a variable, if necessary. Each of these expressions within your for declaration must be separated by a semicolon, even if you decide not to use an incrementing expression, as is the case in this code.

In your for loop, you initialize a new variable called fI of the type JCO.FieldIterator class using the fields() method of the materialList object. Think of the FieldIterator object as a representation of a single row in the table. Using the fI object, your application loops through all of the fields available to it in a given row of data. Don't worry, I will recap this madness momentarily, so just hang on if this doesn't seem to make sense.

The second expression in your for loop is a call to the hasMoreElements() method on the fI object. hasMoreElements() is a standard method name used by most iterator-type Java classes. Again, the purpose of this method is twofold because it not only checks to see whether more records exist (by returning a Boolean of TRUE or FALSE), but it also increments the iteration element, effectively taking you to the next row in the table. Unlike your use of the nextRow() method, which assumes that the application has started at position zero, the hasMoreElements() method always starts at the zero element within the iteration until it has run through each element in the iterator.

> **NOTE** *When dealing with table representations in Java, always make sure you know at what element in the table you are pointing. Most table objects allow you to both increment to the next row in a table and explicitly point to the row using an index value. An enumeration or iterator in Java is a very different beast, usually requiring your application to loop through elements sequentially, until you find the one you need. The only real control you have over an iterator or enumeration is the ability to jump back to the zero element using a* reset() *method.*

After all that, you finally get to pull out some real SAP data!

```
JCO.Field tabField = fI.nextField();
System.out.println(tabField.getName() +
                  (":\t") +
                  tabField.getString());
```

The first line initializes a JCO.Field object call tabField using the nextField() method of the FieldIterator object. Remember, fI contains a list of field names and field values for a single, given row of data in the MATNRLIST table. The JCO.Field class encapsulates methods that allow your application to display the field name and field value for a single field retrieved from the iterator. In this case, you use a System.out.println() statement to display this data back to the command line console. However, in later chapters in this book, you display this information in several different fashions including in a Web browser.

Finally, I have included several other System.out.println() statements in order to better format the output for display. At the start of your do...while loop, the application prints out a simple header line to differentiate between material records.

```
System.out.println("<<<**--------Basic Material Record--------**>>>");
```

I have also added a "new line" directive after the for loop to add some space after each material record.

```
System.out.println("\n");
```

> **NOTE** *Java uses standard escape characters to allow for special formatting. These are implemented using a backslash (\) followed by a single character that indicates the desired special character or formatting. In this example, you have used \n to provide a hard return or new line and the \t to output a tab to the command console. Notice how these escape characters can be intermixed within text strings, but they must always be encased in double quotes.*

If everything has gone according to plan, you should be able to compile this little application, run it from the command line, and get the following output:

```
<<<**--------Basic Material Record--------**>>>

MATERIAL:          Material1
MATL_DESC:         The first material in this SAP system
MATERIAL_EXTERNAL:
MATIERAL_GUID:
MATERIAL_VERSION:

<<<**--------Basic Material Record--------**>>>
MATERIAL:          Material2
MATL_DESC:         The second material in this SAP system
MATERIAL_EXTERNAL:
MATIERAL_GUID:
MATERIAL_VERSION:
....
```

Remember, when you run the application from the command line, you can specify a search parameter, to better limit your results:

```
java MaterialList1 <search term>
```

Your completed application should now look like this:

```
import com.sap.mw.jco.*;
public class MaterialList {
  public static void main(String[] args) {

    final String SAP_CLIENT ="100";
    final String USER_ID ="username";
    final String PASSWORD = "password";
    final String LANGUAGE = "E";
    final String HOST_NAME = "hostname";
    final String SYSTEM_NUMBER = "00";
    String matSearch;
    JCO.Client aConnection;
    IRepository aRepository;
```

```java
            System.out.println("This class looks up materials.");
            try {
              aConnection = JCO.createClient(SAP_CLIENT,
                                            USER_ID,
                                            PASSWORD,
                                            LANGUAGE,
                                            HOST_NAME,
                                            SYSTEM_NUMBER);
              aConnection.connect();
              aRepository = new JCO.Repository("SAPRep", aConnection);

              IFunctionTemplate functionTemplate =
                  aRepository.getFunctionTemplate("BAPI_MATERIAL_GETLIST");

              JCO.Function function = new JCO.Function(functionTemplate);
              JCO.ParameterList tabParams = function.getTableParameterList();
              JCO.Table materials = tabParams.getTable("MATNRSELECTION");

              if (args.length == 0)
                  matSearch = "*";
              else
                  matSearch = args[0];

              materials.appendRow();
              materials.setRow(0);
              materials.setValue("I", "SIGN");
              materials.setValue("CP", "OPTION");
              materials.setValue(matSearch, "MATNR_LOW");
              aConnection.execute(function);

              JCO.ParameterList resultParams = function.getExportParameterList();
              JCO.Table materialList =
                  function.getTableParameterList().getTable("MATNRLIST");

              if (materialList.getNumRows() > 0) {
                  do {
                      System.out.println("<<<**-------Basic Material Record--------**>>>");
                      for (JCO.FieldIterator fI = materialList.fields();
                           fI.hasMoreElements();)
                        {
                          JCO.Field tabField = fI.nextField();
                          System.out.println(tabField.getName() +
                                              (":\t") +
                                              tabField.getString());
```

```
                    }
            System.out.println("\n");
        }
            while(materialList.nextRow() == true);
    }
    else {
            System.out.println("Sorry, couldn't find any materials");
        }
    }
    catch (Exception ex) {
        System.out.println("Call to SAP has failed.");
    }
    }
}
```

Cleaning Up the Application

Before we move on to the next chapter, let's take some time to clean up the code. Doing so will make the code easier and more effective when you go to reuse it in upcoming examples. In this section, you will also take a look at some advanced Java development techniques that enhance the application and introduce some valuable object-oriented programming concepts.

Employing Various Variables

When you look at your existing Java application for SAP, you see that certain variables are used repeatedly throughout the code, while others are used only once or twice. Java recognizes that certain variables might be required by all programming logic within the application, and thus it allows you to elevate key variables from local to class or member level variables.

A *local variable* is one that is declared within the body of a method, such as that of the main method within your application. All local variables can only be used within that method, and two variables of the same name that appear in different methods are always independent of one another.

You can use class or member variables universally throughout your Java class, regardless of the method that is using them. You can consider using member variables to maintain the state of the class because these variables are always initialized before any methods can be called within a class.

```java
public class MyClass {
  public static String myString1;
  public static void main(String[] args) {
    ...
  }
  private static void myMethod1() {
    ...
  }
}
```

This code shows the declaration of a member variable called `myString1` followed by an implementation of this class's `main` method and another method called `myMethod1`. The advantage to using a member variable is that both methods can access this variable, each reading and setting it according to that method's internal logic. In this way, you can determine certain overall class states based on the information contained within a member variable that is accessible by all methods within that class.

Another reason to use member variables is if you want to create visibility around key properties that future developers might need to readily modify. One example of a high profile value is the set of SAP system variables you used earlier to authenticate the application against the R/3 application server.

```java
import com.sap.mw.jco.*;
public class MaterialList {
  public static final String SAP_CLIENT ="100";
  public static final String USER_ID ="username";
  public static final String PASSWORD = "password";
  public static final String LANGUAGE = "E";
  public static final String HOST_NAME = "hostname";
  public static final String SYSTEM_NUMBER = "00";
  private static JCO.Client aConnection;
  private static IRepository aRepository;

  public static void main(String[] args) {
    ...
  }
}
```

So, you have now elevated a bunch of variables that were local to the `main` method and made them available across the entire class. Why did you go to all that trouble?

First off, if you look at the preceding code, you will notice that all of the SAP system variables have been moved and that each line has been prefixed with `public static`. When dealing with variables and methods in Java, you have a great deal of control over who has access to what and how each variable or method can be used. Huh?

Recall that you have initialized, instantiated, and constructed many different JCo objects within the application in order to successfully call SAP. Each time you did so, the application used a method or constructor that had been designated specifically for that use by the JCo application libraries. If the developers of JCo had not wanted you to use a given method, they could have easily restricted you from doing so. Indeed, if you were to look at the source code for the JCo libraries, you would see a number of different variables and methods that are literally inaccessible to this application.

The power of object-oriented development in Java is that various classes, built at varying times by a variety of developers, can happily coexist and interact with one another to create cohesive applications. As a developer of application libraries, you would very likely architect your classes in such a way that you optimized their use by other developers and made it easier to refactor and modify them over time. With such considerations in mind, certain classes and methods in these libraries would only need to be accessible by other classes within the same set of application libraries and not by anyone else. In order to ensure proper use of these classes and methods, Java lets you restrict and regulate access to them through several mechanisms.

Any other class can access a variable declared as `public`, whether that class exists as part of the same application package or anywhere else. Variables declared `private` are only accessible by methods and logic within the current class and are considered invisible to external classes.

This application uses a mix of `public` and `private` variable declarations to illustrate their use within an application. However, were you to generate the Java documentation around this class, you would see the SAP system variables declared `public` as a documented part of the class, whereas the `private` variables would be hidden. This allows the developer to display key variables in the class as a means of describing the use of that class to future developers. In this case, should another developer decide to use this class to call a different SAP system, she would see that the system variables are part of this class and be able to modify it appropriately.

> **CAUTION** *For the sake of this initial example, the system variables have been hard-coded into your class; this means that you must manually modify the application at the code level to call a different SAP system. This practice is highly discouraged because it makes maintenance and support of your applications nearly impossible. In Chapter 5, you will take a look at a way to externalize application attributes so that both developers and users can easily configure your applications.*

The `JCO.Client` and `IRepository` object variables have also been moved to the member level, but for slightly different reasons. Both of these variables have been declared `private` and are only used within the application class. This is because your application uses the `aConnection` instance to maintain an authenticated connection to SAP and the `aRepository` instance to retrieve interfaces from a single version of the SAP repository. You could declare and initialize new local variables each time the application needed to use these classes, but this would add unnecessary overhead to your application and increase the load on the R/3 application server.

Building Classy Methods

At this point, you have only used one method in the application, the `main` method. However, in order to streamline your application, Java lets you break out code blocks into different methods and call those methods from within the `main` method.

Just as with variables, you can use declaration statements to control access at both the method and class level. The current class you are working on must be declared `public` so that the JVM can execute it. However, you also might have created other classes to contain application logic essential to this application package but useless or even dangerous to the outside world.

> **NOTE** *In Java development, an application library is usually comprised of a single package or a group of packages. A Java package is simply a mechanism used to describe a hierarchy of classes, in a directory-style structure. Package names are specified at the top of a Java class, before any other code appears and takes the form of* `package myLib.class;`. *This indicates that the class must be stored in the* `myLib/class` *directory when the library is compiled and archived. Similarly, in order to use this class, you must import that package into your application using the statement* `import myLib.class.*;`.

All of the JCo methods used in this application first had to be declared `public` within the JCo packages or you would not have had access to them. On the other hand, if those methods had been declared `private`, you would not have been able to access or even see them within the Java documentation.

Only classes within the same package can use a class that is not declared `public`. These types of classes are typically used to provide underlying programming logic, which, in turn, supports higher-level, publicly accessible classes within the same package.

In the same way, methods declared `public` are generally accessible by any other class or method, depending on whether the class itself has been declared public. Declaring a method as private means that only other methods within the class itself can access this method. Even if the class is public, a private method declaration restricts the use of that method to solely within that class. Likewise, a method declared public within a class that is not means that only other classes within the same package can access this method, and the outside world cannot access it.

So how do you determine when and whether new methods are appropriate? If you look at the current application, you see three distinct phases within the execution:

1. Authenticate a connection to SAP.

2. Retrieve an SAP interface repository.

3. Call a specific BAPI interface.

Instead of bundling all of this logic into the main method block, you can easily create new methods to house the logic contained within each step.

```
import com.sap.mw.jco.*;
public class MaterialList {
// Menber variables
...
private static void createConnection() {
  try {
    aConnection = JCO.createClient(SAP_CLIENT,
                                   USER_ID,
                                   PASSWORD,
                                   LANGUAGE,
                                   HOST_NAME,
                                   SYSTEM_NUMBER);
    aConnection.connect();
    }
    catch (Exception ex) {
      System.out.println("Failed to connect to SAP system");
    }
  }
  public static void main(String[] args) {
    ...
  }
}
```

You have now added a new method called createConnection() that allows the application to authenticate a connection against the R/3 application server. Notice that your application is using the aConnection variable without having to initialize the instance within the body of the createConnection() method. If you declare this variable at the class level, any method within your application can use and modify the aConnection object.

The second method you need to add will retrieve an SAP repository for the current application. Again, as with the createConnection() method, this method uses a previously declared class-level variable so that the repository can be used throughout the application.

```
private static void retrieveRepository() {
  try {
    aRepository = new JCO.Repository("SAPRep", aConnection);
  }
  catch (Exception ex) {
    System.out.println("Failed to retrieve SAP repository");
  }
}
```

As you can see, both of these methods have been declared as private static. In much the same way that variables can be declared at different levels of access, so too can methods. That both of these methods are private means that only another method within your current class can call them—namely the main method. You declare these as private because no external class should be able to use this class to simply gain a connection or repository to SAP. Rather, your class is designed specifically to call the interface BAPI_MATERIAL_GETLIST and display the results back to the end user. The connection and repository instances are to be used for this purpose and this purpose only, hence the declaration of those methods as private.

Should you decide to make those methods available within your own set of application libraries, you could declare them as package methods. If you needed those methods to be generally available to the world, they would need to be declared public.

You need to call these two methods in order to complete the first two steps of your application. One option is to call these methods within the main method just prior to when the application needs the aConnection and aRepository objects initialized. In the short term, this is perfectly acceptable, but I prefer to take a long-term view if you want to reuse this class in future development.

Although you do not need to fully understand the intricacies of thread behavior in the JVM, you need to be aware of how and when certain types of objects are initialized and used. The JCo object carries just such concerns with it because this is the class designed to maintain the SAP session. If you misuse this class, you place an unnecessary burden on the R/3 application server and leave your BASIS administrator the onerous task of having to clean up system resources in your wake.

A major reason behind declaring and initializing the connection and repository variables at the class level is to ensure that one and only one instance of each is created when the class is accessed or executed. In the current application, where the `main` method is run once and then terminates, you don't really need to worry about multiple instances of these variables being initialized. However, in future chapters, you will be faced with the prospect of multiple users simultaneously running an application, and you need to ensure that they are comfortably sharing the same SAP system objects rather than constantly creating their own. Trust me, this will be made clear in the very near future.

So how are you going to call those methods, if not in the `main` method? Simple; you get to use a static execution block at the class level to initialize the SAP system variables that get used later on in our `main` method. Okay, perhaps it's not really as simple as I make it sound.

```
static {
  createConnection();
  retrieveRepository();
}
```

You have probably noticed by now how I have repeatedly used the `static` declaration, and you are wondering if I am ever going to get around to explaining it. The short explanation is that all `main` methods of every class ever written must be declared `static`, with no exceptions. This has been handed down by the Java specification as an immutable law and has everything to do with how the `main` method is executed within the JVM.

Recall that almost every time we needed an initialized variable in your application, you called a method or default constructor on another Java class. This is known as creating an instance of that class or an instance of the Java class returned by that method or constructor. A class instance gives your application a representation of the original Java class with the ability to use and manipulate the methods and attributes of that class as if it were a native component of this application.

However, in the case of your application (the class containing the `main` method), there is no other class available to create an instance of this class. More precisely, the JVM does not need to create an instance of your application class in order to execute its `main` method. Java uses the `static` declaration to tell the JVM that an instance of the class is not required and that it should be natively executed.

The practical upshot is that any method directly called by a `static` method must also be declared `static` itself. Alternatively, as you have seen within this application, when you create an instance of the class that contains the methods you would like to call, you let your application use those methods within the `static main` method. In order to use the methods you have created in the current class without having to create an instance of that class, you need to use

85

a static block as in the prior code snippet and ensure that all class methods are declared static.

Why bother with all of this? Every time a new instance of a class is instantiated, you create overhead within the JVM. In order to reduce that burden and ensure an optimized application, you should use techniques such as the static declaration. That the JVM has already loaded your application class makes it unnecessary for you to create an instance of that class just to be able to use another method in that class.

Having said all of that, it's time to take a look at the newly optimized application:

```
import com.sap.mw.jco.*;
public class MaterialList {
  public static final String SAP_CLIENT ="100";
  public static final String USER_ID ="username";
  public static final String PASSWORD = "password";
  public static final String LANGUAGE = "E";
  public static final String HOST_NAME = "hostname";
  public static final String SYSTEM_NUMBER = "00";
  private static JCO.Client aConnection;
  private static IRepository aRepository;

static {
  createConnection();
  retrieveRepository();
}

private static void createConnection() {
  try {
    aConnection = JCO.createClient(SAP_CLIENT,
                                   USER_ID,
                                   PASSWORD,
                                   LANGUAGE,
                                   HOST_NAME,
                                   SYSTEM_NUMBER);
    aConnection.connect();
  }
  catch (Exception ex) {
    System.out.println("Failed to connect to SAP system");
  }
}
```

```
private static void retrieveRepository() {
  try {
    aRepository = new JCO.Repository("SAPRep", aConnection);
    }
    catch (Exception ex) {
      System.out.println("Failed to retrieve SAP repository");
    }
  }

  public static void main(String[] args) {

  System.out.println("This class looks up materials.");
  try {
    String matSearch;
    IFunctionTemplate functionTemplate =
        aRepository.getFunctionTemplate("BAPI_MATERIAL_GETLIST");

    JCO.Function function = new JCO.Function(functionTemplate);
    JCO.ParameterList tabParams = function.getTableParameterList();
    JCO.Table materials = tabParams.getTable("MATNRSELECTION");

    if (args.length == 0)
        matSearch = "*";
    else
        matSearch = args[0];

    materials.appendRow();
    materials.setRow(0);
    materials.setValue("I", "SIGN");
    materials.setValue("CP", "OPTION");
    materials.setValue(matSearch, "MATNR_LOW");
    aConnection.execute(function);

    JCO.ParameterList resultParams = function.getExportParameterList();
    JCO.Table materialList =
        function.getTableParameterList().getTable("MATNRLIST");

    if (materialList.getNumRows() > 0) {
        do {
            System.out.println("<<<**--------Basic Material Record--------**>>>");
            for (JCO.FieldIterator fI = materialList.fields();
                fI.hasMoreElements();)
```

```
                {
                   JCO.Field tabField = fI.nextField();
                   System.out.println(tabField.getName() +
                                           (":\t") +
                                           tabField.getString());
                }
                    System.out.println("\n");
                }
                while(materialList.nextRow() == true);
        }
        else {
             System.out.println("Sorry, couldn't find any materials");
        }
    }
    catch (Exception ex) {
        System.out.println("Call to SAP has failed.");
    }
  }
}
```

Summary

In this introduction to JCo, you looked at some fundamental Java development techniques. In addition, you learned how to set up a Java development environment. Here are a few basic reminders that deal with developing, compiling, and running Java applications:

Ensure your CLASSPATH is set properly: Check to see that any external class library used in your application is accurately referenced in the CLASSPATH.

Ensure the Java binaries are in your PATH statement: The directory path <JAVA_ROOT>/bin must appear somewhere in your PATH statement.

Use a text editor you are comfortable with: I used TextPad to build the examples in this book; this text editor can be downloaded and purchased from http://www.textpad.com. UltraEdit is another strong contender; it is available at http://www.ultraedit.com.

This chapter also focused on some Java code syntax and concepts, both basic and advanced. As you build further examples in this book, you will become generally more comfortable with Java. Jumping into concepts such as object instances and the rationale surrounding class and method declarations might seem a bit confusing right now, but this knowledge will pay off in the very near future.

Again, life will get easier as you move on, but I feel that getting right into proper application development is incredibly important when you are dealing with a system like SAP. Hopefully, this will get your engine running and fuel your desire to delve into more extensive Java development outside the confines of this book.

In the next chapter, you will use the streamlined version of this Java application to build out a desktop graphical interface. You will also modify your application to make it easier to deploy to end users, giving them simpler access so that they can search for materials within SAP.

CHAPTER 5

Building a Desktop Interface to SAP

IN THE PREVIOUS CHAPTER, you finally got the chance to develop a Java application for SAP. Granted, the program executes from the command line and has little use in the real world, but it does demonstrate the fundamental concepts involved in using the Java Connector (JCo). However, this tutorial comprised only a fraction of the overall development effort required to create applications for everyday use.

This chapter focuses on Java technologies that extend an application to the end user's desktop. Specifically, this chapter looks at the following:

- Using configuration files to handle system variables

- Providing object-level access to your existing development

- Developing a graphical desktop client to access SAP

Using Configuration Files

Let's assume that you have decided to reuse your existing Java application development. In this case, your first step is to ensure that an end user can configure the program without having to edit and recompile any source code.

The last section of Chapter 4 showed you how to move the system variables from the method level to the class level in order to reduce redundancy in the code and create more visibility for the SAP variables. Unfortunately, a Java developer still needs to modify and recompile this code in order to make any changes to these system variables. Unless you are willing to provide a Java Software Development Kit (JSDK) and appropriate training to each and every user, this is not a viable solution.

Luckily, the Java 2 specification provides a simple-to-use set of libraries that allow you to read data in from a plain text file and use that data as variables within a Java application. Known as *resource bundles,* these text files contain single or multiple text strings associated with keywords. Once you have created them, you can read these resource bundles into an application using the `ResourceBundle` class library that can be found in the `java.util` package.

Internationalizing Java Applications

Java-based resource bundles are designed to house locale-specific information, such as internationalized text strings. This allows developers to build applications in a single written language, which can then be translated over time into any other required language. How is this possible?

Different programming languages and operating systems often provide native methods for passing country- or region-specific information within an application. Java is no exception; it allows the developer to use the java.util.Locale class to represent the region where the end user resides. This localization occurs through the combination of language key and country code, both as listed by the International Organization for Standardization (ISO).

> **NOTE** *The ISO claims that "ISO" is not an abbreviation or acronym. ISO is a word that is derived from the Greek* isos, *which means "equal." The rationale for using this Greek word is to keep the organization's name standard throughout the world. So, despite language and translation differences, the International Organization for Standardization remains ISO in every country across the globe.*

Once the developer determines where the user is from and what language he speaks (usually by asking at the start of the application), the developer creates an instance of the Locale class. This language-specific Locale instance is then used throughout the program wherever the developer needs locale-based formatting or text.

Resource bundles fit into this scheme by providing a plain text file format that houses locale-specific text and can automatically retrieve that text without the developer needing to intervene further. To use a resource bundle, the developer creates a text file with a file extension of *.properties and saves this file somewhere within the Java CLASSPATH. Assuming the default language is English, the properties file is called MyResources.properties and looks something like this:

```
main.welcome=Welcome to the new OpenSource Guru site.
main.articles=Check out the latest in Java technical articles.
main.projects=See the newest OSG projects.
main.contact=Contact OpenSource Guru at:
```

But what if you needed to internationalize this application? If you had designed your application using the Locale class, then you could simply add a new properties file to the Java CLASSPATH that contained the translated language texts.

Assume that you needed to translate the application into German. To do so, instead of changing any of your application code, you would simply create a properties file with the name MyResources_de.properties. Notice that "_de" has been added to the name of the properties file. The two-letter key, DE (meaning

Deutschland), is the code established by the ISO to indicate that German is being used. The new properties file would look like this:

```
main.welcome= Willkommen zum neuen OpenSource Guruaufstellungsort.
main.articles=Überprüfen Sie aus dem spätesten Java in den
                         technischen Artikeln.
main.projects=Sehen Sie die neuesten OSG Projekte.
main.contact=Kontakt OpenSource Guru an:
```

If DE is supplied as the language key within the Locale instance, the ResourceBundle class automatically looks for a properties file named MyResource followed by de, rather than using the default properties file, MyResources.properties.

Perhaps the best way to understand multilingual resource bundles is to develop a quick application that relies on the end user to define the program's language text.

```java
import java.util.ResourceBundle;
import java.util.Locale;
import java.util.Date;
public class LanguageApp {

  public static void main(String[] args){

    String langKey;
    Date currDate = new Date();
    if (args.length > 0)
     langKey = args[0];
    else
     langKey = "";

    Locale currLocale = new Locale(langKey);

    ResourceBundle myResources =
        ResourceBundle.getBundle("MyResources", currLocale);
    System.out.println("<<<***----------------------------***>>>");
    System.out.println(myResources.getString("main.welcome"));
    System.out.println("<<<***----------------------------***>>>" +
                                  System.getProperty("line.separator"));
    System.out.println(myResources.getString("main.articles") +
                                  System.getProperty("line.separator"));
    System.out.println(myResources.getString("main.projects") +
                                  currDate.toString() +
                                  System.getProperty("line.separator"));
```

```
            System.out.println(myResources.getString("main.contact") +
                                  " guru@opensourceguru.com" +
                                  System.getProperty("line.separator"));
    }
}
```

> **NOTE** *This code will not work in anything older than JDK1.4. As of 1.4, the default constructor used to create a new* `Locale` *instance requires only a language key. In earlier releases, in order to utilize this class, this constructor needed both a language key and a country code. If you are using an older JDK, simply hard-code the value "US" as a second parameter in the* `new Locale()` *statement.*

To get this application to work, ensure that the `MyResources.properties` and `MyResources_de.properties` files are located in your development directory. Next, build the preceding application in your text editor, and save it with the file name `LanguageApp.java`. Compile the application and run it from the command line:

```
java LanguageApp
```

By not passing in any parameters on the command line, the `currLocale` instance was initialized with an empty string, "". The `getBundle()` method treats this locale as the default, retrieves the `MyResources.properties` file, and uses it to display the requested fields. You can pass a value for the language key to the Java application by entering it on the command line. Try entering a value of `DE` on the command line.

```
java LanguageApp DE
```

Your application initializes the `currLocale` instance using the ISO language key for German. The `getBundle()` method attempts to retrieve a properties file with "de" at the end of the file name, as in `MyResources_de.properties`, and the German translation displays to the console screen.

Try creating new properties files with the same naming convention, `MyResources_XX.properties`, where *XX* is any standard ISO language key. Then rerun your application, passing in that language key from the command line. This demonstrates how easy it is to support additional languages without having to modify the application code. A list of additional ISO language codes can be found at `http://www.ics.uci.edu/pub/ietf/http/related/iso639.txt`.

The sample application also shows you how to mix static information, such as display formatting, and the email address with the more flexible content of the properties files.

```
System.out.println(myResources.getString("main.contact") +
                 " guru@opensourceguru.com" + "\n");
```

As you can see, this fairly straightforward approach allows you to add new language texts and translations to an application over time, rather than limiting the program to only those language requirements you know of at the time of development. With a little forethought to where language text translations might be appropriate, you can make your Java application an international superstar, or at least you can make it look like one, overnight.

Configuring the Application with Resource Bundles

Having said all of that, I am now going to tell you that you are going to use resource bundles for a slightly different purpose. Instead of needing to add new language translations to your Java application, you need to allow end users to configure the SAP R/3 system variables to suit each local install of the program. You can use the flexibility demonstrated in your properties application to provide configuration files for any Java application. These configuration files are easily modified in any standard text editor and are reinitialized each time the application is started.

First, define the contents of the properties file based on the system variables you are using in the existing application. Those variables include SAP username, password, and language key, as well as R/3 host name, client, and system number.

Now, create a text file called `sapdata.properties` and save this file in your base development directory. Add the following lines to this file:

```
jco.client.user=username
jco.client.passwd=password
jco.client.ashost=sapserver
jco.client.client=100
jco.client.sysnr=00
jco.client.langu=EN
```

As you can see, each line consists of a name/value pair separated by the equal sign (=). You use the name or key attribute within the Java application to specify the value you want retrieved. In this properties file, the key is made up of two terms separated by a period (.). This is not required for the properties file, but it is a convention that developers often use to group similar value sets together. You are not even limited to using a single period because common data groups can take on a more hierarchical structure, as shown here:

```
SAP.system.user=username
SAP.system.password=password
SAP.SALES.salesorg=3000
SAP.SALES.distrchan=10
USER.color=blue
USER.scheme=cornfield
```

In this sample properties file, the SAP-related data has been further broken down into system versus SALES, in addition to the non-SAP fields used to set the color and interface scheme for the end user. This further clarifies the use of various components within the properties file and makes it easier for an end user to configure.

> **NOTE** *The* sapdata.properties *is used in later development to automatically populate the* JCO.Client *object with system values. Because this class relies on specific naming conventions in the properties file, you should stick to the* jco.client.*XXX for the key names in each line.*

Using the sapdata.properties file created earlier, you must now modify the Java program to read in this file and use the values specified as R/3 system variables.

```
import com.sap.mw.jco.*;
import java.util.ResourceBundle;
```

Along with the JCo libraries imported in the first line, the application needs to import the java.util.ResourceBundle class provided by the Java 2 application libraries. The ResourceBundle class gives you the methods you need to read in and extract data from the sapdata.properties file. In the following code snippet, you can see this file read into a ResourceBundle from the file system:

```
import com.sap.mw.jco.*;
import java.util.ResourceBundle;
public class MaterialList1 {
  static ResourceBundle sapProperties = ResourceBundle.getBundle("sapdata");
...
}
```

Now you need to instantiate a new instance of `ResourceBundle` by calling the getBundle() method on the `ResourceBundle` class. The getBundle() method requires the name of the requested properties file to be passed in as a text string. Notice that the *.properties file extension is not required here. The `ResourceBundle` class looks for any file in the Java CLASSPATH that matches the text string parameter passed to getBundle() that has the *.properties file extension.

Once the application has an instance of `ResourceBundle` initialized with the correct properties file, you can pull out `String` variables based on the keys associated with each value.

```
public static final String SAP_CLIENT =
        sapProperties.getString("jco.client.client");
public static final String USER_ID =
        sapProperties.getString("jco.client.user");
public static final String PASSWORD =
        sapProperties.getString("jco.client.passwd");
public static final String LANGUAGE =
        sapProperties.getString("jco.client.langu");
public static final String HOST_NAME =
        sapProperties.getString("jco.client.ashost");
public static final String SYSTEM_NUMBER =
        sapProperties.getString("jco.client.sysnr");
```

Instead of hard-coding every system variable, you need to initialize each `String` instance using the getString() method of sapProperties. The getString() method requires a single text string parameter that indicates the key set to a given value within the sapdata.properties file. Remember, this key is the full text string to the left of the equal sign (=), which separates the name/value pairs in your properties file. In this case, your keys include the "." separator used to group similar pairs together, as in `SAP.client`.

That's all it takes to implement a configuration file for your Java application. This way, the end user can easily utilize his own R/3 user seat to be authorized for use of SAP. Likewise, should the user wish to run your application against a different R/3 system or client, he can make this change simple by modifying the sapdata.properties file.

Modify this sapdata.properties file to suit your specific SAP system:

```
jco.client.user=your user name
jco.client.passwd=your password
jco.client.ashost=your sap hostname
jco.client.client=your sap client
jco.client.sysnr=your sap system number
jco.client.langu=your logon language
```

> **CAUTION** Be aware of the fact that these properties files are plain text. This means that files such as these can be read and changed by anyone who has access to a text editor and your local computer. You can find the best example of this in the SAP.password variable set in the sapdata.properties file, which can be used to determine that R/3 user's name and password. Properties files can be encrypted and the Java 2 specification provides libraries for doing so. However, Java cryptography is outside the scope of this book. For more information on cryptography and general security, check out Java Security *(2nd Edition)*, by Scott Oaks (O'Reilly & Associates, 2001).

As you begin building more complex Java applications, especially integrating with SAP, keep in mind the power and flexibility of resource bundles, not only for configuration but also for internationalization. In fact, SAP has already done much of the translation work for you. By using a language-specific user seat to authorize a user in SAP, the R/3 system automatically formats and translates numeric and text fields into the language designated by the user's language key. Your job is to simply translate any remaining text fields that exist solely within your Java application and provide those translations through locale-based properties files.

Providing Object-Level Access

Up until this point, your application development has combined SAP business logic with execution and display logic (the main method). However, object-oriented programming encourages you to decouple these application components into discreet elements that can be reused in a variety of ways. The MaterialList class that you have been working on up to this point has very few applications in the real world. It is a standalone Java class that executes from the command line and provides very limited display feedback. MaterialList has one very basic feature, and other Java classes that require access to the R/3 system cannot even use it.

Just as you have used Java classes and libraries to easily add new functionality to your application, so too can you create your own class libraries that contain discrete functional components you can reuse throughout your development. By building on the MaterialList class, you can create a new Java class, called InterfaceCaller, which cannot be run by itself but is an integrated component of the application framework.

Creating the Initial Java Class

Start off by creating a new Java class called `InterfaceCaller.java`. You can use the same imports from the `MaterialList` class, including the new line that imports `java.util.ResourceBundle`.

```
import com.sap.mw.jco.*;
import java.util.ResourceBundle;
import java.util.Hashtable;
public class InterfaceCaller {
    ...
}
```

> **NOTE** The third import statement allows your application to use the Java Hashtable class. In Java, the Hashtable allows data to be easily stored and retrieved by your application. This is discussed in more detail later in this chapter.

Likewise, you need to add the SAP system variables and the initialized ResourceBundle so that the application has access to the `sapdata.properties` file you created earlier.

```
ResourceBundle sapProperties = ResourceBundle.getBundle("sapdata");
public static final String SAP_CLIENT =
      sapProperties.getString("jco.client.client");
public static final String USER_ID =
      sapProperties.getString("jco.client.user");
public static final String PASSWORD =
      sapProperties.getString("jco.client.passwd");
public static final String LANGUAGE =
      sapProperties.getString("jco.client.langu");
public static final String HOST_NAME =
      sapProperties.getString("jco.client.ashost");
public static final String SYSTEM_NUMBER =
      sapProperties.getString("jco.client.sysnr");
private JCO.Client aConnection;
private IRepository aRepository;
```

The difference between the variables you initialized here and those in `MaterialList` is that here the `static` declarations have been removed. Throughout the remainder of `InterfaceCaller`, you will see that all `static` declarations have been taken out because they will soon prove to be more of a hindrance than a help.

As you recall, in the previous chapter's development, you needed to declare each method `static` so that the application could call them without needing to instantiate an instance of the `MaterialList` class. You had to make these methods `static` because your program needed to call these methods from within the `main` method of the application's executable class. The new `InterfaceCaller` class does not have a `main` method. Instead, if a class needs to use `InterfaceCaller` it must first instantiate an instance of the `InterfaceCaller` class in order to gain access to its methods and attributes.

Ultimately, the `InterfaceCaller` class is a nonexecutable Java object, designed strictly to house the SAP business logic and JCo connectivity. By removing this class's `main` method, you require another Java class to act as the effective application executable, instantiating and calling methods on `InterfaceCaller` to provide SAP functionality to the end user.

The practical effect of removing all these `static` declarations is that another application can no longer directly access the methods of `InterfaceCaller` without first instantiating an instance of the class. In order to instantiate a Java class, you must make sure that it has at least one default constructor. Remember, you can use the default constructor to create an empty instance of a Java class, and you can then use its methods and attributes as a native part of the application. The simplest default constructor uses the name of the Java class as the method name and doesn't take any parameters.

In the case of the `InterfaceCaller` class, the default constructor would look like this:

```
public InterfaceCaller() {...}
```

However, the default constructor is a great place to put code that must be executed when the class is instantiated. Examples of this type of code include initialization logic required by the methods in this class or variables that are set using the parameters (if any) required to call the default constructor.

If you look at the original `MaterialList` class, you find just such logic in the form of the JCo connection and repository initialization. Whereas before your program called the methods to create both instances at the class level of the application, you can now position them more appropriately within the default constructor. This guarantees that the `InterfaceCaller` attempts to establish a connection and retrieve a repository from SAP before any of the methods that call R/3 BAPIs can be executed.

In the following code, the `createConnection()` and `retrieveRepository()` methods have been moved to the end of the `InterfaceCaller` class. The beginning of the class should look like this:

```
import com.sap.mw.jco.*;
import java.util.Hashtable;
import java.util.ResourceBundle;
public class InterfaceCaller {
```

```
    ResourceBundle sapProperties = ResourceBundle.getBundle("sapdata");
    public static final String SAP_CLIENT =
            sapProperties.getString("jco.client.client");
    public static final String USER_ID =
            sapProperties.getString("jco.client.user");
    public static final String PASSWORD =
            sapProperties.getString("jco.client.passwd");
    public static final String LANGUAGE =
            sapProperties.getString("jco.client.langu");
    public static final String HOST_NAME =
            sapProperties.getString("jco.client.ashost");
    public static final String SYSTEM_NUMBER =
            sapProperties.getString("jco.client.sysnr");

    private JCO.Client aConnection;
    private IRepository aRepository;

    public InterfaceCaller() {
      createConnection();
      retrieveRepository();
    }
    ...
}
```

Implementing the getMaterialList() Method

Next, you need to add a new method, called `getMaterialList()`, to `InterfaceCaller` that implements the SAP logic to call `BAPI_MATERIAL_GETLIST`. When you implement this method, you will see that it looks somewhat different from the methods you developed in Chapter 4. Here is what the opening and closing of this new method looks like:

```
import com.sap.mw.jco.*;
import java.util.Hashtable;
import java.util.ResourceBundle;
public class InterfaceCaller {
  ...
  public Hashtable getMaterialList(String searchParam) {
      ...
      return returnHash;
  }
}
```

This line declares the method to be `public` and to return a `Hashtable` object:

```
public Hashtable getMaterialList(String searchParam)
```

In addition, it declares the method name and a single text string parameter, `searchParam`. By declaring a return object for this method (as opposed to the `void` seen in earlier methods), using an instance of the `InterfaceCaller` class, you tell the application to expect a given Java object to be returned.

In this case, the return is an object of type `java.util.Hashtable`, which is a standard Java class used to store name/value pairs. The last statement in the `getMaterialList()` method, `return returnHash;`, indicates that an instance of the `Hashtable` class populated by this method is returned to the originating Java instance.

The Java `Hashtable` is one of the most widely used mechanisms for quickly storing and retrieving data. It provides very simple methods for setting and getting name/value pairs and can store a wide variety of Java objects. Unlike arrays, the `Hashtable` is not limited to a set number of elements when it is initialized. In Java, when an array is initialized, you have to declare the number of elements in that array, otherwise known as its boundaries. With a `Hashtable`, you simply append new entries to the current instance; this creates additional elements that can be referenced by a key value and modified later in the application.

Understanding HashMaps

Introduced in JDK 1.2, HashMaps are part of the Java Collections Framework. Similar to Hashtables, HashMaps provide highly optimized concrete implementations of the `Map` interface. This simply means that an instance of the `HashMap` class takes advantage of the advanced data structures and algorithms provided by the Java Collections Framework. The major difference is how each class accesses the data stored in it.

Hashtables rely on the `Enumeration` class to retrieve stored values lists, whereas HashMaps return `Collection` views of stored data. These views provide failsafe access to the data via an `Iterator` instance, which has the advantage of allowing elements to be removed during the course of iteration and offers more clarified method names.

The Java Collections Framework deserves a great deal more explanation than can be provided in this book. For more information, check out the excellent tutorials at `http://java.sun.com/docs/books/tutorial/collections/`.

Aside from using the key to retrieve a value from the `Hashtable`, this class provides several methods to pull out a list or enumeration of either key names or values. Table 5-1 lists the various methods in the `Hashtable` class along with a brief explanation of each.

Table 5-1. Synopsis of Methods in Hashtable Class

METHOD NAME	RETURN OBJECT	DESCRIPTION
put(*key, value*)	Object	Stores Java *Object*, *value*, in a hashtable mapped to a specified key.
get(*key*)	Object	Returns a *value* reference by *key* as Java *Object*. *Object* should be cast.
isEmpty()	Boolean	Tests whether a hashtable has no *keys* or *values*.
elements()	Enumeration	Returns a Java *Enumeration* containing all *values* in the hashtable.
keys()	Enumeration	Returns a Java *Enumeration* containing all *keys* in the hashtable.
contains(*value*)	Boolean	Tests whether the hashtable contains a given Java *Object*, *value*.
containsKey(*key*)	Boolean	Tests whether the hashtable contains a given Java *Object*, *key*.

This is not an exhaustive list of all methods in the `Hashtable` class, but it encompasses some of the most commonly used.

So why such a heavy focus on the `Hashtable` class? In Chapter 4, your application used the JCo table structures to retrieve and display data back to the end user. Although these Java classes did get the job done, they are totally reliant on the JCo Java class libraries. In order to build more extensible Java applications, I highly recommended that you allow a certain amount of decoupling to occur between objects and systems in the application framework. Simply put, this means that the Java classes you developed to present an interface to the end user do not need to have specific knowledge of the underlying SAP connector architecture. If you rely on the JCo libraries to display information to the end user, you create a reliance on the SAP connector where none needs to exist.

By using the standard Java `Hashtable` class to store information you want to present to the end user, you create a marked delineation between the various levels of your application. That way, your presentation layer, the desktop client, doesn't need to understand anything about connecting to the R/3 system. This will make more sense as you continue development of the `InterfaceCaller` class.

Adding JCo Logic to getMaterialList()

This part is fairly straightforward because you have already developed much of the functionality for this method in the previous chapter.

```
import com.sap.mw.jco.*;
import java.util.Hashtable;
import java.util.ResourceBundle;
public class InterfaceCaller {
...
  public Hashtable getMaterialList(String searchParam) {
//The getFunction() method is a new method in this class
    JCO.Function function = this.getFunction("BAPI_MATERIAL_GETLIST");
    JCO.ParameterList tabParams = function.getTableParameterList();
    JCO.Table materials = tabParams.getTable("MATNRSELECTION");

    materials.appendRow();
    materials.setRow(0);
    materials.setValue("I", "SIGN");
    materials.setValue("CP", "OPTION");
    materials.setValue(searchParam, "MATNR_LOW");
    aConnection.execute(function);

    JCO.ParameterList resultParams = function.getExportParameterList();
    JCO.Table materialList =
                    function.getTableParameterList().getTable("MATNRLIST");

    Hashtable returnHash = new Hashtable();
    Hashtable rowHash = new Hashtable();
    int i = 0;
    if (materialList.getNumRows() > 0) {
        do {
            for (JCO.FieldIterator fI = materialList.fields();
                fI.hasMoreElements();)
              {
                JCO.Field tabField = fI.nextField();
                rowHash.put(tabField.getName(),tabField.getString ());
            }
              returnHash.put("line" + i, rowHash);
              rowHash = new Hashtable();
              i++;
        }
```

```
                    while(materialList.nextRow() == true);
            }
            else {
                    System.out.println("Sorry, couldn't find any materials");
            }
            return returnHash;
        }
        ...
    }
```

The first difference between this code and the Chapter 4 application is in the statement that follows the method declaration.

```
JCO.Function function = this.getFunction("BAPI_MATERIAL_GETLIST");
```

This line calls another method within the `InterfaceCaller` class, as indicated by the implied class name `this`. Using `this` as the instance against which to call a method tells the Java Virtual Machine (JVM) to look for that method, in this case `getFunction()`, within the current class. The `getFunction()` method provides generic access to the JCo logic required to create a `JCO.Function` object. This method retrieves a `JCO.FunctionTemplate` based on the name of an RFC and then returns a new instance of the `JCO.Function` class. Here is that method:

```
    public JCO.Function getFunction(String name) {
      try {
         return aRepository.getFunctionTemplate(name.toUpperCase()).getFunction();
      }
      catch (Exception ex) {
        ex.printStackTrace();
         return null;
      }
    }
```

If you review Chapter 4, you will see that the JCo logic used to initialize the `function` instance has been extracted and added to the `getFunction()` method. Encapsulating this common technical logic in a method allows you to reuse code throughout the additional methods of your `InterfaceCaller` class.

Likewise, you will notice that the array used to retrieve a search text string from the command line has been removed. Instead, the method uses the `searchParam` text string passed as a parameter when the method is called.

A few lines further down, you see the first use of that much-heralded `Hashtable` class, in the form of two variables that are initialized using the `Hashtable`'s default constructor.

Building a Desktop Interface to SAP

```
Hashtable returnHash = new Hashtable();
Hashtable rowHash = new Hashtable();
```

The rowHash is used to represent individual rows in the table returned from SAP, and returnHash stores all of those rows as a representation of the R/3 table.

Since you have already dealt with using the JCo libraries to pull data out of Java-based SAP tables, now you need only to understand how to put that information into the respective Hashtables. The following code snippet demonstrates how the application populates a Java Hashtable:

```
            do {
                for (JCO.FieldIterator fI = materialList.fields();
                    fI.hasMoreElements();)
                  {
                    JCO.Field tabField = fI.nextField();
//This line uses the field name and value to populate a hashtable
                    rowHash.put(tabField.getName(),tabField.getString ());
                  }
                returnHash.put("line" + i, rowHash);
                rowHash = new Hashtable();
                i++;
            }
            while(materialList.nextRow() == true);
```

Instead of writing the materials records out to the console display using println() statements, the above code snippet adds those field names and values to the temporary rowHash instance, then it appends rowHash to the returnHash Hashtable.

```
rowHash.put(tabField.getName(),tabField.getString());
```

As noted previously, the JCO.FieldIterator provides a representation of all the field names and values in a given table row. Using the getName() and getString() methods on the tabField instance, the application maps the methods' returns to the key and value parameters of the returnHash.put() method. Mapping data to a standard Java object serves to create a Hashtable representation of that same JCO.FieldIterator table row. This new Hashtable record can then be stored in the returnHash instance through the following statement:

```
            returnHash.put("line" + i, rowHash);
```

Having created an integer, i, to act as a counter, the rowHash instance is stored as a value mapped to key "item$X$," where X is the current value of the counter. The `rowHash` instance is then reinitialized to a new `Hashtable` so that it can be used as the next table row, and the line item counter is incremented.

```
rowHash = new Hashtable();
i++;
```

> **NOTE** *The Java programming syntax provides a number of shortcuts for writing expressions. The expression* `i++;` *can also be written as* `i = i + 1;`. *The outcome of either is the same—namely the value of* `i` *is incremented by 1—but the former is preferred for its more widely recognized clarity.*

Once the `do...while` loop has completed, the `getMaterialList()` method returns the newly populated `returnHash` instance, thus finishing the method call.

> **TIP** *Because these examples are meant strictly for educational purposes, much of the recommended error and exception handling that should be part of a more robust development effort has been left out. In the previous example, you would likely add logic to determine whether the call to SAP was successful and to check whether any material records were returned. If the call to SAP was unsuccessful, you would want the* `getMaterialList()` *method to return either a Java exception or a* `null` *value rather than an empty* `Hashtable` *instance. The type of return or exception would depend on how this class needed to interact with your overall application framework.*

Your `InterfaceCaller` class should now look something like this:

```
import com.sap.mw.jco.*;
import java.util.Hashtable;
import java.util.ResourceBundle;
public class InterfaceCaller {

  ResourceBundle sapProperties = ResourceBundle.getBundle("sapdata");
  public static final String SAP_CLIENT =
        sapProperties.getString("jco.client.client");
  public static final String USER_ID =
        sapProperties.getString("jco.client.user");
  public static final String PASSWORD =
        sapProperties.getString("jco.client.passwd");
  public static final String LANGUAGE =
```

```java
            sapProperties.getString("jco.client.langu");
    public static final String HOST_NAME =
            sapProperties.getString("jco.client.ashost");
    public static final String SYSTEM_NUMBER =
            sapProperties.getString("jco.client.sysnr");

    private JCO.Client aConnection;
    private IRepository aRepository;

    public InterfaceCaller() {
        createConnection();
        retrieveRepository();
}

    public Hashtable getMaterialList(String searchParam) {
        JCO.Function function = this.getFunction("BAPI_MATERIAL_GETLIST");
        JCO.ParameterList tabParams = function.getTableParameterList();
        JCO.Table materials = tabParams.getTable("MATNRSELECTION");

        materials.appendRow();
        materials.setRow(0);
        materials.setValue("I", "SIGN");
        materials.setValue("CP", "OPTION");
        materials.setValue(searchParam, "MATNR_LOW");
        aConnection.execute(function);

        JCO.ParameterList resultParams = function.getExportParameterList();
        JCO.Table materialList =
            function.getTableParameterList().getTable("MATNRLIST");

        Hashtable returnHash = new Hashtable();
        Hashtable rowHash = new Hashtable();
        int i = 0;
        if (materialList.getNumRows() > 0) {
            do {
                for (JCO.FieldIterator fI = materialList.fields();
                    fI.hasMoreElements();)
                  {
                    JCO.Field tabField = fI.nextField();
                    rowHash.put(tabField.getName(),tabField.getString());
                  }
                returnHash.put("line" + i, rowHash);
                rowHash = new Hashtable();
                i++;
            }
```

109

```java
                while(materialList.nextRow() == true);
    }
    else {
            System.out.println("Sorry, couldn't find any materials");
    }
    return returnHash;
}

public Hashtable checkPassword(String username, String password) {

    JCO.Function function = getFunction("BAPI_CUSTOMER_CHECKPASSWORD");
    JCO.ParameterList listParams = function.getImportParameterList();
    listParams.setValue(username, "CUSTOMERNO");
    listParams.setValue(password, "PASSWORD");

    aConnection.execute(function);

    JCO.ParameterList resultParams = function.getExportParameterList();
    Hashtable returnHash = new Hashtable();
    returnHash.put("RETURN.TYPE",extractField("RETURN","TYPE",resultParams));
    returnHash.put("RETURN.CODE",extractField("RETURN","CODE",resultParams));
    returnHash.put("RETURN.MESSAGE",
                    extractField("RETURN","MESSAGE",resultParams));
    return returnHash;
}

public String extractField(String structure,String field,
                                    JCO.ParameterList parameterList)
{
    return ((JCO.Structure)parameterList.getValue(structure)).getString(field);
}

public JCO.Function getFunction(String name) {
    try {
        return
aRepository.getFunctionTemplate(name.toUpperCase()).getFunction();
    }
    catch (Exception ex) {}
    return null;
}
```

```java
private void createConnection() {
  try {
    aConnection = JCO.createClient(SAP_CLIENT,
                                   USER_ID,
                                   PASSWORD,
                                   LANGUAGE,
                                   HOST_NAME,
                                   SYSTEM_NUMBER);
    aConnection.connect();
    }
    catch (Exception ex) {
      System.out.println("Failed to connect to SAP system");
    }
  }

private void retrieveRepository() {
  try {
    aRepository = new JCO.Repository("SAPRep", aConnection);
    }
    catch (Exception ex) {
      System.out.println("Failed to retrieve SAP repository");
    }
  }
}
```

Run the Java compiler and you should get back a new Java class, InterfaceCaller.class. In order to test InterfaceCaller, you need to build a quick little test class. This class contains simply a main method that calls a specific method on InterfaceCaller. The following class uses the getMaterialList() method to demonstrate that InterfaceCaller can retrieve materials from SAP.

```java
import java.util.Hashtable;
import java.util.Enumeration;
public class SapTest {

public static void main(String[] args) {
//Change this variable to narrow search criteria
  String materialSearch = "*";
  InterfaceCaller iCaller = new InterfaceCaller();
  Hashtable resultHash = iCaller.getMaterialList(materialSearch);
  Hashtable tempRow;
```

```
      for (Enumeration e = resultHash.elements(); e.hasMoreElements();) {
        tempRow = (Hashtable)e.nextElement();
        System.out.println("Material: " +
            (String)tempRow.get("MATERIAL") +
            System.getProperty("line.separator"));
        System.out.println("Material description: " +
            (String)tempRow.get("MATL_DESC") +
            System.getProperty("line.separator"));
      }
    }
  }
```

Save and compile this file as `SapTest.java` in the same directory as your compiled `InterfaceCaller` class. Execute `SapTest` and your results should look something like this:

```
Material: MATERIAL1

Material description: Material 1
Material: MATERIAL2
Material description: Material 2
Material: MATERIAL3
Material description: Material 3
Material: MATERIAL4
Material description: Material 4
```

The next section details how to use `InterfaceCaller` to provide SAP connectivity from a graphical user interface.

Developing a Graphical User Interface

The final section in this chapter deals with developing a desktop client application that can be deployed across different computers within your company's local area network (LAN). The graphical user interface (GUI) refers to the visual representation of information and how a user interacts with it through accepted metaphors, such as buttons, menus, and scroll bars. In contrast, your earlier Java application required the user to enter and view all application data through a command line, relying solely on the keyboard for input and text characters for output.

Times have changed—green screens and dumb terminals are a thing of the past. Most end users are not hardened terminal-heads and they expect applications to adhere to general windows-like conformity. Certainly, as you develop new Java classes, you conduct initial unit testing and debugging from a command line interface. In fact, I recommend that you become more comfortable with the command line because it provides a very ready and incredibly useful way to quickly build prototype applications or experiment with new programming techniques.

However, you must always keep end users in mind; regard them as your ultimate customers, upon whose satisfaction your position likely rests. Visual interface or GUI development can often be very frustrating, particularly when you are dealing with the Java 2 programming specification. This is due more to the current lack of available strong visual development tools, including the list of integrated development environments (IDEs) mentioned in Chapter 4. On the positive side, Java 2 has (re)introduced a strong set of application libraries that ease the development effort around GUI programming and, with a little practice, can even be fun to work with.

Even if you don't think GUI development is in your near future, you will find that having experience with these Java application libraries is invaluable. Although you are very likely eager to move on to Web application programming, which seems to be the stuff of many high profile corporate projects these days, you need to cover the basics first. In the process, you will very likely need some level of GUI development, even if it just means providing a user-friendly interface for configuring the properties files.

Managing the Graphical User Interface

Developing an application in Java Swing may seem daunting at first, but you can break it down into several manageable pieces. In order to grasp the overall picture, you must understand the various pieces in a Swing application.

> **NOTE** *Sun provides the Java Swing API as part of its Java Foundation Classes (JFC). The JFC is used to support graphical interface design and functionality across a variety of operating system platforms. You can find more information on JFC at Sun's Java Foundation Classes Website* (http://java.sun.com/products/jfc/).

At the most basic level, Swing, and most GUI application development, is comprised of two major framework components—windows and buttons. You use windows to take data from the end user and display it back throughout the process of the application. Buttons provide interactivity—they allow the end user to tell the program when to begin certain processes, and they provide access to the underlying functions of the application.

Windows can be display only, entry only, or both. The most basic window displays text strings to the end user, commonly in the form of error, warning, or informational dialogs. These types of windows require little underlying logic and provide no interaction other than to close the dialog box, that is. However, every windows-based application inherits from the very simple premise of a dialog window and expands on it until you are left with overly complicated, multilayered, button-laden applications that require a master's degree just to get through the user license during installation. Of course, your new Java GUI application for SAP suffers under no such onus.

Unbeknownst to the end user, most GUI applications comprise a series of nested windows, visible or otherwise, that can be used to build a cohesive application front end. Grouping tabbed windowpanes within a larger window frame is a very common mechanism for providing quick access to a wide range of information, which can be bundled logically within each individual pane. Although not a subject in this book, Java Swing provides some very sophisticated windowing mechanisms that have been used to build commercial grade desktop applications. To learn more, visit the excellent tutorial on Java Swing development at http://java.sun.com/docs/books/tutorial/uiswing/.

Windows can also be input fields, which are designed to allow text-based entry of field data. Similar to the example provided later in "Building a Java GUI for SAP," the material search parameter provides a window in which the user can enter a full or partial material identifier to search against SAP's material master database. Windows can also be text areas, such as the white space in a text editor where you enter text to be saved to a file in the file system. You will also see an example of a text area in the following application, specifically used as a display mechanism, rather than as a means to take data entry from the end user.

Figure 5-1 depicts a diagrammatic user interface and represents some of the most commonly used elements in UI design.

Buttons, in their many forms, allow the user to interact with data on the screen and describe how that data can be manipulated. The general class of buttons we deal with here go far beyond the more usual idea of the vaguely rectangular, slightly gray, text- or picture-enhanced icons that you see in everything from Web pages to the SAP GUI. Buttons can be radio style (multiple, small, and circular), check boxes, highlighted text, menu bars, and so forth.

The definition of a button is really just a visual representation of underlying application logic. Better representations lead to easier-to-use applications, which lead to happier end users. Of course, the major challenge surrounding GUI development is not the language syntax or your conceptual understanding of it, but the ultimate implementation of the user interface, as evidenced by the myriad of painfully designed Websites you are forced to visit every day.

Building a Desktop Interface to SAP

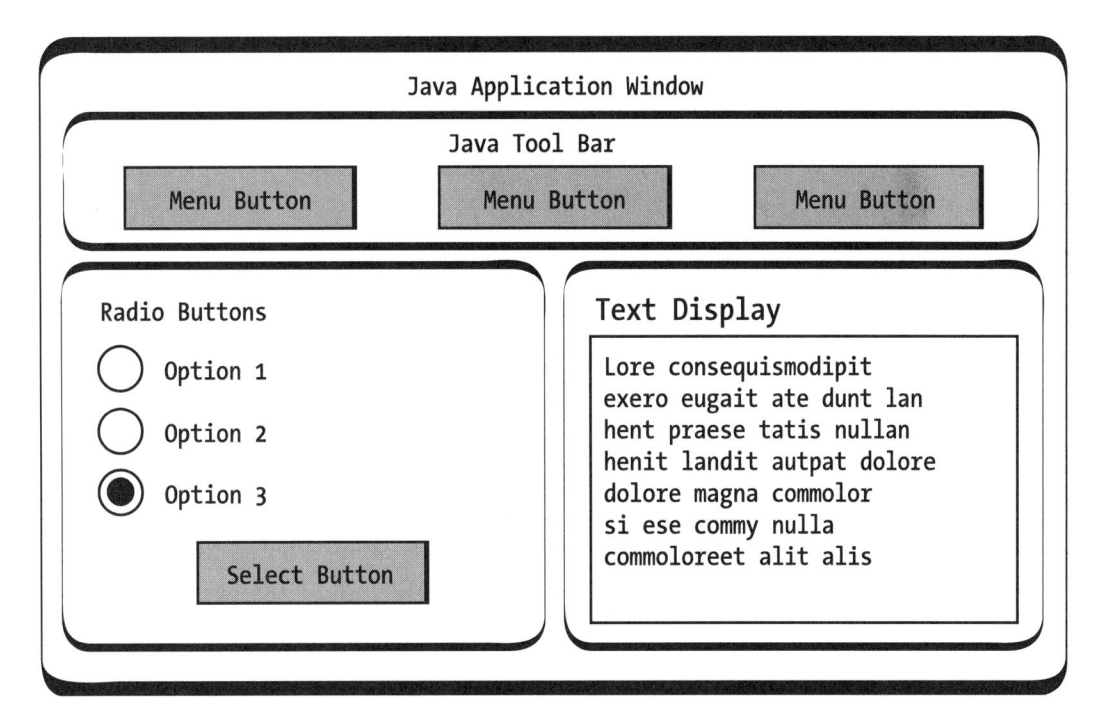

```
┌─────────────────────────────────────────────────────────┐
│                 Java Application Window                  │
│  ╭───────────────────────────────────────────────────╮  │
│  │                   Java Tool Bar                    │  │
│  │  ┌────────────┐  ┌────────────┐  ┌────────────┐   │  │
│  │  │Menu Button │  │Menu Button │  │Menu Button │   │  │
│  │  └────────────┘  └────────────┘  └────────────┘   │  │
│  ╰───────────────────────────────────────────────────╯  │
│  ╭─────────────────────╮  ╭──────────────────────────╮  │
│  │ Radio Buttons       │  │ Text Display             │  │
│  │   ○  Option 1       │  │  ┌────────────────────┐  │  │
│  │                     │  │  │Lore consequismodipit│ │  │
│  │   ○  Option 2       │  │  │exero eugait ate dunt lan│  │
│  │                     │  │  │hent praese tatis nullan │  │
│  │   ●  Option 3       │  │  │henit landit autpat dolore│ │
│  │                     │  │  │dolore magna commolor │  │  │
│  │   ┌─────────────┐   │  │  │si ese commy nulla    │  │  │
│  │   │Select Button│   │  │  │commoloreet alit alis │  │  │
│  │   └─────────────┘   │  │  └────────────────────┘  │  │
│  ╰─────────────────────╯  ╰──────────────────────────╯  │
└─────────────────────────────────────────────────────────┘
```

Figure 5-1. Overview of GUI windowing components

The button can be the user's best friend or her worst enemy. As the developer, your goal is to make your application as simple and user friendly as possible, a prospect that Java Swing does not always aid.

Building a Java GUI for SAP

Now that you have a better idea of the conceptual basics that underlie the JFC and the Swing application libraries, it is time to start building the application.

This section demonstrates a different type of user interface and Java class definition than the command line interface introduced in Chapter 4. Although your new class still relies on a `main` method, much of the actual GUI implementation resides in a default constructor.

Introducing the MaterialGui Class

Start off by creating a new Java class called `MaterialGui.java` and save this file into your development directory.

Next, import the appropriate Swing application libraries along with the standard Java libraries you need to support interaction with the `InterfaceCaller` class.

Remember, you need the `java.util` package to return the `Hashtable` that the methods of `InterfaceCaller` send back.

```
import javax.swing.*;
import java.awt.*;
import java.awt.event.*;
import java.util.*;

public class MaterialGui implements ActionListener {
   ...
}
```

Similar in appearance to previous class declarations, the `MaterialGui` class implements an interface that allows your program to receive action events and process them according to your internal application logic. The `ActionListener` interface provides you with a key method that you need to implement within the application. Where and why this method is used becomes clear very shortly.

Like the `InterfaceCaller` class, certain variables in `MaterialGui` are declared at the class level to make them easier to use throughout the application. In order to develop a graphical interface in Java, the developer must use key objects to build the visual framework and provide the end user with interaction and display.

```
...
public class MaterialGui implements ActionListener {
   JFrame sapFrame;
   JPanel sapPanel;
   JTextField matSearch;
   JButton retrieveList;
   JTextArea resultText;
   JPanel selectPane;
   JPanel displayPane;
   ...
}
```

Table 5-2 gives a quick overview of each instance and describes its responsibility.

Building a Desktop Interface to SAP

Table 5-2. Java Swing Application Components

COMPONENT NAME	DESCRIPTION
JFrame *sapFrame*	Overall window frame. Contains all subsequent GUI components.
JPanel *sapPanel*	Top-level panel used to house and organize content panels.
JTextfield *matSearch*	Single text field that allows user to enter material search criteria.
JButton *retrieveList*	Clickable button that initiates a call to SAP.
JTextArea *resultText*	Scrollable text area that displays a list of materials that match search criteria.
JPanel *selectPane*	Panel that organizes a text field and a button.
JPanel *displayPane*	Panel that provides layout for a text area display.

This table does not describe all of the possible Swing components or their various uses within a graphical development framework. Rather, it describes the components you will use in application developed in this chapter and how they specifically relate to the functionality provide by the MaterialGui class.

In order to execute the MaterialGui class from a command line, you must implement the main method to house the application start-up logic.

```
public class MaterialGui implements ActionListener {
  ...
  public static void main(String[] args) {
    try {
      UIManager.setLookAndFeel(
      UIManager.getCrossPlatformLookAndFeelClassName());
    }
    catch (Exception e) {
        e.printStackTrace();
    }
    MaterialGui matGui = new MaterialGui();
  }
}
```

This is a very basic implementation of the main method that could be used in GUI development, but you would likely want to expand or refactor it before you used it in a real-world application. For now, it demonstrates the basic requirements that surround setting up the application's look and feel, as well as calling a second method in your class to provide the visual components for the end user.

Defining Look and Feel with the UIManager

The UIManager is part of the javax.swing.* package and its purpose is to define and organize the look and feel of your application. Generally speaking, Java Swing development allows your application to instantly conform to a variety of cross-platform visual interfaces. This means that your application can run just as effectively within a UNIX environment as it can within the MS Windows operating system.

The *look and feel* of an application describes the visual properties such as the Maximize, Minimize, and Close buttons, in addition to overall button, field, and display formatting. That Java 2 is a platform-independent language means that your application tries to determine the default look and feel of the operating system and use those visual elements to conform to that system's standard graphical representation.

Normally, you can allow the UIManager to determine the default look and feel from a properties file found in the Java installation. If this file cannot be found, the UIManager uses the look and feel defined by the Java 2 specification, otherwise known as the Java Look and Feel (JLF). In this case, the statement

```
UIManager.getCrossPlatformLookAndFeelClassName();
```

tells the application to use the JLF by default and not to worry about determining or allowing the user to define the application's look and feel.

The last line of the main method creates a new instance of the MaterialGui class (yes, the same class that is currently being executed) using its default constructor.

```
MaterialGui matGui = new MaterialGui();
```

You will recall that using the default constructor is a great way to execute application logic as soon as the class is instantiated, and it does not require any further developer interference. Using the default constructor is appropriate when you are creating a GUI application because you must create the visual components before any user interaction can take place.

Interacting with the User Through ActionListener

Before you jump into using the default constructor, however, there is one other method that you must implement in order to provide SAP functionality for the end user. This is the method mentioned earlier as part of the `ActionListener` interface; you need it to translate the user's interaction with the GUI into an actual call to your `InterfaceCaller` class.

```
public class MaterialGui implements ActionListener {
  ...
  public void actionPerformed(ActionEvent event) {
  InterfaceCaller iCaller = new InterfaceCaller();
  Hashtable returnHash = iCaller.getMaterialList(matSearch.getText());
  Hashtable rowHash;
  for (Enumeration e = returnHash.elements(); e.hasMoreElements();) {
    rowHash = (Hashtable)e.nextElement();
    resultText.append("Material: " +
        (String)rowHash.get("MATERIAL") + "\n");
    resultText.append("Material description: " +
        (String)rowHash.get("MATL_DESC") + "\n\n");
    }
  }
  ...
}
```

The `actionPerformed()` method is automatically called when the user interacts with a visual component, such as a button, that the application has registered as an action listener. In this case, your application has only one such component, the `retrieveList` button, which is registered as an action listener within the `MaterialGui` class's default constructor. The `actionPerformed()` method takes a single parameter, an `ActionEvent` object. This object simply tells the `actionPerformed()` method about the event and its source, details that are hidden in the Swing library classes so that the developer doesn't need to worry about the code-level implementation.

Within the `actionPerformed()` method, the first step is to instantiate a new instance of your `InterfaceCaller` class. Remember that all of the SAP connection logic buried in that class's default constructor? That is handled automatically through the simple instantiation of `InterfaceCaller` and requires no specific knowledge of SAP, the JCo connector, or even the type of ERP system used on the backend.

```
InterfaceCaller iCaller = new InterfaceCaller();
Hashtable returnHash = iCaller.getMaterialList(matSearch.getText());
Hashtable rowHash;
```

The only knowledge of InterfaceCaller the developer needs at this point is the name of method, the parameter(s) required, and the type of Java object returned. Currently, InterfaceCaller has only one method to call SAP, getMaterialList(). This method takes a single text string as its sole parameter and returns a standard Java Hashtable. Notice that using InterfaceCaller does not require the use of any JCo application libraries or any specific knowledge of the underlying SAP connectivity. By encapsulating the R/3 data returns in a standard Java Hashtable, you effectively release the developer using InterfaceCaller from having to learn the JCo connector, thereby making any future development around this class much simpler.

Populating Data in a Hashtable

The returnHash instance is populated by the object returned from the call to the getMaterialList() method on the iCaller instance of InterfaceCaller. In the following line, you initialize a Hashtable called rowHash, which is used as temporary storage for each individual row contained in the returnHash instance.

```
for (Enumeration e = returnHash.elements(); e.hasMoreElements();) {
  rowHash = (Hashtable)e.nextElement();
  resultText.append("Material: " +
          (String)rowHash.get("MATERIAL") + "\n");
  resultText.append("Material description: " +
          (String)rowHash.get("MATL_DESC") + "\n\n");
}
```

Once the application has a populated instance of returnHash, you can use the for loop to loop through the Hashtable and write the results back to the JTextArea, resultText. The for loop instantiates a new Enumeration, e, using the elements() method of returnHash. This Enumeration instance contains strictly a list of Hashtable elements, which are the values in the name/value pairs contained within returnHash.

At this point, you are not concerned with the order in which the line items are returned by SAP, so using the elements() method to retrieve an unordered list of the values in returnHash will suffice. The for loop also specifies the termination expression e.hasMoreElements(), which tests whether the enumeration contains additional elements, and ends the loop when this method returns a Boolean value of FALSE.

Ordering Data in a Hashtable

Retrieving data from a Hashtable using the elements() method does not guarantee a list ordered in the way the data was originally stored. If you need to pull out the elements in the same order in which they were stored, that is, the line item order returned by SAP, you must retrieve each value individually, using the name stored as a key.

In the Chapter 4 code examples, these keys were stored as item*XX*, where *XX* represents the individual line number of each item. You could increment an integer variable, then use the Hashtable.get() method, and pass in a String parameter of ""item" + integer" to incrementally retrieve the elements of that Hashtable. Here is an example of that code:

```
int i = 0;
while (i < 100) {
   (String)myHash.get("item" + i);
   i++;
}
```

Additionally, the Java Collections Framework offers abstract and concrete implementations of sort and store algorithms to provide ordered list functionality. See the "Understanding HashMaps" sidebar earlier in this chapter for more information.

The first line in the for loop sets the value of rowHash equal to the result of a call to the nextElement() method on the Enumeration, e. Again, you must cast the Java object returned by this method as a Hashtable, otherwise the JVM is unable to determine how to treat this object.

```
resultText.append("Material: " +
         (String)rowHash.get("MATERIAL") + "\n");
resultText.append("Material description: " +
         (String)rowHash.get("MATL_DESC") + "\n\n");
```

> **TIP** *As you saw in the previous chapter, escape characters can be used to provide limited character formatting in the text strings. Escape characters, specified as a backslash (\) followed by a reserved character, are a simple mechanism to make the output text more legible to the end user. Try using the tab escape, \t, to line up the field name columns, or \" if you need to place printed quotes around a text string. Likewise, you can add additional text to better delineate the difference between material records, such as dashes, asterisks, and hash marks.*

As stated earlier, the rowHash instance is used as temporary storage for a given SAP table row retrieved from returnHash. The rowHash instance now contains a list of name/value pairs, each representing a different field name and field value of a given row in the table. For this simple application, you need to display only the MATERIAL and MATL_DESC fields contained in rowHash, so using the get() method on this instance and passing in the field name as key parameter is sufficient.

Displaying Information Using JTextArea

In order to display this information to the end user in a text area, the application uses the resultText instance initialized as a class-level variable. Remember, by using a class-level variable, any logic you build into your application can access and modify this instance. Through this mechanism, you do not need to worry about passing variables to the actionPerformed() method, which you cannot do, regardless, because ActionEvent is the only valid parameter that can be passed to this method.

By using the append() method of resultText, you can easily push strings of text back to the text area. This is a very basic approach to displaying lists of data back to the end user, but it suffices for this relatively simple application. As you explore the Java Swing libraries, you will find much more advanced mechanisms to providing more creative and interactive display results to the end user.

The JTextArea class provides several different methods that are used to set the way text characters are displayed and how the user interacts with the text area. Table 5-3 shows a few of these methods and provides a brief description for each. Feel free to try out these methods on the resultText instance and see how they affect your application.

Table 5-3. Methods of `JTextArea`

METHOD NAME	DESCRIPTION
`append(String text)`	Adds the *text* string specified to the end of the current JTextArea document.
`insert(String text, int pos)`	Inserts the specified *text* string at the position of the integer value.
`replaceRange(String text, int start, int end)`	Replaces the characters specified by the *start/end* integers with the value of the *text* string.
`setFont(Font f)`	Uses a Java Font instance to set the font display; check out the Java documentation on the API class `java.awt.Font` for more information.
`setLineWrap(boolean wrap)`	Sets the text area to wrap text based on a boolean value of TRUE or FALSE
`setTabSize(int size)`	Sets the number of characters to which the tab key expands.
`new(String text, int rows, int cols)`	Uses the default constructor to set the initial *text* string entry in text area. This is in addition to the text area set using integer values for rows and columns.

After implementing the `actionPerformed()` method, you are ready to build the GUI interface and use the `InterfaceCaller` logic built into this method, as shown here:

```
public class MaterialGui implements ActionListener {
    ...
    public MaterialGui() {
//Initialize and set visual framework components
    sapFrame = new JFrame("Material Search for SAP R/3");
    sapPanel = new JPanel();
    sapPanel.setLayout(new BorderLayout());
    selectPane = new JPanel();
    displayPane = new JPanel();
```

Chapter 5

```
//Initialize and set input and output components
    matSearch = new JTextField(20);
    resultText = new JTextArea(10,30);
    resultText.setEditable(false);
    JScrollPane resultPane = new JScrollPane(resultText,
                                    JScrollPane.VERTICAL_SCROLLBAR_ALWAYS,

JScrollPane.HORIZONTAL_SCROLLBAR_ALWAYS);
//Implement button with keyboard access and set listener
    retrieveList = new JButton("Get materials...");
    retrieveList.setMnemonic(KeyEvent.VK_ENTER);
    retrieveList.addActionListener(this);
//Add individual panels to overall application frame
    selectPane.add(matSearch);
    selectPane.add(retrieveList);
    displayPane.add(resultPane);
//Define panel layout within frame
    sapPanel.add(selectPane, BorderLayout.NORTH);
    sapPanel.add(displayPane, BorderLayout.SOUTH);
    sapFrame.getContentPane().add(sapPanel);
    sapFrame.getRootPane().setDefaultButton(retrieveList);
//General cleanup for close and frame implementation
    sapFrame.setDefaultCloseOperation(JFrame.EXIT_ON_CLOSE);
    sapFrame.pack();
    sapFrame.setVisible(true);
  }
  ...
}
```

Housing Visual Components with JFrame

You are finally ready to implement the default constructor that houses the application logic for building the visual interface. As seen previously, public MaterialGui() {...} *declares the constructor using the name of the Java class,* MaterialGui.

Next, you initialize the various GUI components that were declared as class-level variables.

```
//Initialize and set visual framework components
    sapFrame = new JFrame("Material Search for SAP R/3");
    sapPanel = new JPanel();
    sapPanel.setLayout(new BorderLayout());
    selectPane = new JPanel();
    displayPane = new JPanel();
```

The sapFrame instance is a new instance of the JFrame class, to which you pass the title displayed above the menu bar in the application's window. Similarly, you instantiated a new instance of JPanel, called sapPanel, which houses the subpanels of the GUI. Through the setLayout() method of sapPanel, the application is able to determine the method by which subsequent components are displayed in this panel. Java Swing provides a number of different layout mechanisms, each serving a slightly different purpose for displaying components.

BorderLayout gives the panel five distinct areas in which components can be placed: north, south, east, west, and center. This is a very straightforward means to layout components, enabling you to use commonly known directional terms to specify component placement. You only need to pass a newly instantiated instance of the BorderLayout class to the setLayout() method, with no parameters, so using the expression new BorderLayout() will suffice.

The last two lines instantiate the content panels, selectPane and displayPane, that are to be contained within the main panel, sapPanel. Nesting panels is a very common practice in Swing because it allows the developer more exact control over the placement of various components within the graphical user interface. Figure 5-2 shows the various user interface components as represented by their Java class names.

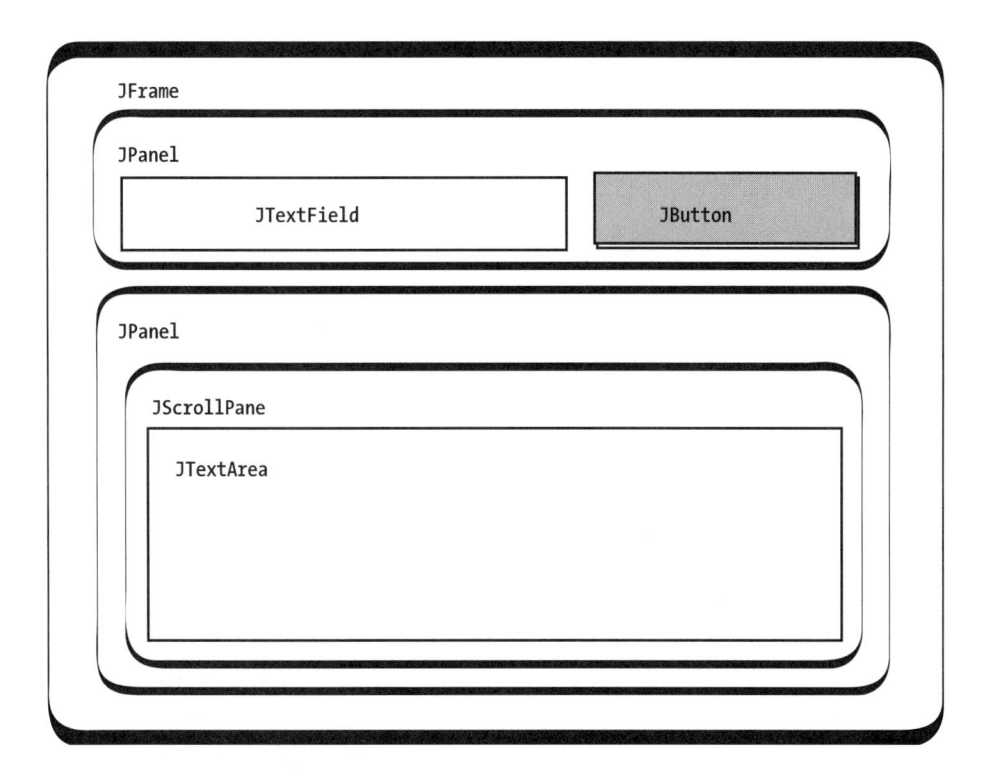

Figure 5-2. Java Swing layout used by the MaterialGui *class*

The next block of code initializes the various Java UI variables that were declared previously:

```
//Initialize and set input and output components
    matSearch = new JTextField(20);
    resultText = new JTextArea(10,30);
    resultText.setEditable(false);
    JScrollPane resultPane = new JScrollPane(resultText,
                                JScrollPane.VERTICAL_SCROLLBAR_ALWAYS,

JScrollPane.HORIZONTAL_SCROLLBAR_ALWAYS);
```

The application initializes a new `JTextField` called `matSearch`, which serves as a means for gathering input from the end user. Recall that this instance is used within the `actionPerformed()` method to retrieve the text string the user entered and pass it to the `getMaterialList()` method of `InterfaceCaller`. The single parameter used by `JTextField`'s default constructor is an integer value that specifies the display length of the field box in the GUI. This value does not limit the number of characters that can be entered into the `JTextField` instance, `matSearch`, rather, it limits the length of the field box displayed to the end user.

The subsequent statement instantiates a new `JTextArea` instance, called `resultText`, that is used to display the material list return from SAP. Like the `matSearch` instance, you have also seen `resultText` accessed in the `actionPerformed()` method, in this case to display text results back to the end user. This instance is also created using two integer values to limit the display size of the text area. The first value specifies the number of rows, and the second specifies the number of columns. As with `JTextField`, these values do not limit the amount of data displayed, only the amount of screen real estate used by the text area.

You will also likely want to restrict the text area display so that the end user cannot edit the list of materials that SAP returns. Regardless, this editing ability cannot affect SAP, only the user's ability to edit the display on the local computer. By passing a parameter of `FALSE` to the `setEditable()` method of `resultText`, you make it impossible for the user to change the text of the material list. The default behavior for a `JTextArea` allows the user to modify any text displayed here, so be sure you use the `setEditable()` method to turn this capability off.

Lastly, in order to make the display contents of `resultText` scrollable, you must instantiate an instance of `JScrollPane`, passing in `resultText` and two field attributes. The field attributes define certain characteristics of the scroll bar, such as whether or not to use horizontal and vertical scroll bars. Looking at the application library documentation for the `JScrollPane` class gives you a more comprehensive look at what fields are available for use in the default constructor.

Building a Desktop Interface to SAP

```
//Implement button with keyboard access and set listener
    retrieveList = new JButton("Get materials...");
    retrieveList.setMnemonic(KeyEvent.VK_ENTER);
    retrieveList.addActionListener(this);
```

In this code snippet, the application instantiates a new `JButton` instance, `retrieveList`, passing in the text string displayed on the button's face as the sole parameter. `JButton` also has several methods that the application calls on the `retrieveList` instance. The `setMnemonic()` method creates a keyboard shortcut so that the button can be clicked using ALT-*XX* from the keyboard, where *XX* is a predefined key. In this case, the application passes a field attribute, `KeyEvent.VK_ENTER`, which sets the shortcut to ALT-Enter on the keyboard.

Finally, the `retrieveList` instance uses its `setActionListener()` method to register this object as an action listener on the class `this`. Remember, `this` is a reserved keyword in Java that points to the current class. In effect, you are telling the `setActionListener()` method to look in the `MaterialGui` class for the appropriate methods to handle an action event sent from the `retrieveList` button. By implementing the `ActionListener` class within the class declaration for `MaterialGui`, you allow `MaterialGui` to be registered as an action listener. Furthermore, by implementing the `actionPerformed()` method of the `ActionListener` class as part of `MaterialGui`, when you click the Get Materials button, any logic built into this method is automatically invoked.

```
//Add individual panels to overall application frame
    selectPane.add(matSearch);
    selectPane.add(retrieveList);
    displayPane.add(resultPane);
```

You are now ready to add the newly populated content components to their respective application panels. The text field and button need to be housed in the `selectPane`, which is the panel displayed at the top of the application. Using the `add()` method on `selectPane`, the application passes in `matSearch` and `retrieveList` as two different calls to this method. Likewise, the pane containing the display text area `resultPane` needs to be added to `displayPane` using that instance's `add()` method.

```
//Define panel layout within frame
    sapPanel.add(selectPane, BorderLayout.NORTH);
    sapPanel.add(displayPane, BorderLayout.SOUTH);
    sapFrame.getContentPane().add(sapPanel);
    sapFrame.getRootPane().setDefaultButton(retrieveList);
```

Now things get a little more complicated. Recall that the application has used the `setLayout()` method on `sapPanel` to set the layout to an instance of `BorderLayout`. In order to use the layout management features of the `BorderLayout` class, you must specify one of five areas in which to place a given component: north, south, east, west, and center. As you add each pane to `sapPanel`, you must also tell the instance in which quadrant to locate that component. Using the `add()` method of `sapPanel`, you pass two parameters: the `JPanel` instance that maintains the application's content components, and a field attribute that specifies where to place that pane. In the first line or this code, `selectPane` is being added to `sapPanel` and placed in the north quadrant of that pane. Then similar to `selectPane`, on the next line, `displayPane` is also added to `sapPanel`; however, it is being placed in the south quadrant.

Once the content panes have been populated, you are ready to add the main pane into the window frame. Using a straightforward nested method call series, you retrieve the `sapFrame` instance's `contentPane` object using the `getContentPane()` method. Then, you call the `add()` method on this object, passing in the `sapPanel` instance populated earlier. Ultimately, these methods allow you to push content panes out to the main `JFrame` instance, `sapFrame`, which then displays those panes and their content components back to the end user.

```
//General cleanup for close and frame implementation
    sapFrame.setDefaultCloseOperation(JFrame.EXIT_ON_CLOSE);
    sapFrame.pack();
    sapFrame.setVisible(true);
```

Now that the panes and frame have all been populated, formatted, and set, the final detail is to tell the Java Swing libraries to kick them off to the end user. However, before you do that, you might also want to set a close operation so that the user can exit cleanly from the application.

The `setDefaultCloseOperation()` sets the default action that occurs when the user clicks the Close button on the current window. Because this is a single window application, you probably want the application to exit completely when the user clicks the Close button. By passing the field attribute `JFrame.EXIT_ON_CLOSE` to this method, you cause the JVM to exit the application and shut down.

Calling the `pack()` method on `sapFrame` causes the window to be sized appropriately and made displayable if it is not already. The `setVisible()` method simply tells the JVM whether to make the window visible or not based on the value of the boolean passed as a parameter. In this case, you set this value to TRUE so that the window and all of its components are visible to the end user.

Bringing all of that together, your application should look something like this:

```
import javax.swing.*;
import java.awt.*;
import java.awt.event.*;
import java.util.*;
```

```java
public class MaterialGui implements ActionListener {
    JFrame sapFrame;
    JPanel sapPanel;
    JTextField matSearch;
    JButton retrieveList;
    JTextArea resultText;
    JPanel selectPane;
    JPanel displayPane;

    public MaterialGui() {
        sapFrame = new JFrame("Material Search for SAP R/3");
        sapPanel = new JPanel();
        sapPanel.setLayout(new BorderLayout());
        selectPane = new JPanel();
        displayPane = new JPanel();

        matSearch = new JTextField(20);
        resultText = new JTextArea(10,30);
        resultText.setEditable(false);
        JScrollPane resultPane = new JScrollPane(resultText,
                                        JScrollPane.VERTICAL_SCROLLBAR_ALWAYS,
                                        JScrollPane.HORIZONTAL_SCROLLBAR_ALWAYS);

        retrieveList = new JButton("Get materials...");
        retrieveList.setMnemonic(KeyEvent.VK_ENTER);
        retrieveList.addActionListener(this);

        selectPane.add(matSearch);
        selectPane.add(retrieveList);
        displayPane.add(resultPane);

        sapPanel.add(selectPane, BorderLayout.NORTH);
        sapPanel.add(displayPane, BorderLayout.SOUTH);
        sapFrame.getContentPane().add(sapPanel);
        sapFrame.getRootPane().setDefaultButton(retrieveList);
        sapFrame.setDefaultCloseOperation(JFrame.EXIT_ON_CLOSE);
        sapFrame.pack();
        sapFrame.setVisible(true);
    }
```

```java
    public void actionPerformed(ActionEvent event) {
      InterfaceCaller iCaller = new InterfaceCaller();
      Hashtable returnHash = iCaller.getMaterialList(matSearch.getText());
      Hashtable rowHash;
      for (Enumeration e = returnHash.elements(); e.hasMoreElements();) {
        rowHash = (Hashtable)e.nextElement();
        resultText.append("Material: " +
                (String)rowHash.get("MATERIAL") + "\n");
        resultText.append("Material description: " +
                (String)rowHash.get("MATL_DESC") + "\n\n");
      }
    }
    public static void main(String[] args) {
      try {
        UIManager.setLookAndFeel(
        UIManager.getCrossPlatformLookAndFeelClassName());
      }
      catch (Exception e) {}
      MaterialGui matGui = new MaterialGui();
    }
}
```

For the sake of brevity, all of the comments used to describe the code snippets have been removed. Remember, single-line comments are indicated with double forward slashes, //, and are totally ignored by the Java compiler and executable.

Compile the new `MaterialListGui` application and execute it from the command line as you have done previously with the `MaterialList` class:

`java MaterialListGui`

Figure 5-3 depicts a screenshot of the `MaterialListGui` after the end user has retrieved a list of materials from SAP and selected one for display.

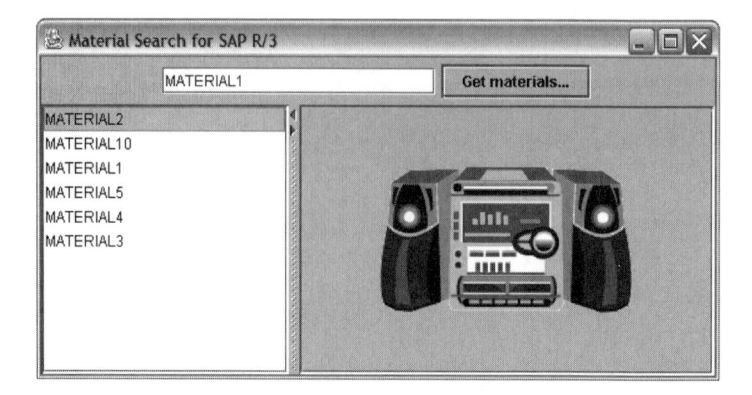

Figure 5-3. `MaterialListGui` *screenshot*

Summary

Having worked through the `MaterialGui` application tutorial, you should now be familiar with the fundamental concepts surrounding the development of a desktop client using a visual interface. Likewise, this chapter demonstrated how to use properties files to configure the system variables of your SAP application; it also helped you broaden your understanding of internationalization in Enterprise Java.

Here are a few points to keep in mind:

- Be very careful when you are hard-coding information within your applications; consider using properties files or other methods unless hard-coding is absolutely required.

- Using Java locales and resource bundles to specify static text strings in your application makes it much simpler to internationalize, should the need to do so ever arise.

- Graphical desktop clients provide an intuitive way for users to work with your SAP functionality; however, if you must deploy to a large number of users, consider the Web application development proposed in the next two chapters.

CHAPTER 6
Extending SAP to the Web

Chapter 6

IN THE LAST TWO CHAPTERS, you looked at building Java applications for SAP that deployed directly to the end user's desktop. Although this gives your end users a break from navigating the SAP GUI, it does not really make life easier for the Information Technologies (IT) department. This is because every time the application is updated, whether through a bug fix or functional enhancement, your IT group has to manually reinstall or update the code on each machine. Thankfully, the company intranet provides an easier way to deploy and maintain these Java-based applications.

This chapter focuses on building applications that can be run within a Java application server and accessed via a standard Web browser. In using such applications, you not only wield the flexibility of a single desktop interface, but you also centralize the application logic to guarantee that your end users have the most current version of your code.

This chapter looks at the following:

- Basic application server concepts

- Installing the Tomcat application server

- Building a sample Web application

Looking at the Application Server

The introduction of client/server technology in the 1980s was a huge step forward from the dumb terminal/mainframe model. The client/server model allowed you to move much of the computing load off the mainframe server and into more readily available and less expensive desktop computers. However, this came at the price of decentralizing the store of application logic into discrete units represented as a single end user on the network. Although this may have made sense from a purely hardware economic perspective, the move inadvertently created and required two entirely new company departments: Information Systems and Desktop Support.

As the cost of centralized server hardware and software has rapidly diminished over time, companies have begun to reevaluate their purpose and place within the corporate infrastructure. Of course, there can be no stemming the tide of powerful desktop machines and notebook computers, which allow users to process text, spreadsheets, and presentation documents at unprecedented speeds. But for key business processes and mission critical applications, companies have grown more and more leery of relying on the vagaries of assuming that each user's software version is current or even running at any given moment.

Enter the application server. Many of you are apt to be familiar with the concept of an application server, and if you are SAP users, than everything you do requires an application server. The R/3 architecture uses a three-tier model, which calls for a database system to house information, an application server to run applications that affect this information, and a client desktop application that displays this information to the end user. Everyday, you use the SAP GUI to access business transactions within the R/3 system, whether you are creating sales orders, looking up materials, or even creating a new SAP application.

The major limitation of the SAP GUI is simply that it requires around 40 megabytes of hard drive space and must be installed on a user's desktop before that user can access the R/3 system. For regular, internal users of your SAP instances, SAP GUI is required. But what about the occasional users of the system—those who run a small number of transactions and don't need the flexibility of the SAP GUI? Or perhaps your company needs to let key business partners have access to a limited number of R/3 transactions and reports. Loading SAP GUI on their machines is out of the question. Couldn't you build a Java application designed specifically around their needs and let them access it from a centralized application server?

The answer, of course, is yes. The Java 2 Platform, Enterprise Edition (J2EE) introduces the specification for an incredibly powerful Java application server that allows you to easily develop and deploy Java applications across the network. The remainder of this chapter shows you how to install your own application server and walks you through an example of an application that you can access through a standard Web browser.

Installing Tomcat

Offered by the Apache group as part of their Jakarta project, Tomcat is a limited implementation of the Enterprise Java application server specification with some additional capabilities thrown in for good measure. For those of you unfamiliar with Apache, it is a loosely formed group of developers who are dedicated to contributing and supporting open source software development. Open source applications are those in which the source code, as well as platform specific binaries, are released free of charge to the world. Any developer can use or modify this source code, under the condition that any modification or enhancement must also be released as open source.

I say that Tomcat is a limited implementation of the Enterprise Java specification because it does not include support for the more advanced J2EE standards such as Enterprise JavaBeans (EJB). However, it definitely suits the purposes of this book, and anything you build to run in Tomcat can be easily deployed by any J2EE-compliant application server. In addition, you can also use Tomcat as a Web server; this lets you build Java applications with a Web front end and lets your users access those applications through a Web browser. The obvious advantage of this type of interface is that most end users already have a favorite Web browser installed and require little in the way of direct desktop or network support.

> **NOTE** As mentioned previously, this book assumes that you are developing on a Microsoft Windows-based platform and will direct you to the Tomcat binaries accordingly. On the other hand, if you are looking for an alternative, you will find a good cross section of UNIX-based operating systems to which Tomcat has already been ported.

To get started with the installation, first download the application server binaries from the Apache Website. Go to http://jakarta.apache.org/tomcat/ and select the Binaries link underneath the Download section in the left column. This takes you to a list of all the current release builds in the Jakarta project. In this list, you will find a link to Tomcat 4.0, which will take you to an FTP server. Under the bin/ directory, you will find a series of archived files, each with a slightly different purpose. You should download the JDK1.4 light version—jakarta-tomcat-4.0.4-LE-jdk14.zip—although any of the Tomcat 4.0 versions will work for your application.

Now that you have saved the archived file to disk, simply unzip the archive into your development directory (or the root drive, such as C:\).

> **NOTE** When you unzip Tomcat using the default directory name, you end up with an obscenely long path name—C:\jakarta-tomcat-4.0.4-LE-jdk14, for example. For the sake of simplicity, I prefer to rename the directory to something like: C:\Tomcat. As long as you rename it immediately after unzipping the server, you won't have any problems with system variables and registry settings.

The next step is to set a system variable to locate the installation directory of the Tomcat server. Again, open the autoexec.bat file located in your boot drive (usually c:\autoexec.bat) and add the line:

```
set CATALINA_HOME=C:\dev\tomcat
```

Be sure to use the directory where you unzipped the application server if you didn't rename it to \dev\tomcat. You need to reboot your computer to initialize this new system variable.

> **NOTE** From Windows NT forward, you can set environment variables through the Control Panel. From the Start menu, open the Control Panel and double-click the System icon. In this dialog box, select either the tab or the button labeled Environment Variables and set the name/value pairs as indicated.

Extending SAP to the Web

You are now ready to test the Tomcat installation. First, open the `bin` directory found directly underneath the Tomcat install path (for example, `c:\dev\tomcat\bin`). This directory contains all the server executables, but you are only interested in `startup.bat`. Run `startup.bat` and you will see a command console window pop up displaying the text `Apache Tomcat/4.0.4` or whatever version of Tomcat you are running.

Load your Web browser and enter: `http://localhost:8080` as the URL. Your browser will display the Tomcat welcome page, indicating that the server has been installed successfully. Notice that you had to specify a port number in the URL line. As a Web server, Tomcat can be configured to use different ports so it does not interfere with any other Web server software you might be running. For the sake of convenience, let's configure Tomcat to run on port 80, the standard port for serving Web pages. In doing so, you won't have to specify a port in the URL, which is behavior more consistent with the Websites you encounter on a daily basis.

> **NOTE** *The term* `localhost` *used in a URL statement refers to the internal domain name assigned to your computer. When using TCP/IP, each machine on a given network must be assigned a unique, external IP address, such as* `192.168.1.10`. *However, each machine also has an internal IP address, known as the loopback address. This is an address assigned to the network interface, such as an Ethernet card, and it is used to test the TCP/IP connection within the operating system before any traffic is sent across the network. The loopback address is* `127.0.0.1` *and is the same on nearly any machine designed to deal with TCP/IP network traffic. Just as IP addresses on the Internet often have an easy-to-remember domain name, so too does the loopback IP address. Instead of typing in* `127.0.0.1` *every time you want to call a service on your own computer, you can simply use the domain name* `localhost` *to achieve the same results.*

Alongside the `bin` director underneath your Tomcat home, you will also find a directory named `conf`. The `conf` directory contains both configuration and policy files you need to run Tomcat. Using your text editor, open the `server.xml` file. Search for the text string "8080" within this file.

The search brings you to a block of XML code similar to this:

```
<!-- Define a non-SSL HTTP/1.1 Connector on port 8080 -->
<Connector className="org.apache.catalina.connector.http.HttpConnector"
           port="8080" minProcessors="5" maxProcessors="75"
           enableLookups="true" redirectPort="8443"
           acceptCount="10" debug="0" connectionTimeout="60000"/>
```

137

```
<!-- Note : To disable connection timeouts, set connectionTimeout value
    to -1 -->
```

Change the text string "8080" to "80", save the file, and exit. You now need to shutdown your Tomcat server using the file `shutdown.bat` found in the `bin` directory. Restart the server using `startup.bat` as you did previously. Enter the URL http://localhost. You should see the same Tomcat welcome page, but this time you do not need to remember the port to get to the local Tomcat Website.

> **CAUTION** *The default installation of Microsoft Windows often includes the Personal Web Server or Microsoft Internet Information Services (IIS). These products both use port 80 to serve Web pages. Either shut down these servers, or leave Tomcat configured to use port 8080. If you prefer the latter, simply change any* http://localhost/ *reference to* http://localhost:8080/.

Building a Sample Application

You are finally ready to start developing your Web application for SAP. First, you need to create a deployment directory for the Web application in Tomcat.

Under the Tomcat home directory, find the directory called `webapps`. Create a directory under `webapps` called `sap`. You also need to create a directory called `WEB-INF` underneath the `sap` directory. After you have created both directories, restart the Tomcat server using the `shutdown.bat` and `startup.bat` files found in the `bin` directory. You should now have a directory structure similar to this:

```
C:\dev\tomcat\webapps\sap\WEB-INF
```

You also need to add an initial XML configuration file for the Web application. The file is called `web.xml` and it is based on a more robust version found under `tomcat/conf`. You will use `web.xml`, later on to control and fine-tune certain aspects of your application. For now, you just need to have a version of the file in the `webapps/sap/WEB-INF` directory. Your `web.xml` should look like this:

```
<?xml version="1.0" encoding="ISO-8859-1"?>

<!DOCTYPE web-app
    PUBLIC "-//Sun Microsystems, Inc.//DTD Web Application 2.3//EN"
    "http://java.sun.com/dtd/web-app_2_3.dtd">

<web-app>
</web-app>
```

Extending SAP to the Web

Let's create a simple Web page, called `testpage.html` to deploy and test within the `webapps/sap` directory.

```
<HTML>
  <BODY>
    <H1>Why is Austin making me write boring HTML?</H1>
  </BODY>
</HTML>
```

Enter the URL: `http://localhost/sap/testpage.html`. You should see the message you entered into the HTML page displayed in big, thick, bold letters. Not drastically exciting, but it does show that *any* HTML page you put in your `webapps/sap` directory is automatically deployed without you having to restart the Tomcat server. However, you are not here to learn HTML, so it's time to throw some Java into the mix.

The J2EE specification allows you to mix HTML display tags and Java application code into something known as JavaServer Pages (JSP) technology. The great thing about JSP pages is that you can modify them on the fly, even when the application server is still running, and see the work reflected when you refresh the page in your Web browser.

Creating a Dynamic JSP

So what exactly does a JSP page do? Using special JSP tag directives in a normal Web page, you can define blocks of Java code that are read by the Java application server before the page is displayed to the end user. The Java application server, in this case Tomcat, recognizes and differentiates between HTML and Java, leaving the HTML alone, while compiling the Java into actual bytecode. Recall that in previous chapters you had to explicitly compile the Java classes before they could be executed. When dealing with JSP pages, the application server does that for you automatically, saving the bytecode on the server for future reuse. Sun's in-depth tutorial on JavaServer Pages can be found at: `http://java.sun.com/j2ee/tutorial/1_3-fcs/doc/JSPIntro.html`.

I think it's time for a hands-on look at a JSP page.

```
<%@ page language="java"
<%@ page import="java.util.*" %>

<HTML>
  <HEAD>
    <TITLE>Simple Date Page</TITLE>
  </HEAD>
```

```
    <BODY>
      <H1>Simple Date Page</H1>
      <B><I><%= new Date().toString() %></B></I>
    </BODY>
</HTML>
```

Again, enter this code into a text editor, but this time save the file as `date.jsp`. By giving the file an extension of `.jsp`, you are telling the application server to pull out and compile any Java tags, and then display the result as a Web page.

Save the `date.jsp` file into your `webapps/sap` directory, and then enter the URL `http://localhost/sap/date.jsp`. You will see a very basic title with a time and date string displayed below it. So where does the Java code come in? Refresh your Web browser, and each time you do, notice the time stamp dynamically incrementing. Figure 6-1 depicts the results from a successful call to `date.jsp`.

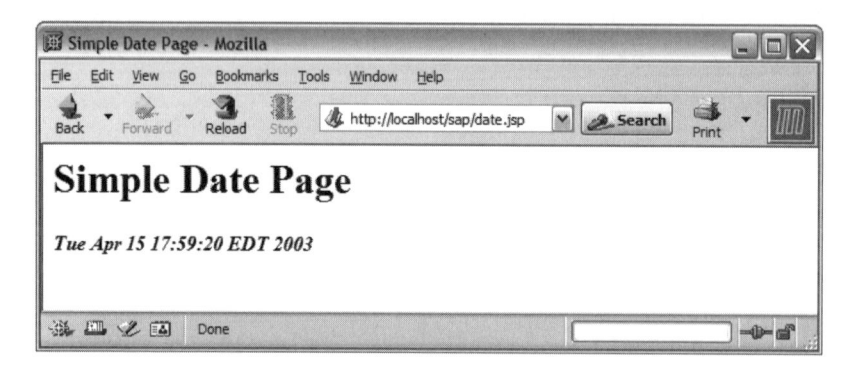

Figure 6-1. A successful call to `date.jsp`

Using JSP Tags

Before moving on, let's dissect this sample JSP page, demonstrated in the previous section, to better understand its components? The

```
<%@ page language="java" %>
```

line simply tells the application server that you have built this page using Java as the programming language. Next, you have an `import` statement similar to those found in the earlier applications:

```
<%@ page import="java.util.*" %>
```

This statement gives your JSP page access to any of the Java class libraries that are part of the `java.util` package.

The next line of Java code is the date routine, which is the essence of this little Web application:

```
<%= new Date().toString() %>
```

The Java code is very simple, in that you are creating a new instance of the Date class using its default constructor. The JSP page then calls the toString() method of this new Date instance, which returns a text string with the time and date set to when the object was created. Every time you refresh this page, you create a new instance of the Date object, and every time this happens, the default constructor sets the time and date of that instance to current. This behavior allows you to see the time dynamically incrementing each time the page is refreshed within your Web browser.

Of perhaps more interest is how you are able to embed Java code directly into a Web page and use standard HTML tags to format the result. Any Java code used in a JSP must be bracketed with an opening tag, <%, and a closing tag, %>. These tags tell the application server to treat anything between them as Java code, and attempt to compile it accordingly.

In this example, you used two different types of basic JSP tags. The first is the <%@ page...%> tag, otherwise simply known as a page tag. This type of tag applies to everything within the current JSP page. In this case, you define the language of the Web page, Java, and import a Java package for use within this JSP page. Both attributes are applied to the entire page, allowing any Java code built into the JSP page to be able to use the java.util.* package.

The <%=...%> tag can contain any valid Java expression, such as a String variable, or any method or expression that evaluates to a text string. This tag is mainly used to dynamically display data contained within the various Java objects used or created by the JSP page.

Handling User Input from a Web Page

The next JSP example comprises both an inbound page to take data from the end user and an outbound page to display results. This is your first step toward building a truly interactive Web application.

Retrieving Data with an HTML Form

First, you need to take data from the end user. You can accomplish this easily by using a standard HTML form. Moreover, most users should already be familiar with how to use this type of interface to interact with a Web application.

The following code is a straightforward HTML document that describes two input fields and a Submit button:

```
<%@ page language="java" %>

<HTML>
  <HEAD>
    <TITLE>User Login</TITLE>
  </HEAD>
  <BODY>
    <H1>User Login</H1>
    <FORM ACTION="loginResult.jsp" METHOD="post">
    Username: <INPUT TYPE="text" NAME="username">
    <P>
    Password: <INPUT TYPE="password" NAME="password">
    <P>
    <INPUT TYPE="submit" VALUE="Login">
    </FORM>
  </BODY>
</HTML>
```

Copy this code into your text editor and save the file as `login.jsp` in the `webapps/sap` directory. For the remainder of this chapter, you may assume that any JSP files you are working with should be saved in the `webapps/sap` directory, unless specified otherwise.

This JSP page contains an HTML form and three input elements. The beginning of the form is defined by the following statement:

```
<FORM ACTION="loginResult.jsp" METHOD="post">
```

This line tells the Java application server which JSP page to hit after processing the data in this form. Notice that the `ACTION=` attribute points to a relative URL indicating only the name of the JSP page. Relative URLs tell the Web server to remain at the current directory level on the server when attempting to retrieve a given page. In contrast, a fully qualified URL explicitly spells out the page name and absolute file path of the document page on the server.

> **CAUTION** *Any URL defined with* `localhost` *as the domain name is only accessible through the machine where the application server is running. This means that you are limited to running your Web application through a browser that exists on the application server and nowhere else on the network. As you expand your development effort, be sure to strip out any* `localhost` *references so that the application can be accessed from across the network.*

The METHOD= attribute describes how data should be transferred back to the application server. The two applicable values for this attribute are get and post. When you use the get value, any data you enter into the form is sent as legible text within the string of the URL. Not the greatest idea when you are dealing with sensitive information such as passwords. The post value requests that the server enclose the data in some type of subordinate resource. The application server determines what that resource is and how it should be stored. The practical use for the post value is to keep data effectively hidden from human eyes, at least at the URL level. Needless to say, I recommend using the post value, unless you wish to risk prying eyes and unauthorized users.

> **CAUTION** *Although using the* post *value effectively prevents casual snooping from a Web browser, a hacker can easily get at this information. A network sniffer is one tool that can intercept packets sent over the network and decode them as plain text. In a production environment, data should be encrypted and sent via a Secure Sockets Layer (SSL) connection using the secure version of the Hypertext Transfer Protocol (HTTPS).*

Your JSP page uses three different types of field tags to actually take input from the end user. The line

```
<INPUT TYPE="text" NAME="username">
```

specifies the use of a plain text form field with a key assigned to it called "username". The TYPE= attribute defines the type of form field, and the NAME= attribute assigns a field key so that you can easily retrieve the data within subsequent Web pages.

The following statement is similar, except now your JSP page is using an input type of "password".

```
<INPUT TYPE="password" NAME="password">
```

Whereas typed characters are visible to the end user when the input type is set to "text", a series of Xs are used to mask the user's input when the input type is set to "password".

Finally, the following line describes the HTML version of a Submit button, instructing the application server to process the form data and proceed to the Web page specified in the <FORM ACTION=...> attribute.

```
<INPUT TYPE="submit" VALUE="Login">
```

Changing the VALUE= attribute changes the text displayed on your form button. Figure 6-2 shows the basic login screen with username and password fields as input.

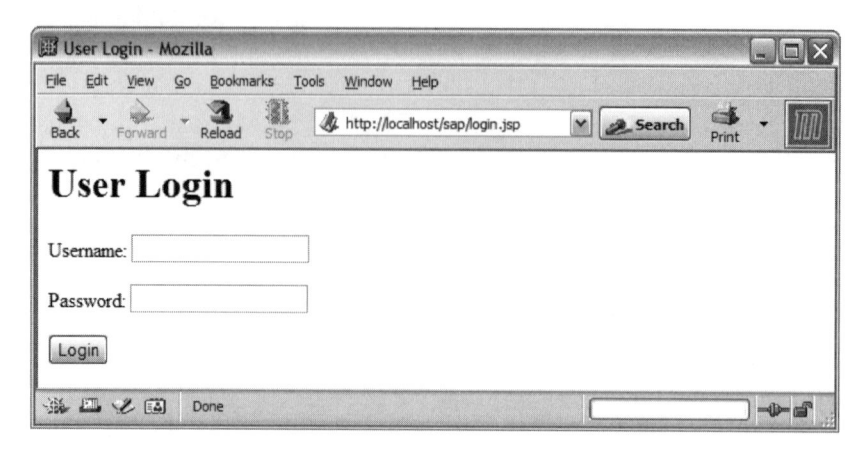

Figure 6-2. Basic Web browser login screen

Now that the inbound JSP page is complete, you are ready to move on to displaying the results of your login back to the end user. To do so, you need a slightly more complex JSP page in which you have added Java code to handle the authentication and end user display. At this point, you will not actually authorize the end user against a database, rather, you are going to use Java code within the JSP page to spoof such a login.

Displaying Stored HTTP Session Data

The following code demonstrates the use of a user's Web session to store and display data. Although this page does not connect to an authentication system, it does provide a starting point for building a working login to a real system.

```
<%@ page language="java" %>
<%@ page import="java.util.*" %>

<HTML>
  <HEAD>
    <TITLE>User Login</TITLE>
  </HEAD>
  <BODY>
  <%
    String username = (String)request.getParameter("username");
    String password = (String)request.getParameter("password");
```

```
      if ("password".equals(password)) {
   %>
      <H1>Welcome, <%= request.getParameter("username") %></H1>
      You have logged in at: <%= new Date().toString() %>
   <%
      }
      else {
        out.println("<H1> Password incorrect, please try again.</H1>");
      }
   %>
   </BODY>
</HTML>
```

As you can see, this JSP page is somewhat more complicated than the first one because it introduces some valuable JSP techniques that you will use later on.

The top of the JSP page still contains two page tags: one defines the language used in this Web page, and the other imports a specific Java package. The next JSP tag is a new one that you haven't used yet; it is known as a *scriptlet tag*.

As the name implies, the scriptlet tag allows you to build Java code, or scripts, directly into the body of the JSP page. You use the syntax <%...%> to tell the application server to treat any text contained within as Java code that the server should pull out and attempt to compile.

```
   <%
      String username = (String)request.getParameter("username");
      String password = (String)request.getParameter("password");
      ...
   %>
```

The first scriptlet block in this JSP page deals with retrieving the username and password fields that were populated by the end user in the login.jsp page. In order to do so, the JSP page must access the ServletRequest object that gets populated by the Java application server.

Without even asking, the Java application server has gone behind your back and created an instance of the javax.servlet.ServletRequest class in order to house the data coming from the end user. The ServletRequest class is the part of the J2EE specification that allows you to retrieve data coming in from a Web browser over the HTTP stream. This means that you can easily use information captured by standard HTML forms to feed variables in your Java applications.

Using this ServletRequest instance is so necessary that the JSP specification has given it a reserved identifier called request. Rather than having to manually retrieve the ServletRequest object from the application server, you can seamlessly use the request object that has already been made available to the JSP page.

Using the `getParameter()` method of the `request` object, the JSP page initializes two `String` instances: `username` and `password`. In order to use this method, you must pass it a text string parameter that indicates the key value that was used to store the field value in the `ServletRequest` object. Sounds complicated? Not at all, this is simply the value you used in the `NAME=` attribute of the HTML form input tags.

Next, you begin an `if...else` block, bearing in mind that it differs from the usual Java syntax.

```
<%
...
if ("password".equals(password)) {
%>
```

In the preceding conditional, your JSP page checks to see that the string "password" equals the value of `password`. Remember, every text string in Java is treated as a `String` object and has certain methods that you can use to check and manipulate the value of that object. Here, you call the `equals()` method, passing in the `String` object you wish to check against as the single parameter. If the value of `password` equals "password", then whatever follows in the {...} block is executed.

However, you now need to combine some static HTML with dynamic, conditional data. You must first close off the Java code block with a scriptlet end tag, `%>`. This puts your JSP page back into standard HTML mode, where you can define several lines of HTML code.

```
<H1>Welcome, <%= request.getParameter("username") %></H1>
You have logged in at: <%= new Date().toString() %>
```

Again, notice that the JSP page has combined HTML tags such as `<H1>` with JSP tags, like the expression tag `<%=...%>`. Your JSP page is also using the `request` object to retrieve and display the username within the `<H1>...</H1>` block. Likewise, you could have used the `username` variable that was initialized earlier because the values are the same. However, I wanted to show you another use of the JSP expression tag as a way to displaying dynamic data.

Finally, you need to reopen the scriptlet block to define the `else` condition within the JSP page.

```
<%
}
else {
    out.println("<H1> Password incorrect, please try again.</H1>");
}
%>
```

Extending SAP to the Web

When you are using the <%...%> scriptlet block, you must first close off the `if` block from the previous scriptlet. If you fail to do so, the Java application server is unable to compile this application because you have not followed proper Java syntax by ending the `if` block. After you close this block, you can then add an `else` block, which contains the Java code to be executed if the `if` condition has not been met.

Rather than exiting out of this scriptlet, the JSP page includes the HTML display tags directly within your Java code. This is simply an alternative way of ending the scriptlet block to execute standard HTML; you can then reopen the scriptlet to complete the `else` block. Here, you use another reserved identifier described by the JSP specification—the `out` instance.

The `out` object is an instance of the `javax.servlet.jsp.JspWriter` class, which you can use to write the output stream to the Web browser. As with the case of the `request` object, `out` is used so frequently that it has been made available as a reserved instance, meaning you do not need to manually initialize or mange it.

In this case, the JSP page simply calls the `out.println()` method, passing in the text string you wish to send to the browser. That the JSP page also includes HTML tags in the text string means that the browser interprets and displays those tags as part of the standard Web page. Figure 6-3 shows the results from a login using any username and a password of "password".

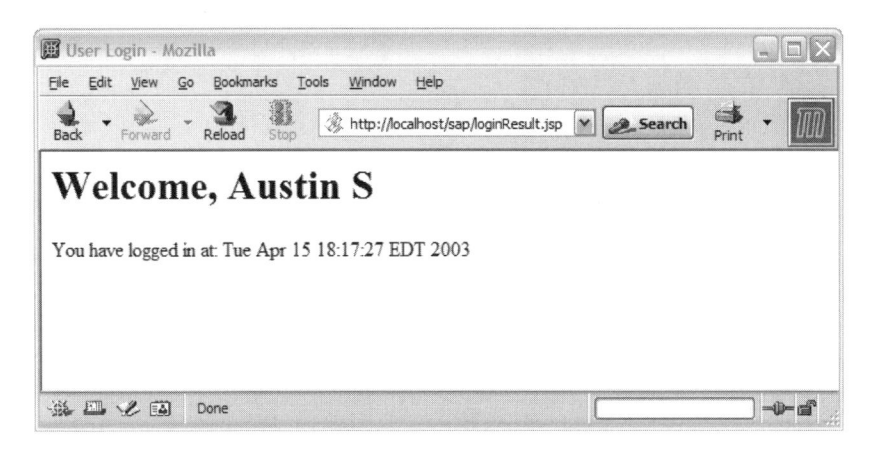

Figure 6-3. Displaying session data through the login screen

You have explored the basics of JSP page development and created the skeleton for a basic login Web application. This is a "quick and dirty" technique for quickly building Web applications. Chapter 7 looks at a more sustainable development approach using Java servlets and a commonly recognized design pattern. With that said, the next section demonstrates the ability to directly access your SAP logic from within a JSP page.

Authenticating a User with SAP

You are now ready to build a real-world application that uses the R/3 database to authenticate the user, rather than using the faux authentication from the previous example. Assuming that all of your users have preassigned SAP user seats, you could simply modify the R/3 system variables used to create the JCo connection and determine authority based on whether the call to `JCO.Client` succeeds or fails. Unfortunately, this method limits access to your Web application based on existing R/3 users. Likewise, the expense associated with purchasing new user seats can quickly get out of hand as your company adds new users to this application.

Thankfully, SAP has provided a convenient mechanism for authenticating users who would normally not require a full SAP user license. Known as the Internet User facility, this functionality allows anyone with a record as a customer, vendor, employee, and so on in SAP to also have an Internet username and password. For the purposes of this application, you are going to assume that each of the users has a customer profile in SAP, so you will create your Internet users using the customer type. To accomplish this, you need to work with your BASIS administrator to create such an account. Tell them that you need an Internet user created for your chosen customer profile and they will give you a username and password. The username will be the same as that assigned to the customer identifier in SAP's customer master database.

Once you have the Internet user set up, you need to determine which BAPI allows the application to correctly authenticate the customer in SAP. Again, use the Function Builder to find a BAPI called `BAPI_CUSTOMER_CHECKPASSWORD`, whose sole purpose is to check the authority of an Internet user account assigned with a customer profile.

Next you need to add a new method, called `checkPassword()` to the `InterfaceCaller` class that you created in the last chapter. This is the method your Java applications will use to authenticate the Web user against SAP's Internet User facility.

```
package com.apress.ejsap;

import com.sap.mw.jco.*;
import java.util.Hashtable;
import java.util.ResourceBundle;
public class InterfaceCaller {
  ...
  public Hashtable checkPassword(String username, String password) {

    JCO.Function function = getFunction("BAPI_CUSTOMER_CHECKPASSWORD");
    JCO.ParameterList listParams = function.getImportParameterList();
    listParams.setValue(username, "CUSTOMERNO");
    listParams.setValue(password, "PASSWORD");
```

```
        aConnection.execute(function);

        JCO.ParameterList resultParams = function.getExportParameterList();
        Hashtable returnHash = new Hashtable();
        returnHash.put("RETURN.TYPE",extractField("RETURN","TYPE",resultParams));
        returnHash.put("RETURN.CODE",extractField("RETURN","CODE",resultParams));
        returnHash.put("RETURN.MESSAGE",
                        extractField("RETURN","MESSAGE",resultParams));
        return returnHash;
    }
    ...
}
```

This `checkPassword()` method takes two text strings as parameters: String username and String password. The code in this new method is similar to the `getMaterialList()` method, except that instead of retrieving and populating a table from the metadata interface, you simply set the values for two single parameters.

```
        JCO.ParameterList listParams = function.getImportParameterList();
        listParams.setValue(username, "CUSTOMERNO");
        listParams.setValue(password, "PASSWORD");
```

Notice that you are still using an instance of the `ParameterList` class, but the application is calling a different method on the `function` object. Rather than needing to retrieve a list of tables from the BAPI interface, you only need a list of the single parameters required to make this call. The `getImportParameterList()` method returns a `ParameterList` object containing these parameters' keys, which you then set in the following two lines. Remember, the `setValue()` method requires that its parameters be formatted with a field value followed by a field name.

Finally, as with the `getMaterialList()` method, the application returns a `Hashtable` back to originator of the method call. Unlike `getMaterialList()`, you don't really have any data that needs to be returned, just the state of authentication—success or failure, for example. To check the login status, you grab several key fields from the BAPI structure returned by SAP, specifically the return type and code as well as any message text from the R/3 system. This gives you the ability to not only check the status of authentication, but also to display any error messages that SAP may have sent back.

Let's make sure that you have all of these changes straight with a look at the newly and heavily modified `InterfaceCaller` class:

```java
package com.apress.ejsap;

import com.sap.mw.jco.*;
import java.util.Hashtable;
import java.util.ResourceBundle;
public class InterfaceCaller {

  ResourceBundle sapProperties = ResourceBundle.getBundle("sapdata");
  public static final String SAP_CLIENT =
        sapProperties.getString("jco.client.client");
  public static final String USER_ID =
        sapProperties.getString("jco.client.user");
  public static final String PASSWORD =
        sapProperties.getString("jco.client.passwd");
  public static final String LANGUAGE =
        sapProperties.getString("jco.client.langu");
  public static final String HOST_NAME =
        sapProperties.getString("jco.client.ashost");
  public static final String SYSTEM_NUMBER =
        sapProperties.getString("jco.client.sysnr");

  private JCO.Client aConnection;
  private IRepository aRepository;

  public InterfaceCaller() {
    createConnection();
    retrieveRepository();
  }

  public Hashtable getMaterialList(String searchParam) {
    JCO.Function function = getFunction("BAPI_MATERIAL_GETLIST");
    JCO.ParameterList tabParams = function.getTableParameterList();
    JCO.Table materials = tabParams.getTable("MATNRSELECTION");

     materials.appendRow();
     materials.setRow(0);
     materials.setValue("I", "SIGN");
     materials.setValue("CP", "OPTION");
     materials.setValue(searchParam, "MATNR_LOW");
     aConnection.execute(function);

     JCO.ParameterList resultParams = function.getExportParameterList();
     JCO.Table materialList =
         function.getTableParameterList().getTable("MATNRLIST");
```

```java
    Hashtable returnHash = new Hashtable();
    Hashtable rowHash = new Hashtable();
    int i = 0;
    if (materialList.getNumRows() > 0) {
        do {
            for (JCO.FieldIterator fI = materialList.fields();
                fI.hasMoreElements();)
              {
                JCO.Field tabField = fI.nextField();
                rowHash.put(tabField.getName(),tabField.getString());
              }
              returnHash.put("line" + i, rowHash);
              rowHash = new Hashtable();
              i++;
        }
        while(materialList.nextRow() == true);
    }
    else {
         System.out.println("Sorry, couldn't find any materials");
    }
    return returnHash;
}

public Hashtable checkPassword(String username, String password) {

    JCO.Function function = getFunction("BAPI_CUSTOMER_CHECKPASSWORD");
    JCO.ParameterList listParams = function.getImportParameterList();
    listParams.setValue(username, "CUSTOMERNO");
    listParams.setValue(password, "PASSWORD");

    aConnection.execute(function);

    JCO.ParameterList resultParams = function.getExportParameterList();
    Hashtable returnHash = new Hashtable();
    returnHash.put("RETURN.TYPE",extractField("RETURN","TYPE",resultParams));
    returnHash.put("RETURN.CODE",extractField("RETURN","CODE",resultParams));
    returnHash.put("RETURN.MESSAGE",
                    extractField("RETURN","MESSAGE",resultParams));
    return returnHash;
    }

public String extractField(String structure,String field,
                                    JCO.ParameterList parameterList)
```

```
        {
            return ((JCO.Structure)parameterList.getValue(structure)).getString(field);
        }

        public JCO.Function getFunction(String name) {
          try {
                return aRepository.getFunctionTemplate(name.toUpperCase()).getFunction();
          }
          catch (Exception ex) {}
            return null;
          }

    private void createConnection() {
      try {
        aConnection = JCO.createClient(SAP_CLIENT,
                                      USER_ID,
                                      PASSWORD,
                                      LANGUAGE,
                                      HOST_NAME,
                                      SYSTEM_NUMBER);
        aConnection.connect();
      }
      catch (Exception ex) {
        System.out.println("Failed to connect to SAP system");
      }
    }

    private void retrieveRepository() {
      try {
        aRepository = new JCO.Repository("SAPRep", aConnection);
      }
      catch (Exception ex) {
        System.out.println("Failed to retrieve SAP repository");
      }
     }
    }
```

You also may have noticed an additional statement at the top of the InterfaceCaller class—package com.apress.ejsap;. As mentioned in previous chapters, Java packages provide a simple mechanism for organizing similar Java classes. In order to differentiate the InterfaceCaller class from other Java objects in this Web application, this class has been moved to the com.apress.ejsap package. The only real impact that this has on your development effort is that you need to ensure that certain Java classes and libraries required by the JSP technology can be found in the right place.

Open the `webapps/sap/WEB-INF` directory that you created earlier. Add a directory called `classes` under `WEB-INF`. This is the directory where all the supporting Java classes and packages should go, such as the `InterfaceCaller.class`. You also need to create the `com/apress/ejsap` directory structure under `classes` due to the fact that the `InterfaceCaller` class is part of the `com.apress.ejsap` package. Copy the `InterfaceCaller.class` file into the `com/apress/ejsap` directory. You also need to copy the `sapdata.properties` file into the `WEB-INF/classes` directory, so that `InterfaceCaller` can read your R/3 system variables.

In order to deploy the JCo libraries, you need to create another directory under `webapps/sap` called `lib`. The `lib` directory contains the archived Java libraries that should be deployed for use in this Web application once the Tomcat server is started. Copy the `sapjco.jar` file from the JCo zip file into the `webapps/sap/WEB-INF/lib` directory. At this point, you need to restart the Tomcat server so that these new libraries will be deployed with your Web application.

Building the Customer Login JSP

You can reuse the `login.jsp` that was built in the earlier example to pass in HTML form parameters. The `loginResult.jsp` needs to be modified to include a call to the `checkPassword()` method of the `InterfaceCaller` class.

Your `loginResult.jsp` should now look like this:

```
<%@ page language="java" %>
<%@ page import="java.util.*" %>
<%@ page import="com.apress.ejsap.*" %>

<HTML>
  <HEAD>
    <TITLE>User Login</TITLE>
  </HEAD>
  <BODY>
  <%
    String username = request.getParameter("username");
    String password =request.getParameter("password");
    InterfaceCaller ifCaller = new InterfaceCaller();
    Hashtable userCheck = ifCaller.checkPassword(username, password);
    if (!userCheck.get("RETURN.TYPE").equals("E")) {
  %>
```

```
      <H1>Welcome, <%= request.getParameter("username") %></H1>
      You have logged in at: <%= new Date().toString() %>
  <%
    }
    else {
       out.println("<H1> Password incorrect, please try again.</H1>");
       Enumeration enum = userCheck.keys();
       while ( enum.hasMoreElements() ){
                String nextKey = (String)enum.nextElement();
                     out.println( nextKey + "=" + userCheck.get(nextKey) +
"<br/>");
       }  }
  %>
  </BODY>
</HTML>
```

A new line has been added at the top, which imports the com.apress.ejsap package that contains the InterfaceCaller class. The call to InterfaceCaller's checkPassword() method is made in this line:

```
Hashtable userCheck = ifCaller.checkPassword(username, password);
```

Here, the JSP page has initialized a new Hashtable object using the return from checkPassword(). Because you had defined in the InterfaceCaller class, this method requires two text strings as parameters and returns an instance of a Hashtable.

The next line modifies the if conditional to check whether or not the value associated with the RETURN.TYPE key in the userCheck Hashtable equals "E".

> **NOTE** *Using an exclamation point or "bang" in front of a Java expression tells the Java Virtual Machine (JVM) to evaluate the result of that expression as "not equal to." So, whereas the expression x == y evaluates to* TRUE *if x and y are the same value, x != y evaluates to* TRUE *if the value of x does not equal the value of y.*

SAP uses the RETURN.TYPE field to indicate the status of the BAPI call, with a blank or "S" value indicating success and an "E" value indicating failure. For this simple login application, you can assume that if SAP returns an "E" error code, the user was not successfully authenticated. The `else` condition is then executed by your application, resulting in the "Password incorrect" error message. You could also have displayed the error message coming from SAP because the checkPassword() method stored that message in its return Hashtable.

```
else {
  out.println(userCheck.get("RETURN.MESSAGE"));
}
```

However, if the RETURN.TYPE field does not equal "E", you know that the user has been successfully authenticated as a customer within the R/3 system. The JSP page then displays a welcome message to the user, along with the current date and time.

Note that the InterfaceCaller class is currently being called outside of the Java application server. Importing a Java class directly into the JSP page causes a new instance of that class to be created each time the page is loaded. Depending on the level of traffic and the configuration of the application server, this can lead to a great deal of redundancy and system overhead.

Figure 6-4 provides a top-down perspective of the components running in the JVM at this stage in the development. This diagram shows a high number of InterfaceCaller instances being created outside of the Tomcat server, which are completely out of the server's control. The last section in this chapter focuses on enhancing performance and reducing wasted resources in the JVM by bringing control on the InterfaceCaller class within the Tomcat application server.

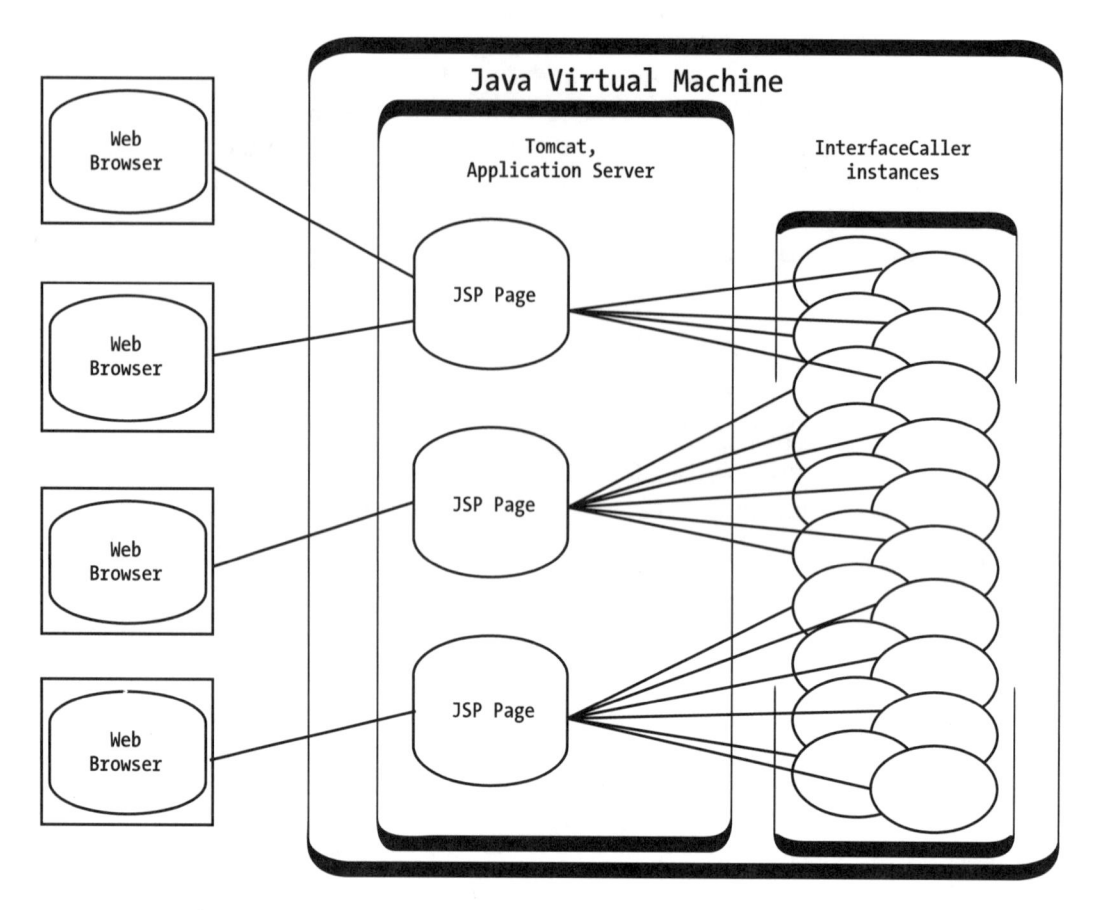

Figure 6-4. Current outlay of objects within the JVM

Maintaining SAP User Authority

The next step you want to take is to ensure that the user only needs to log in once to access the various functions provided by your Web application. To do so, you need to set a variable in the user's session that indicates that the user has been authenticated and should be granted access to all SAP functionality in this Web application.

The J2EE specification provides a mechanism for identifying a user across hits to multiple pages. The HTTP used by Web servers is inherently stateless. This means that the server does not maintain a constantly open session with a given end user when that user is accessing pages from the Web server. Rather, each time a Web browser requests a page from the server, it is as if the browser were doing so for the first time. A stateless interface has no means for recognizing or remembering the information a user has entered into one page from another.

To overcome this liability, the J2EE specification introduces the concept of an HTTP session, which stores information about the user either through URL rewriting or writing a cookie to the user's computer. The preferred technique is that of writing cookies, which saves your application from dealing with the character limitations that surround the length of a valid URL.

However, users may have turned off cookies for security reasons, so using URL rewriting as a fallback is always a good idea. Depending on the Java application server, certain methods can be used to check to see if a user will accept a cookie first and, if she will not, automatically switch to URL rewriting. For the scope of this book, I am assuming that cookies are turned on and URL rewriting is unnecessary.

The Java session class can be found in the package `javax.servlet.http.*` and is called `HttpSession`. Again, because an instance of this class is so important, the JSP specification has a reserved identifier for it—session. Similar to the request object you saw earlier, the session object contains all of the stored information for a unique HTTP or Web end user. This guarantees that a user cannot inadvertently steal another user's session; this allows for a certain level of security between the Web browser and server.

> **CAUTION** *The* `HttpSession` *object relies on a unique key generated by the Web server for each single Web browser instance requesting access. A malicious user or hacker could intercept a user's key from the HTTP stream and use it to spoof that user's identity to the Web server. If you are concerned about this, make sure that your application server is capable of serving secure Web pages over the encrypted protocol, HTTPS. This way, all information passed between server and browser is encrypted while in transit over the Internet. There is no absolute guarantee that a hacker will not intercept and decode the encryption, but by the time they are finished, the user will likely have ended his own session.*

Let's go ahead and store the user's SAP customer ID in the session and retrieve it within a subsequent JSP page.

First, modify the `loginResult.jsp` to look like this:

```
<%@ page language="java" %>
<%@ page import="java.util.*" %>
<%@ page import="com.apress.ejsap.*" %>

<HTML>
  <HEAD>
    <TITLE>User Login</TITLE>
  </HEAD>
```

```
    <BODY>
    <%
      String username = request.getParameter("username");
      String password = (String)request.getParameter("password");
      Hashtable userCheck = InterfaceCaller.checkPassword(username, password);
      if (!userCheck.get("RETURN.TYPE").equals("E")) {
/*
   If the user is authenticated in SAP, we set an attribute in the session
   called 'username' which is equal to the ID they used to log in
*/
      session.setAttribute("username", username);
    %>
      <H1>Welcome, <%= request.getParameter("username") %></H1>
      You have logged in at: <%= new Date().toString() %>
      <P>
<!-- This URL takes us to the materials lookup page -->
      <A HREF="materialList.jsp">Look up materials</A>
    <%
      }
      else {
        out.println("<H1> Password incorrect, please try again.</H1>");
      }
    %>
    </BODY>
</HTML>
```

After the JSP calls SAP and authenticates the end user, it uses the setAttribute() method on the session object to add the text string value of username to the user's session. The setAttribute() method takes two parameters: the first is a string key value and the second can be any Java object. Future JSP pages can use that key field to retrieve whatever Java object has been stored in the session.

> **TIP** *A very powerful but potentially dangerous ability of the session object is that it can store* any *type of Java object associated with a key value. This means that you could create a Java object to specifically model the user's profile, populate it, and then store in within the session object. This saves you from having to manually store and retrieve each key/value pair for the user profile within the session object. However, be aware of the memory size that each given object occupies in the session space. Make sure your application server can handle the load of hundreds or even thousands of simultaneous users, all writing and storing these Java objects into the server's memory.*

The initial version of your materialList.jsp simply retrieves the username from the session and displays it in a new Web page. It also checks to see whether that field is set to NULL, meaning the user hasn't logged in or been properly authenticated. If this is the case, the user sees a different message—one that requests that she log in to the system before she is able to continue.

Create a file called materialList.jsp and enter the following code:

```jsp
<%@ page language="java" %>
<%@ page import="java.util.*" %>
<%@ page import="com.apress.ejsap.*" %>

<HTML>
  <HEAD>
    <TITLE>Look up materials</TITLE>
  </HEAD>
  <BODY>
  <%
    String username = (String)session.getAttribute("username");
    if (username != null)
    {
  %>
    <H1>You are still logged in as: <%= username %></H1>
  <%
    }
    else {
      out.println("You are not logged in.  Please try again.");
    }
  %>
  </BODY>
</HTML>
```

In this code, the line following initializes a String object called username and populates this object using the getAttribute method of the session object.

```
lineString username = (String)session.getAttribute("username");
```

This is fairly straightforward, but what if you weren't retrieving a String object? The HttpSession class can be used to store any type of Java object, which means that you need to explicitly tell the JVM about the type of object you want it to retrieve from the session. In Java-speak, this is called *casting an object*, and it means that you specify the object class that you expect as a return from the method. In order to cast an object, you prefix the object method call with the object's class name.

In this example, seen in the following line

```
(String)session.getAttribute("username");
```

the (String) prefix tells the JVM that the object being retrieved from the session is a String so that the JVM can set the String variable, username, accordingly. This may seem a little obtuse, but the casting mechanism gives you the power and flexibility to store Java objects on the fly, without the method or class needing to know what that object is beforehand.

You can now verify that the following are true:

- The user has been authenticated against the R/3 system.

- Your JSP pages know who the user is throughout subsequent page hits.

This comes in handy should you ever need to track a user's activity outside of SAP or ensure that he has access within SAP based strictly on his customer profile.

Adding a Material List Lookup

The last piece of SAP functionality you will add in this chapter is that of a material list lookup. If she reuses the code developed in previous chapters, the user will be able to search for a list of materials by entering in either all or part of an SAP material number.

To make this happen, let's first modify the existing materialList.jsp to include a form text field.

```
<%@ page language="java" %>
<%@ page import="java.util.*" %>
<%@ page import="com.apress.ejsap.*" %>

<HTML>
  <HEAD>
    <TITLE>Look up materials</TITLE>
  </HEAD>
  <BODY>
  <%
    String username = (String)session.getAttribute("username");
    if (username == null)
      out.println("You are not logged in.  Please try again.");
    else {
  %>
```

```
    <H1>SAP Material List Lookup</H1>
    <FORM ACTION="materialResult.jsp" METHOD="post">
    <INPUT TYPE="text" NAME="material">
    <P>
    <INPUT TYPE="submit" VALUE="Get Materials">
    </FORM>
  <%
    }
  %>
  </BODY>
</HTML>
```

The first thing you probably noticed is that the conditions in the if...else block have been reversed. This means that when username is set to NULL, the JSP page immediately tells the user to log in again and will not allow further execution of the application code. This has been done mainly for the sake of clarity and to ensure that your JSP page does not allow any unauthorized use of the SAP Web application.

Your JSP page then displays a very simple HTML form that contains a text field for the material search and a Submit button. The ACTION= attribute is set to materialResult.jsp, which contains the logic required to call SAP.

The materialResult.jsp takes the user's material search parameter and executes a call to SAP.

```
<%@ page language="java" %>
<%@ page import="java.util.*" %>
<%@ page import="com.apress.ejsap.*" %>

<HTML>
  <HEAD>
    <TITLE>Look up materials</TITLE>
  </HEAD>
  <BODY>
  <%
    String username = (String)session.getAttribute("username");
    if (username == null)
      out.println("You are not logged in.  Please try again.");
    else {
      InterfaceCaller ifCaller = new InterfaceCaller();
      Hashtable materialsHash =
        ifCaller.getMaterialList(request.getParameter("material"));
      Hashtable rowHash;
```

```
            if (materialsHash.isEmpty())
                out.println("<H2>Your search has returned zero results</H2>");
            else {
              out.println("Here are the list materials based on a search criteria of " +
                "<B>" + request.getParameter("material") + "</B><P>");
              for (Enumeration e = materialsHash.elements(); e.hasMoreElements();) {
                rowHash = (Hashtable)e.nextElement();
                out.println("Material: " +
                            (String)rowHash.get("MATERIAL") + "<BR>");
                out.println("Material description: " +
                            (String)rowHash.get("MATL_DESC") + "<P>");
              }
            }
         }
    %>
   </BODY>
</HTML>
```

Again, your JSP page first checks the user's session object to ensure proper authentication, asking her to log in if this check fails. Next, it initializes a Hashtable object using the getMaterialList() method in the InterfaceCaller class, passing in the material search value retrieved from the request object.

Recall that you used nested Hashtables to store the table data, rows and fields, returned from the call to BAPI_MATERIAL_GETLIST. This means that you need to declare a second Hashtable in addition to the one returned from the call to the getMaterialList() method. You use the second Hashtable like a temporary storage location; it should contain a single row in the table at any given moment.

To display the materials list back to the end user, first create a for loop with the initialization expression Enumeration e = materialsHash.elements() and the termination expression e.hasMoreElements(). The initialization expression declares and populates an Enumeration object by calling the elements() method on your materialsHash Hashtable instance. The elements() method essentially returns a list of all the values in a given Hashtable. Despite the fact that a Hashtable contains key/value pairs, you are only interested in retrieving the field data (values) and not the line numbers stored as keys in the Hashtable.

The termination expression tests to ensure that the Enumeration contains additional elements to read through, hence the call to the hasMoreElements() method on our Enumeration instance, e. The hasMoreElements() method returns a boolean of TRUE, indicating that elements exist beyond the current; otherwise the expression evaluates to FALSE, and the JSP page exits from the for loop.

The Enumeration object was designed to allow your application to quickly iterate through a set of data or Java objects. In this case, each value in the Enumeration will be another Hashtable object, stored within the original materialsHash instance. To get at the Hashtable object stored in a given element of our enumeration, the JSP page initializes the rowHash variable using the nextElement() method on the Enumeration instance, e. The nextElement() method returns an uncast Java Object, which the application must cast by explicitly declaring the object to be a Hashtable. As seen previously, you simply prefix the call to the nextElement() method with a (Hashtable) declaration; this tells the JVM to cast this object as a Hashtable when the rowHash instance is initialized.

The next two lines retrieve the key/value pairs that were stored in the nested Hashtable and format them for display within the Web browser.

```
out.println("Material: " +
            (String)rowHash.get("MATERIAL") + "<BR>");
out.println("Material description: " +
            (String)rowHash.get("MATL_DESC") + "<P>");
```

Notice that the JSP is using the reserved identifier out to write directly to the HTTP stream, combining standard HTML tags with calls to the get() method of the rowHash instance. Similar to the put() method, the get() method requires you to pass the text key assigned to the value when rowHash was originally populated by the InterfaceCaller instance. This returns an uncast Java Object, which requires you to prefix the method call with (String) before it can be displayed to the end user. Figure 6-5 depicts the materials search results through a Web browser.

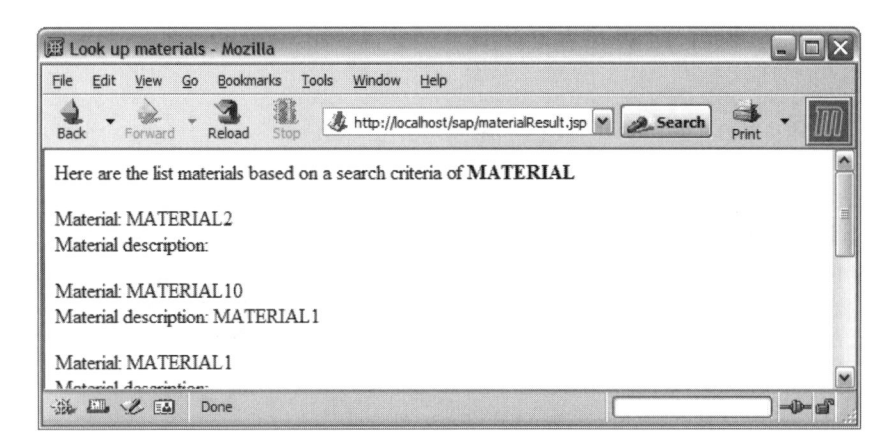

Figure 6-5. Results of a material search in SAP

Your first official Web application is now complete. This example demonstrated the basic steps involved in building JSP pages, chained several JSP pages together, and integrated Internet user authentication into the material search application. What else could possibly be left?

Sharing JCo System Resources

So far, your SAP Web application has likely been used by only one user—you. However, the whole point of developing Web-based server-side components is so that anyone with a Web browser and the right authority can access and use this functionality. Imagine deploying the GUI client application developed in Chapter 5 to a thousand end users across the Internet. Now imagine each user accessing the application at the same time, all requesting SAP connections simultaneously—no order, no organization, just chaos. You can see how quickly the R/3 application server would get overloaded—it might even shut down—just because of one innocent, little desktop application that you had developed for SAP.

Of course, the Java application server does bring some order to this chaos by virtue of its Web serving capabilities. However, there is a fatal flaw in the application developed so far that cannot be accounted for by the application server. The flaw is that each time a new user accesses your Web application, a totally new instance of the JCo connection object gets created within the application server. In fact, this happens not only for each new user, but also anytime a user stops and restarts their Web browser; this is because the Web application must reauthenticate the user.

Remember, you are relying on two different types of authentication within the Web application. At the top level, a user must log on with an SAP Internet User customer name and password. Your application uses the results of this authentication to determine whether the user can have access to other functional areas. At a deeper level, the JCo connector requires your application to pass a valid, licensed SAP username and password in order to gain access to the RFC and BAPI interfaces. This is the system information that you stored in the `sapdata.properties` file in Chapter 5. The result of this basic authorization for the use of the R/3 system is the JCo connection object, of which you currently create a unique instance for every user of the application.

Whereas the Internet User authentication needs to vary by individual user, the JCo system connection remains the same. This means that your existing application creates numerous redundant system connection objects, each exactly the same as the other, endlessly filling up the memory space of the Java application server. Isn't there some mechanism that allows users to share the same system connection?

Optimizing Performance with the ServletContext

The J2EE specification provides a mechanism that allows users of the same Web application to transparently share object-level resources. In this way, the application can deliver a centralized, consistent base of information, resources, and so on, that is easy to maintain and is highly optimized.

Known as the `ServletContext`, this Java class defines a series of methods to set and retrieve Java objects that are accessible to any user within a given Web application.

> **NOTE** *I have used the term "Web application" somewhat loosely up to this point. However, in the case of the `ServletContext` class, this term takes on a more specific meaning. In this context, a Web application is a collection of JSP pages and servlets that have been installed under a specific namespace in the Java application server. A namespace refers to the URL identifier assigned to allow users access via a Web browser, such as the `/sap` used by your application. A Web application can also refer to the installation of a Web Archive (WAR) file. Similar to the JAR files discussed in Chapter 4, WAR files compress and deploy Web applications using a single file and minimal application server configuration.*

Like the `session` object introduced in "Displaying Stored HTTP Session Data," earlier in this chapter, the `ServletContext` lets you to store and retrieve Java objects to use in the JSP pages. However, whereas the `session` object stores objects unique to each Web browser, the ServletContext provides generally accessible Java objects, regardless of the individual user. Ultimately, this is the mechanism you will use to share SAP system resources across the entire Web application, rather than the limited, per-user access available through the `session` object.

The first step is to develop a Java servlet that loads automatically at the start of the Java application server. This servlet instantiates an instance of your `InterfaceCaller` class, then stores it within the `ServletContext` with a unique attribute identifier.

The Java servlet specification is part of the J2EE, defining a series of libraries to create precompiled server-side components. You have already used a subset of this specification through the development of JSP pages. When you create and deploy a JSP page, the Java application server acts behind the scenes to compile and execute a Java servlet. This servlet is based on any Java logic built into the JSP page as well as the HTML tags used to format information for display.

Are you curious about these mystery servlets being automatically created with your JSP pages? Check out the `<TOMCAT_HOME>/work/Standalone/localhost/sap` directory and open any of the `*.java` files you find there. This directory is also a great place to view the raw Java code of the JSP page before it gets compiled into a servlet, in case any of your JSP pages need to be debugged at the code level.

In order to instantiate a Java object on server startup, you need to create a servlet instance that can be automatically loaded by Tomcat. Using your text editor, start a new document and save it as `InterfaceServlet.java` in the `webapps/sap/WEB-INF/classes` directory.

Now you need to copy the Java servlet libraries into the Java extension framework directory so that the javac compiler can find them. You could download the full J2EE SDK from http://java.sun.com, but the Tomcat application has already provided them for you. In the directory `<TOMCAT_BASE>/common/lib`, you will find the file `servlet.jar`. This contains all of the Java libraries you need to create and compile a Java servlet. I recommend copying the JAR file directly into the `<JAVA_ROOT>/jre/lib/ext` directory. Make sure you copy it and do not just move it because the Tomcat server needs this Java archive to execute the JSP pages and servlets you have developed.

The `InterfaceServlet` class also needs to use the `InterfaceCaller` class developed previously in Chapter 5. Because `InterfaceServlet` exists in the same path structure as the `com/apress/ejsap/InterfaceCaller.class` library, you only need to ensure that you compile the `InterfaceServlet` class at the same path level that the `com/apress/ejsap` directory exists.

Once the `servlet.jar` file is accessible through the Java extension framework, you can import the packages you must have to build and compile the `InterfaceServlet` class. Add the following `import` statements to the `InterfaceServlet.java` file.

```
import com.apress.ejsap.*;
import java.io.*;
//These are the servlet libraries
import javax.servlet.*;
import javax.servlet.http.*;

public class InterfaceServlet
            extends HttpServlet{
   ...
}
```

You should be familiar with the first two `import` statements, which give the servlet access to Java classes under the `com.apress.ejsap` and `java.io` packages, respectively. The next two imports build the foundation for developing a Java servlet by letting your application employ the existing Java servlet architecture.

In order for your Java class to behave as a servlet, it must first implement the `HttpServlet` class. To make this happen, you need to use the `extends` declaration in the `public class` line to tell the JVM that this class inherits all of the methods and attributes of the `HttpServlet` class. Again, the `public class` statement declares the name of your Java class, `InterfaceServlet`, but this time you are using `HttpSerlvet` as your class's superclass with the declaration `extends HttpServlet`.

Now that the application has access to all of the functionality provided by the `HttpServlet`, it's time to build a Java servlet that loads `InterfaceCaller` into the `ServletContext`.

```
public class InterfaceServlet
            extends HttpServlet{
    public void init(ServletConfig servConfig) throws ServletException{
      ServletContext servContext = servConfig.getServletContext();
      InterfaceCaller infCaller = new InterfaceCaller();
      servContext.setAttribute("ifaceCaller", infCaller);
    }
}
```

Even though `HttpServlet` has a number of different methods, you are only interested in the `init()` method. Why? This is the method that is automatically accessed when the servlet class is executed, and any logic built into this method gets kicked off as well. Since the whole point of this servlet is to load an instance of `InterfaceCaller` when the application server is started, the `init()` method is the only one you need to use.

Notice that the `init()` method requires a `ServletConfig` instance as its sole parameter. `ServletConfig` is a configuration object that is used to pass information from the Java application server to the servlet during its initialization phase. You need the `ServletConfig` instance, `servConf`, in order to retrieve the `ServletContext` from the application server. The `ServletContext` instance you retrieve is specific to the Web application in which the servlet exists. Remember, this Java object is accessible only to those classes deployed within a given Web application. This restricts use of that context so that other Web applications deployed by the same server will not inadvertently access it.

In order to call the `init()` method of your servlet, the Java application server must pass in an instance of the `ServletConfig` class, called `servConf`. The next statement retrieves the `ServletContext` instance from `servConf` using the `getServletContext()` method. This method requires no parameters and returns an instance of `ServletContext`. Your servlet initializes `servContext` using the return from the `getServletContext()` method and proceeds to set values to the `ServletContext` instance.

```
InterfaceCaller infCaller = new InterfaceCaller();
servContext.setAttribute("ifaceCaller", infCaller);
```

Next, a new instance of the `InterfaceCaller` class is instantiated, called `infCaller`. Recall that `InterfaceCaller` provides a default constructor to initialize the connection to SAP as well as to retrieve an R/3 repository. As a result, the application only needs to create a new instance of this class and then store that instance within servContext.

The last line uses the setAttribute() method of servContext to map a key name to infCaller and then store that instance into the servlet context. Once that instance is stored, a JSP page or servlet within this Web application can easily retrieve it. Moreover, it is that single instance that is retrieved over and over again rather than requiring each subsequent JSP page or servlet to create a new instance of the InterfaceCaller class. Rather than creating a new instance, the application server provides a single instance of the InterfaceCaller class to each subsequent JSP request.

Configuring the Application Server

Before your Web application can use the InterfaceServlet, you must configure Tomcat to load that servlet when the application server starts. To do so, you need to create a new file, web.xml, which must be stored in the <TOMCAT_HOME>/webapps/sap/WEB-INF directory. This file acts as a mechanism by which you can configure each individual Web application deployed by the Tomcat server.

Tomcat provides a default version of web.xml under the directory <TOMCAT_HOME>/conf; however, I have provided the following simplified version:

```xml
<?xml version="1.0" encoding="ISO-8859-1"?>

<!DOCTYPE web-app
    PUBLIC "-//Sun Microsystems, Inc.//DTD Web Application 2.3//EN"
    "http://java.sun.com/dtd/web-app_2_3.dtd">
<web-app>
<!-- InterfaceServlet to load shared resources -->
  <servlet>
    <servlet-name>sap</servlet-name>
    <servlet-class>InterfaceServlet</servlet-class>
    <init-param>
      <param-name>debug</param-name>
      <param-value>0</param-value>
    </init-param>
    <init-param>
      <param-name>listings</param-name>
      <param-value>true</param-value>
    </init-param>
    <init-param>
      <param-name>readonly</param-name>
      <param-value>false</param-value>
```

```
        </init-param>
        <load-on-startup>1</load-on-startup>
    </servlet>
</web-app>
```

Based on standard XML document notation, this specific file maintains a single servlet that should be loaded on startup. Without going into too much detail regarding XML and its usage, let me explain this. `web.xml` contains an open and close tag for the servlet to be loaded, `<servlet>...</servlet>`; a `<servlet-name>...</servlet-name>` tag as a unique identifier for the servlet within the application server; and a `<servlet-class>...</servlet-class>` that indicates the actual servlet to be loaded. The following `<init-param>...</init-params>` allow you to set a series of different parameters that affect the behavior of the servlet within the application server. Finally, the `<load-on-startup>...</load-on-startup>` tag specifies the order in which servlets should be loaded if `web.xml` contained multiple servlets.

By adding it to the startup configuration, `InterfaceServlet` is loaded each time you start the Tomcat application server, and an instance of `InterfaceCaller` will be stored in the servlet context automatically.

Using the Servlet Context in JSP Pages

The last step involves modifying your JSP pages so that they use the `InterfaceCaller` instance stored in the servlet context, rather than creating a new instance each time the page is loaded.

This is not as difficult as it sounds. Open the `loginResult.jsp` and locate the following lines:

```
InterfaceCaller ifCaller = new InterfaceCaller();
Hashtable userCheck = ifCaller.checkPassword(username, password);
```

Replace this line with the following code:

```
InterfaceCaller ifCaller =

    (InterfaceCaller)application.getAttribute("ifaceCaller");
Hashtable userCheck = ifCaller.checkPassword(username, password);
```

So what's the difference? In the original JSP page, each time you accessed this page, you caused a new instance of `InterfaceCaller` to be created and a new connection to SAP to be initialized. With one or two users of your Web application, the memory overhead on the application was negligible. But as users were added to the system, this redundant use of InterfaceCaller was magnified many times over, until the application slowed to a crawl.

In the new version of this JSP page, you initialize the ifCaller instance using the InterfaceCaller object that was stored in the servlet context. The reserved keyword, application, provides your JSP page with access to the servlet context without having to specifically initialize an instance of it. This is the shared servlet context that is available to any JSP page or servlet residing within the current Web application, that is, any of the components under the /webapps/sap directory. Your application calls the getAttribute() method on application, passing the text string parameter that maps to the appropriate Java object in the servlet context. In this case, InterfaceServlet stored an instance of the InterfaceCaller class as "ifaceCaller" in the servlet context, so using this value in the getAttribute() method retrieves the shared instance of InterfaceCaller.

At this point, ifCaller is no longer a new instance of the InterfaceCaller class; rather, it acts as a local pointer to the global instance of InterfaceCaller that was stored in the servlet context when the application server was started. Each time a JSP page needs to use the methods of InterfaceCaller, it simply grabs a local pointer to the global instance, thus greatly reducing the overhead on the application server.

Figure 6-6 shows a component-level view of this new arrangement. Notice that every Java component used by this application is contained within the Tomcat application server.

You now need to modify the materialResult.jsp in the same way. The current JSP page instantiates a new instance of InterfaceCaller, as seen here:

```
InterfaceCaller ifCaller = new InterfaceCaller();
Hashtable materialsHash =
    ifCaller.getMaterialList(request.getParameter("material"));
```

Instead, your application should retrieve a local pointer to the global instance so that your code looks like this:

```
InterfaceCaller ifCaller =
    (InterfaceCaller)application.getAttribute("ifaceCaller");
Hashtable materialsHash =
    ifCaller.getMaterialList(request.getParameter("material"));
```

Once you have made the modifications to your JSP pages, restart the Tomcat application server and login using

http://localhost/sap/login.jsp

Extending SAP to the Web

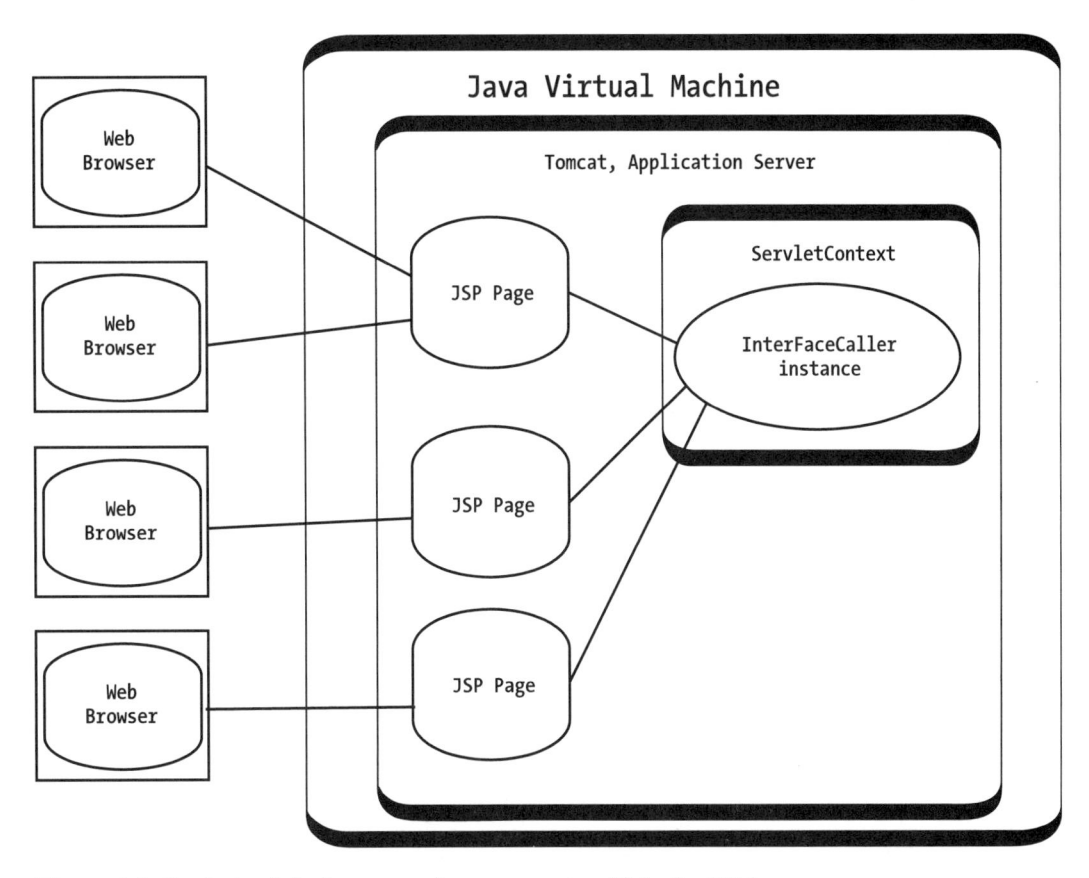

Figure 6-6. Optimized deployment of components within the JVM

If everything works exactly as it has in the past, your changes are successful! Multiple users can now effectively share the resources of one JCo connector and one `InterfaceCaller` instance without too much danger of overloading the system.

> **CAUTION** *Since you will likely use these examples for tutorial purposes, I just want to warn you that I can't guarantee that sending thousands of users to your new SAP Web application won't crash the Tomcat server. The later chapters of this book focus on techniques for building high-volume Web applications. The application presented in this chapter would certainly be suitable for intranet or strict LAN-based applications, but it is not appropriate for wider usage across the Internet.*

Summary

This chapter introduced the concept of Java application development for the Web and explained some of the supporting technologies. It demonstrated several basic JSP applications that use a combination of Java code and HTML formatting to build a simple Web-based front end for SAP.

The Java application server, Tomcat, allows you to quickly develop and deploy JSP pages and servlet applications directly from your computer. Building on previous development, this chapter showed you how to integrate SAP functionality into your Web applications.

Here are a few points to remember:

- JSP pages provide a quick way to deploy and modify dynamic SAP content.

- Use the `session` object to store and retrieve data across multiple Web pages; you might store the results from multiple material queries or allow the user to bring up a "favorites" material list during the session.

- Provide clear separation of Java and HTML code within your JSP pages; this allows Web designers to change the look of the Web page without changing your Java code.

CHAPTER 7

Developing Web Applications with Struts

THROUGHOUT THE COURSE OF THIS BOOK, the term "Web application" has been used to denote a software program or suite that is fully accessible within a Web browser. As opposed to a single Web page, a Web application comprises multiple functions or at least different views of a dataset. The Web application relies on Web pages to define how the user interacts with its functionality. Beyond the user interface, however, the Web application specifies the logic and screen flow that are needed to form a complete picture for the end user.

You have already built much of the connection logic you need to communicate with an R/3 application server. Likewise, in Chapter 6, you also learned how to build a very basic Web-based user interface. The next step is to refine the front-end screen flow so that your Web application can be easily supported and maintained over time. As an application's functionality grows in complexity, so does the interaction between the various screens that make up its user interface. The most effective way to handle this growth is by building your Web application within a predefined screen flow framework. This chapter introduces Struts, an open source framework for Java that eases the development and deployment of a graphical user interface (GUI) over the Web.

This chapter looks at the following:

- The Model-View-Control design pattern

- Using the Struts framework

- Creating a Struts-based Web application for SAP

Design patterns allow you to build on proven development solutions. The first section in this chapter deals with the most popular design pattern for developing user interfaces.

The Model-View-Control Design Pattern

By now you should be somewhat familiar with the concept of a design pattern. The Model-View-Control (MVC) pattern is highly recommended for tiered, Web-based application development. As implied by the name, this pattern breaks up an application into three logical units: the model, the view, and the controller. Because your Web application utilizes SAP's business application layer, it just uses the MVC pattern to handle the user interface.

MVC Components

MVC was originally created to map the more traditional, transaction-based roles of input, processing, and output into the arena of GUI development. The input became the model, the output became the view, and processing became the controller. Respectively, the data model or state and the graphical feedback to the user are mapped to the model and view objects of the system. These components are separated and handled by the controller, which brokers requests and responses between the various objects in the system.

When users interact with the mouse and keyboard, these components supply input that initiates the appropriate action by the controller. The controller houses a centralized mapping mechanism that interprets the user request and sends it off to the model or datastore. The model responds with the requested information, which the controller then forwards to a display layer or view. The view visually formats the data in addition to displaying any required user inputs, such as form fields or buttons. Figure 7-1 illustrates the basic interaction between these components.

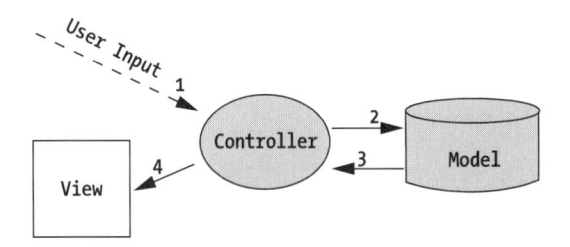

Figure 7-1. Interaction between Model-View-Control components

The model typically represents an abstraction of a real-world process or underlying business logic. This object should be able to respond to queries regarding its state, manage an internal data set, and change its data set according to external instructions. By providing one or more of these attributes, the model component can be readily integrated into a larger architecture. In the case of an R/3 system, the Business Application Programming Interface (BAPI) layer provided through the application server represents the model. Specifically, the business application interface defined by SAP BAPIs meet the criteria of a model within the MVC architecture. BAPIs allow an application to retrieve the status of the R/3 system and perform data queries against the database. You can also use BAPIs to create new records and process transactions within the R/3 application server. The BAPI_MATERIAL_GETLIST used in Chapter 4 demonstrates a predefined search query contained in an abstracted interface that is accessible from within a development framework.

The model component might seem a little confusing at first. Remember, it is not the database store or the R/3 tables themselves. Rather, it is a mechanism defined by the system programmers that can be used to gain access to information maintained in the database. If you were building an application from scratch that relied on an underlying database, you would need to code these model objects. Because your Web application taps into the existing SAP business application layer, you are saved the time and expense of having to develop model components. However, this luxury can also be a bit of a limitation when you are dealing with a restricted set of RFC and BAPI interfaces. Should you need to create or expose new functionality out of SAP, you could create custom RFC interfaces that would then act as the model components. This book assumes that you will rely on existing BAPIs to act as model objects, but you can always add your own through the SAP RFC layer.

Whereas the model determines how data is stored and accessed, the view component formats that data for display to the end user. In the larger picture (no pun intended), the view is responsible for mapping any graphical output to an end user device. This means that the view must understand how to render the display, and it must depend on the hardware and software layers to do so. Fortunately, the Web browser handles the bulk of rendering and display roles and provides a native, graphical interface layer to which your Web application can write. As in Chapter 6's tutorial, in this chapter, you continue to use JavaServer Pages (JSP) and HTML to format the data you display to the end user. The browser interprets the HTML generated by a JSP page and creates a human-legible screen based on your specifications.

You can also automatically update the view whenever the model changes. Depending on your application's configuration, the user interface might refresh on a scheduled basis or only when the user requests an update. Such an update queries the model for its current state and then rerenders the view with this new data. Multiple views of the same dataset are also possible through the Model-View interaction. One example of this multiview architecture is the popular use of customizable Web portal sites. Different users can generate Web pages relying on the same data in the backend but with highly variable front-end views. This might be as simple as using a different color scheme or as complex as compiling dynamic reports based of multiple combinations of the same data. Figure 7-2 depicts three different views based on the same model. Notice that the third view represents a view combined with a second model or data source.

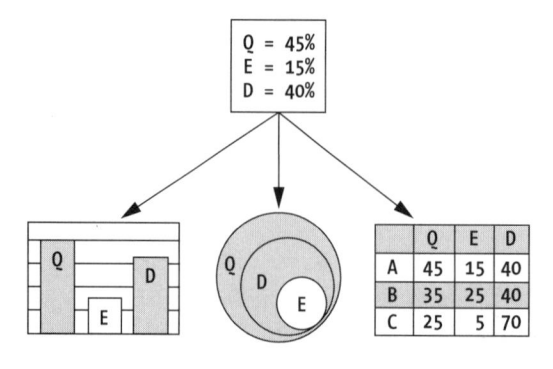

Figure 7-2. Three views derived from a common model

The controller is a centralized configuration mechanism used to separate the model and view components. It also provides you with a way to interact with the end user. When a request comes in, the controller maps that request to a given model based on the predefined system configuration. Your SAP Web application uses an XML file to define this configuration. XML provides a human-readable document that any standard text editor can view and modify.

Based on the mappings in this centralized configuration, the controller sends the end user to the appropriate view. The view then retrieves and displays any data received through the controller. In essence, the controller houses all component relationships within the MVC framework. Think of the controller as a traffic cop at an unlit intersection. Every driver moving through that intersection recognizes the police officer's authority to direct traffic at the appropriate time and place. Similarly, the controller directs objects in the MVC framework so that they can respond and coordinate when functional requests enter the system.

The controller's importance will become more evident as you explore the power of a decoupled user interface framework. In the next section, you will learn why MVC is such an important design concept and look at how this type of development compares to development within an SAP environment.

Built-in Flexibility with MVC

The previous section highlighted the different components of an MVC framework and how each interacts with the others. However, it did not answer the question of why MVC is so vital when you are developing a Web application or, indeed, any type of user interface.

Consider an application another developer wrote using the ABAP Workbench that you have been asked to modify. When you open the application in SAP's Screen Painter, you see some of the visual components in the application in addition to various Process Before Input (PBI) and Process After Input (PAI) directives. You drill into a PBI and note that before it paints the current screen, the application calls an R/3 function module. You then open a new SAP GUI screen and display that module in the Function Builder. Once you understand its purpose, you go back to the Screen Painter and continue to delve into the application's screen flow.

Time and time again, you are forced to look at various places within the ABAP Workbench to try to figure out the ultimate flow and purpose of the application. Whether you are drilling into some aspect of hotkey functionality through the Menu Painter or are checking the next screen's dynpro code, you must constantly deal with many different application aspects just to understand the screen flow. The ultimate task of modifying the application is made much more challenging because no clear delineation of responsibility exists between screen flow, workflow, and application logic. For instance, what if all of the screen flow logic was housed in a single, centralized controller component?

The MVC design pattern reduces these complex interrelationships through two aspects of its system solution. The first is a strong decoupling of computational logic between the view and the model. Certainly, you could build business logic within the view of an application and the remainder of your MVC components would continue to function. However, this would be a direct violation of the strictures set forward in the MVC design pattern. Moreover, any changes you made to the view or display layer might inadvertently affect the underlying application functionality provided through the model components. This strong decoupling of objects also means that a future developer can more accurately predict where application logic will be housed.

In a very real sense, the model and view layers have no direct connection to one another. By separating business and display logic, you reduce the number of dependencies that exist within the application framework. Fewer dependencies translate into an application that can be more easily modified and maintained by future developers.

The second major feature of the MVC pattern is a centralized configuration and control mechanism contained in the controller component. Depending on the actual programmatic implementation of this pattern, the controller configuration can take on several different flavors. As mentioned previously, Struts relies on an XML-based configuration file to handle the mappings between view and model components. This single XML file can be used to describe an entire set of screen flow logic within a Web application. Using a text editor, you can quickly modify this file to completely revise the control logic of an application as well as add or update model components on the backend. This high level of flow visibility allows developers to

- Easily add new functionality or modify existing functionality for an existing application.

- Quickly track the screen flow between various pages.

- Review the underlying functional components used in an application.

- Tag special features that require further clarification with comments.

Figure 7-3 shows the control relationship between the controller component, the XML file, and the other system components.

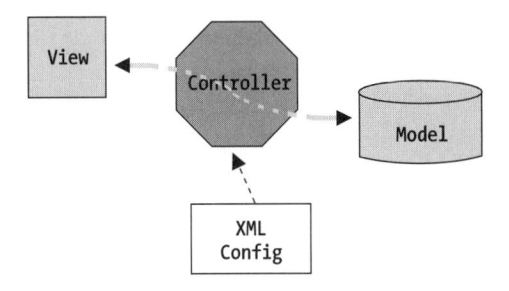

Figure 7-3. The controller uses an XML file to map the view to the model

When you implement the MVC pattern within an application, you create a logical separation between system components. This pattern makes it much easier for you to change the presentation layer without modifying the underlying business logic because the two are not natively interrelated. As the application grows, you can add new screens and new functionality through the centralized control and configuration mechanism.

MVC and SAP

So how can you use the MVC design pattern to build Web applications for SAP? The best way to answer this question is through a mock scenario that relies on SAP for backend connectivity. This example does not deal with any specific MVC implementation; rather it demonstrates how to use a design pattern as a system solution.

The scenario outlined here is that of a user logging on to an SAP system over the Internet via a Web browser. Later tutorials in this chapter flesh out this solution using a Java-based implementation of the MVC pattern.

The four key requirements of this system are as follows:

- Grant authority to Web functionality based on a preexisting SAP Internet User account.

- Retrieve the user name and password from a Web page form.

- Authenticate the user within the R/3 system.

- Forward the user to the appropriate Web page based on the result from the SAP authentication.

Figure 7-4 diagrams this scenario using the MVC design pattern.

179

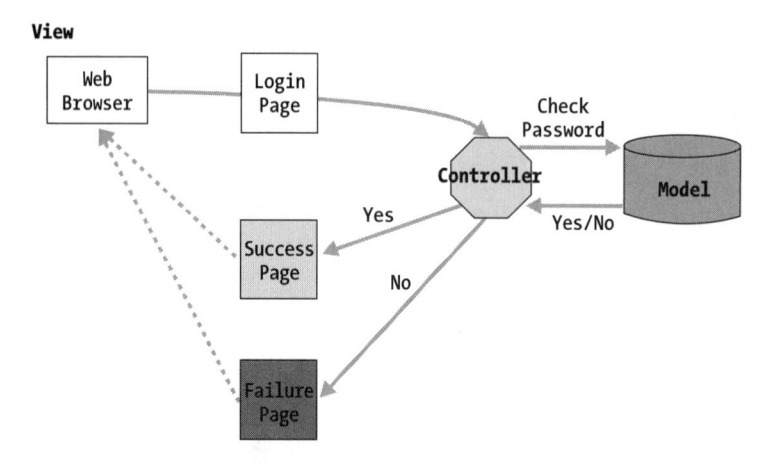

Figure 7-4. MVC diagram of the SAP login process

The view is presented here as a standard, form-based Web page. Using HTML tags and form directives, this page describes both a user name and a password field as well as a Submit button. When the user hits the Submit button, the controller processes and forwards the login information to the model. The controller relies on predefined mapping to indicate which model component should be used. In this case, the model is the BAPI interface responsible for checking a Web user's password.

JCo classes form the basis for connectivity to the R/3 system. The user name and password are passed to SAP via the prescribed interface. SAP responds with either a success or failure indicator and returns control of the call back to the controller. Depending on this indicator, the controller forwards the user to the appropriate Web page. Again, this forwarding is based on mapping described in a configuration routine or file. If the call succeeds, the controller sends the user to the next page in the Web application's screen flow. If the call fails, the user is sent to an alternate page in which he is asked to reenter a user name and password for another attempt.

The value of MVC in this limited example shows the division of labor between the model, the view, and control components. Notice that the view, or Web page, layer has no direct knowledge of the R/3 system. Neither the initial login page nor the two result pages need to understand the JCo connector or the interface layer used to call SAP. This means that a strict HTML developer with little knowledge of the backend system can modify the Web front end.

In the same way, the model components have no direct connection to the presentation layer. The model defines data access and transactional routines with little or no consideration for how the content is used (Web view, desktop application, and so on). By developing data objects that do not describe their own presentation, model components can be independently reused throughout many different applications. This layer provides consistent access to information regardless of where that request might come from.

When it ties the view and presentation layers together, the control object brokers requests from the view and responses from the model. If SAP changes a return code that indicates success or failure, that change needs only to be reflected within the controller's configuration. The view layer remains untouched. Likewise, if the screen flow needs to be redirected from one Web page to another, the controller can simply be updated to point to this new Web page without affecting the model.

This decoupling of responsibility for system objects is also reflected in the division of labor among developers and designers. The login scenario requires an SAP developer to provide discrete access to the key R/3 interface via published object methods. It also needs a Web designer to craft the front end using standard HTML technologies. Once these components are available, the controller can be configured to maintain the proper screen flow based on the application's functional specifications. Notice that there is relatively little need for a superguru type who maintains knowledge of both types of development. Certainly, programmers should be versed in several different programmatic aspects of the solution, but by using the MVC pattern this responsibility is not wholly centered in one or two individuals.

Of course, the MVC pattern is only a pattern. Remember, this is not the actual language implementation, but it foreshadows what this eventual system will look like. However, you could build your own Java-based solution system matching the specifications of the MVC pattern. Such a system might use a different configuration mechanism or deal with a presentation layer other than a Web browser. In fact, because the Web is such a popular medium for distributing applications, the Apache Group has already done so with its Jakarta project. It has developed an MVC-based framework for building Web applications called Struts. The next section introduces the Struts toolkit and details its extended feature set for deploying sustainable user interface designs across the Web.

Using the Struts Framework

Developed by Craig R. McClanahan, the Struts framework was donated to the Apache Software Foundation in May of 2000. Struts became an open source toolkit as part of Apache's Jakarta project. Because it is open source, new developers can customize and explore the Struts' components at the source code level. The Struts framework was developed as a Java-based implementation of the MVC design pattern, relying on standard Enterprise Java technologies for connectivity to external systems. These technologies include, but are not limited to, JavaServer Pages (JSP), servlets, XML stylesheets, and Java Database Connectivity (JDBC).

Struts includes a binary, servlet-based controller component that uses XML configuration files to support mapping between model and view objects. The framework also comes with a series of application libraries designed to enable Java-based development of these model and view objects. The MVC design pattern is technically complex, requiring a high degree of discrete authority among system components. This is not to say that you couldn't develop your own MVC implementation similar to that of Struts; you might choose to do so in a future application development. Struts provides a great way for you to kick start your current Web application development without investing a lot of time building a strong user interface framework.

Because every specific implementation of the MVC pattern is slightly different, I will now introduce the key features and language elements of the Struts framework. Struts is made up of three individual layers and each layer has several subcomponents. At the core of this framework is the Struts Controller (discussed in the next section)—a well-defined binary and application programming interface (API) that greatly simplifies the task of building MVC-based applications.

Java Servlet Architecture

The Java Servlet Architecture is designed to interact directly with the HTTP requests and responses that come through a Web server. Servlets let a developer put Web traffic into a more object-oriented context so that other Java classes and applications can easily process it.

Chapter 6 introduced a basic servlet that used only the `init()` method from the superclass `javax.servlet.http.HttpServlet`. Recall that this method is automatically called each time the servlet is loaded. This superclass also contains two methods for handling data sent to the servlet via a Web browser or other HTTP-capable client. The `doGet()` and `doPost()` methods take the same two parameters, `HttpServletRequest` and `HttpServletResponse`. Respectively, these objects represent the information a Web browser sends when it makes a request and the response the Web server sends back.

The `HttpServletRequest` object contains information about the HTTP request as well as the methods you can use to access that data, including the following:

> **Parameters:** Request parameters can either be retrieved from the URL query string or derived from embedded message content. The `getParameter()` method is used to retrieve the value associated with a given name of a request parameter.
>
> **Headers:** HTTP headers that come through with the request can also be accessed by name from the `HttpServletRequest` object.
>
> **Cookies:** Cookies, or small pieces of information written to the client, can be retrieved from the request using the `getCookies()` method.

The `HttpServletResponse` object maintains the data to be routed back to the HTTP client. Using this object, a developer can do any of the following:

Set cookies: Write cookies back to the Web browser or client. These cookies can then be retrieved and modified by a later HTTP request.

Set headers: Headers are generally used to indicate the type of content being sent to the HTTP client. For instance, `text/html` indicates a standard Web page whereas `application/doc` indicates a word processing document.

Return error messages: Instead of writing messages back to the page content, a servlet can use the standard HTTP error statuses (404, 500, and so on) to indicate the nature of a problem.

Send redirect: The servlet can indicate some type of content or Web page to which the HTTP client should be redirected. This is useful for automatically forwarding the Web browser to different pages based on logic built into the servlet.

You have already seen `SerlvetContext` used to share resources among different users of the same Web application. This object can also be used by a servlet to set and retrieve common values in conjunction with other servlets and JSP pages in a Web application. The methods `getAttribute()`, `setAttribute()`, `getAttributeNames()`, and `removeAttribute()` provide access to attributes that are accessible across the Web application.

The `HttpSession` object provides a unique, per-user storage space for servlets and JSP pages. Because HTTP is a stateless protocol, the Web server cannot recognize a single user across multiple pages. As seen in Chapter 6, the `HttpSession` object can be used to "remember" whether a user has been authenticated in the system and to retrieve any attributes associated with that user. By using a unique session ID stored as a cookie or in the URL, the `HTTPSession` object ensures that a given user can only access information stored in her session.

The Struts Controller

The Struts Controller is comprised of several different objects and libraries. These include a Java servlet, a set of application libraries, and an XML configuration file. As mentioned in the "Java Servlet Architecture" sidebar, Java servlets are precompiled objects that deploy when the Java server is initialized. Unlike JSP pages, servlets cannot be readily modified while the application server is running. If a servlet is changed, the Java application server must be stopped and restarted for those changes to take effect. However, the servlet has a slight speed advantage over JSP pages because it never needs to be compiled on the fly. On the other hand, most application servers precompile JSP pages into servlets, so the speed differential for a client tends to be negligible or nonexistent.

Remember that each implementation of the MVC pattern has its own language and terminology for system components. Struts is no exception. Much of the Struts Controller functionality is housed in a Java servlet known as the `ActionServlet`. This servlet is responsible for processing all incoming HTTP requests sent via the user's Web browser or an intermediary Web server and directing HTTP responses back to the appropriate source.

> **NOTE** *In production deployments of Java applications, your environment would likely consist of separate Java application servers and Web servers. Distributing the workload generated by Web traffic allows a separate server to host static Web pages. You allow any deployed Java applications to run more efficiently by offloading this static page traffic from the Java server. In such a scenario, you configure the Web server to pass only certain types of requests or traffic to the Java application server.*

Based on the originating source, the `ActionServlet` matches an inbound HTTP request to the mapping definitions from an external XML configuration file. This file delineates the difference between the source of a request and where that request should be sent in the Struts framework. It also determines how to deal with responses sent back by the Struts Model component. Figure 7-5 shows the mapping relationship between the XML configuration file and the Struts system components.

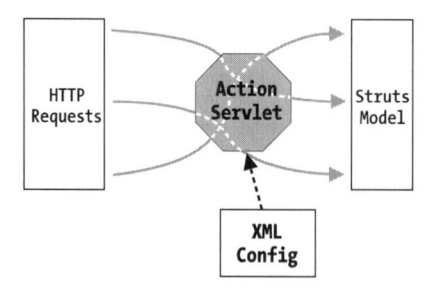

Figure 7-5. The XML configuration file

The `ActionServlet` is configured through the use of a set of `ActionMappings`. An `ActionMapping` is a predefined path that maps an incoming Uniform Resource Identifier (URI) request to a Struts Model component.

Developing Web Applications with Struts

> **NOTE** *A URI is a mechanism used to identify various types of content on the Internet. A URI path could refer to an FTP file server address, an SMTP mail server, or even streaming audio and video. The most common URI is that of a Web page address, which is designated by a subset of URI called the Uniform Resource Locator (URL). Because Struts can handle different types of content, I have chosen to use the term URI to deal with any type of file accessible over the Internet. Typically, most of your application's interaction with users occurs via the Hypertext Transfer Protocol (HTTP), as indicated by the* `http://` *used at the beginning of each address statement.*

The Struts XML configuration file shown in Figure 7-5 maintains these `ActionMappings`.

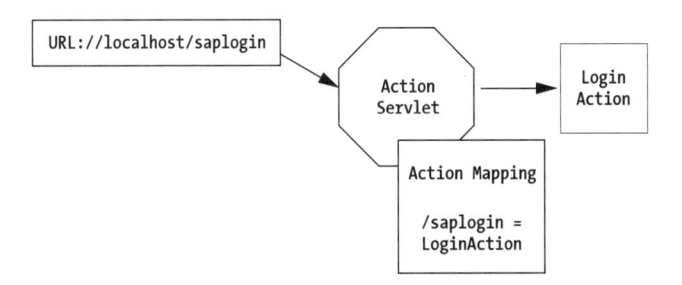

Figure 7-6. Using `ActionMapping` *to define a URI path*

Demonstrated in Figure 7-6 and the following XML snippet, an `ActionMapping` can be used to map almost any URI name and extension to functionality housed in a Struts Model component. Note that the line numbers are used for reference only and should not be included as part of the configuration file.

```
1    <action path="/saplogin"
2            type="LoginAction"
3            name="saplogin"
4            scope="session"
5            input="/userlogin.jsp">
6      <forward name="success"    path="/sapmain.jsp"/>
7      <forward name="error"      path="/tryagain.jsp"/>
8    </action>
```

Line 1 defines the inbound URI path as /saplogin. Any HTTP request made using this path (for example, `http://localhost/saplogin`) will be forwarded by the

185

ActionServlet to the Java class indicated in line 2. Lines 6 and 7 define the ActionMappings for the HTTP response, which depends on whether the LoginAction class returns an indicator of "success" or "failure". The tutorial application later in this chapter allows you to further explore the use of ActionMappings within an XML configuration file.

The ActionServlet resides at the heart of the Struts framework. It acts as the essential mediator between other objects in the system, based on a wide variety of technologies. The plain text XML configuration file can be easily modified by anyone who somewhat understands the document standard and uses human legible tags and attributes. ActionMappings provide a powerful and flexible mechanism for defining relationships between screen and workflow (business logic) components. The next section defines the Struts Model layer, and it specifically focuses on tapping into SAP business applications.

The Struts Model

In the Struts framework, the model layer can be comprised of both Java classes and the adapters those classes use to access backend systems. Struts defines a specific superclass, called the Action class, for developing Java classes that can be accessed by the ActionServlet. The Action class is used to process and convert data from an HTTP client into information that can be utilized by other Java classes.

Action classes make up the system connection logic of a Web application. These classes act as a type of adapter to middleware and backend systems. Consider SAP's BAPI/RFC layer as the business application interface, with JCo providing the underlying Java connectivity. The Action class acts as a wrapper around calls to the Java classes that connect to the R/3 system via JCo.

Figure 7-7 illustrates the grouping of different system objects and interfaces as part of the model component. Notice that only part of the Action class is considered to truly be a model component. You need to have the other part of that class to handle incoming Web requests over an HTTP stream, so it is somewhat tied to the protocol interface.

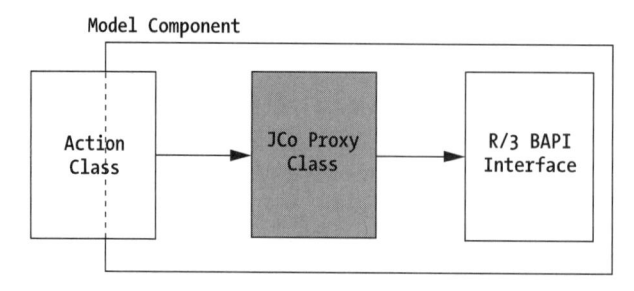

Figure 7-7. Classes and interfaces of the model component

Strictly speaking, the Action class has a stronger role in the control layer than it does in the model. However, because this class is responsible for providing communication back to the true model components, in this case the BAPIs and RFCs, it is simpler to consider it as part of the model layer. More accurately, the Action class represents model objects and provides control components with accessibility to them. Again, due to the varying nature of platform and language semantics, the MVC design pattern may not map exclusively to a single object or sets of objects within the solution system. Rather, as with Struts, the MVC pattern illustrates proven and fundamental concepts that should be adhered to from an architectural perspective. The actual implementation details are based on the specific needs and requirements of the framework.

As you will see in the tutorial, model components in this framework look more like the InterfaceCaller class developed earlier. This class implements JCo libraries and calls to different BAPI and RFC interfaces in a way that is completely removed from the user interface. It is not tied to a given protocol or message interface such as HTTP or a Web browser. In the idiom of the MVC solution pattern, you have already developed a model-style component that you can reuse later as part of your Web application development for SAP.

The Struts View

The last and most visible layer of the Struts framework is the view layer. This layer comprises all of the front-end components that display and define user interaction with an application. Although Struts can be used with different types of user interfaces, the focus of this book is on the Web, so the only client we deal with is a Web browser. Given this, Struts's view layer must be implemented largely around standard HTML and Web page directives. Fortunately, both Enterprise Java and the Struts framework provide libraries that simplify and extend Web page development to deliver more dynamic content to your end users.

Much of the view or presentation layer in Struts is deployed using JSP pages. You have already seen JSP pages in action, and you successfully deployed a material search application using them in the Chapter 6. Struts takes JSP pages to the next level, by applying another Enterprise Java technology called the JavaServer Page Standard Tag Library (JSTL).

Similar in look to standard HTML tags, the JSTL allows developers to create custom tags that can be used within any compliant JSP page. This custom tag is backed by Java code to provide complex data interactions without needing to embed extraneous Java code into a Web page. Java developers who need to provide more extensive functionality to Web page designers commonly use tag libraries. These designers utilize the Java tags as if they were standard HTML directives, without needing to understand the complexities of the code behind them. JSTL reinforces the notion of a strong division of labor by allowing a Java domain expert to create and maintain presentation logic that can be used by a variety of Web programmers within the enterprise.

> **TIP** You can find the code for this chapter in the Downloads section of the Apress Website (http://www.apress.com).

The following two examples illustrate the same Web page functionality before and after a custom Java tag is implemented.

```
<%@ page language="java" %>
<HTML>
<HEAD>
<TITLE>Hello World</TITLE>
</HEAD>
<BODY>
<%
   if (request.getParameter("username") == null)
   {
    out.println("Hello World!");
   }
   else
   {
    out.println("Hello, " + request.getParameter("username"));
   }
 %>
</BODY>
</HTML>
```

This very simple JSP page checks whether the parameter "username" has been sent in the HTTP request message. If it has, the page outputs a personalized greeting; if it does not, then the generic "Hello, World!" message is displayed. Note the amount of highlighted Java code required to implement this logic.

```
<%@ page language="java" %>
<%@ taglib uri="/WEB-INF/lib/mytag.tld" prefix="mytag" %>
<HTML>
<HEAD>
<TITLE>Hello World</TITLE>
</HEAD>
<BODY>
<mytag:helloworld />
</BODY>
</HTML>
```

A modified version of this JSP page using a custom Java tag gets rid of the need to directly embed Java code in the Web page. All of the Java code in the previous JSP page has been reduced to the highlighted line, `<mytag:helloworld />`. This line encapsulates the code logic of the first JSP page in an HTML-style tag. The functionality and output are exactly the same, but in the second example, the Web designer didn't need to know Java or the programmatic logic behind the `helloworld` tag.

Using custom Java tags is a great way to centralize Java development and even further decouple display logic from the HTML-based presentation layer. However, this book does not need to focus on building custom tags because Struts provides a refined set of tags based on the JSTL specification that you can use immediately within your application development.

Tag libraries are integral to development with Struts because they allow the JSP page to become part of the MVC application framework. Struts uses Java tags to pass dynamic data back and forth between Web pages and `Action` classes. Users can also use these tags to populate and repopulate data fields when they encounter an error page or must modify data stored as part of a current session, as in the case of a shopping cart.

Based on a combination of static HTML, Java code, and custom Java tags, the Struts View layer relies on JSP technology to deliver front-end functionality to the user. The next section demonstrates how to install the Struts framework and get your Struts Web application development off the ground.

Deploying an Initial Application with Struts

Learning how to reuse your existing development effort is key in object-oriented programming. You have already deployed a basic application using the Tomcat Java application server and are ready to build components for the Struts framework. Fortunately, much of this earlier effort can be reused as you begin learning the Struts application suite.

This section takes you through the process of installing Struts and converts the existing login application into the Struts framework. The first step is to download and install the Struts toolkit.

Installing Struts

The Struts framework is available from the Apache Web site as part of their Jakarta project. The Jakarta project builds and maintains open-source, server-side development for the Java and Enterprise Java platforms.

You are welcome to download any of the latest nightly builds of Struts; however, this book uses the 1.0.2 build for all tutorials. This version is available from http://jakarta.apache.org/struts/doc-1.0.2/index.html, under the "Acquiring Struts" section.

Once you have downloaded the "Struts 1.0.2 Binary Distribution," unzip the file into a temporary directory. You will need to copy a number of files from this directory, so I will refer to it as <STRUTS_TEMP> through the remainder of this chapter.

Open the directory where you installed the Tomcat server and navigate to the /webapps/sap directory. You will be using the same deployment directory and some of the application components from Chapter 6. Copy all of the files in the <STRUT_TEMP>/lib directory to <TOMCAT_HOME>/webapps/sap/WEB-INF/lib. This gives your Web application all of the basic Struts binaries and application libraries it needs to operate within the Struts framework.

You will also need to make the struts.jar file accessible to the Java compiler. Unfortunately, you cannot simply add a path to this file in your existing CLASSPATH. Having this Java archive in both your CLASSPATH and deployed in the Tomcat server may cause the wrong set of libraries to be loaded by your Web application. The best way to use struts.jar when you are compiling is to compile with the following command line option:

```
javac -classpath <TOMCAT_HOME>/webapps/sap/lib/struts.jar;%CLASSPATH%
myStrutsClass
```

The next step is to configure your existing SAP Web application to use the Struts components.

Configuring Struts

In Chapter 6, recall that you used the web.xml file to configure the Web application to utilize shared resources among different JSP pages. In Tomcat, the web.xml file is responsible for maintaining the entire configuration specific to a given Web application. Your web.xml should look something like this:

```
<?xml version="1.0" encoding="ISO-8859-1"?>

<!DOCTYPE web-app
    PUBLIC "-//Sun Microsystems, Inc.//DTD Web Application 2.3//EN"
    "http://java.sun.com/dtd/web-app_2_3.dtd">
<web-app>
<!-- InterfaceServlet to load shared resources -->
  <servlet>
    <servlet-name>sap</servlet-name>
    <servlet-class>com.apress.ejsap.InterfaceServlet</servlet-class>
```

```xml
    <init-param>
      <param-name>debug</param-name>
      <param-value>0</param-value>
    </init-param>
    <init-param>
      <param-name>listings</param-name>
      <param-value>true</param-value>
    </init-param>
    <init-param>
      <param-name>readonly</param-name>
      <param-value>false</param-value>
    </init-param>
    <load-on-startup>1</load-on-startup>
  </servlet>
</web-app>
```

You will use this file to implement connectivity between the Tomcat application server and the Struts framework.

Mapping the ActionServlet

In order for the Struts `ActionServlet` to broker requests within the framework, the Web application must be configured to intercept a specific type of request and send those requests to the `ActionServlet`. This configuration is based on the file extension used as part of the URI request path. You are probably familiar with the `.html` extension that indicates a standard Web page request, as in `http://www.mydomain.com/welcome.html`. The Tomcat server can be modified to handle almost any file extension sent via the URI path and map requests with that extension to different types of system components, such as Java servlets and JSP pages.

Because requests coming into the Struts framework must be handled differently than standard Web pages, you must configure the `web.xml` file to recognize and forward these requests to the `ActionServlet`. Modify your `web.xml` to look like this to allow the `ActionServlet` to take over when needed:

```xml
<?xml version="1.0" encoding="ISO-8859-1"?>
<!DOCTYPE web-app
    PUBLIC "-//Sun Microsystems, Inc.//DTD Web Application 2.3//EN"
    "http://java.sun.com/dtd/web-app_2_3.dtd">
<web-app>
<!-- InterfaceServlet to load shared resources -->
  <servlet>
    ...
```

```xml
  </servlet>
  <!-- ActionServlet Configuration -->
  <servlet>
    <servlet-name>action</servlet-name>
    <servlet-class>org.apache.struts.action.ActionServlet</servlet-class>
    <init-param>
      <param-name>application</param-name>
      <param-value>com.apress.ejsap.ApplicationResources</param-value>
    </init-param>
    <init-param>
      <param-name>config</param-name>
      <param-value>/WEB-INF/struts-config.xml</param-value>
    </init-param>
    <init-param>
      <param-name>debug</param-name>
      <param-value>2</param-value>
    </init-param>
    <init-param>
      <param-name>detail</param-name>
      <param-value>2</param-value>
    </init-param>
    <init-param>
      <param-name>validate</param-name>
      <param-value>true</param-value>
    </init-param>
    <load-on-startup>2</load-on-startup>
  </servlet>
  <!-- ActionServlet Mapping -->
  <servlet-mapping>
    <servlet-name>action</servlet-name>
    <url-pattern>*.do</url-pattern>
  </servlet-mapping>
</web-app>
```

The ActionServlet Configuration loads the ActionServlet class automatically at the start of the Tomcat server. Without detailing each parameter, this configuration looks for the class org.apache.struts.action.ActionServlet, assigns it the name action, and loads the file /WEB-INF/struts-config.xml as an initial parameter. In doing so, the Tomcat server loads the ActionServlet class and tells it to retrieve all ActionMapping configurations from the struts-config.xml file.

The ActionServlet Mapping defines the URI path extension that any incoming requests use for the ActionServlet. This extension can be an arbitrary string value, but it shouldn't conflict with standard or known extensions such as .html, .pdf, and so on. The Struts documentation recommends the use of .do as the extension that should map to the `ActionServlet`, so this is the convention I followed in this book.

Very simply, Tomcat maps any requests using the `.do` extension to the servlet specified by the name `action`. So a call to `http://www.mydomain.com/login.do` will be directed to the `ActionServlet` rather than going to a Web page or physical file named `login.do`.

Adding Java Tag Libraries

You must also configure your application's access to Java tag libraries using `web.xml`. A tag library is composed of a Tag Library Descriptor (TLD) and the Java class(es) that make up its functionality. Before an application can use a tag library in Tomcat, that library must be deployed through `web.xml`. Because Struts provides a series of canned tag libraries, this deployment is fairly simple; only a few lines need to be added to `web.xml`.

You have already copied the Struts tag libraries into the `/webapps/sap/WEB-INF/lib` directory. Now add these libraries to your `web.xml` with the following lines:

```
<!DOCTYPE web-app
    PUBLIC "-//Sun Microsystems, Inc.//DTD Web Application 2.3//EN"
    "http://java.sun.com/dtd/web-app_2_3.dtd">
<web-app>
  <!-- InterfaceServlet to load shared resources -->
  <servlet>
  ...
  </servlet>
  <!-- Action Servlet Configuration -->
  <servlet>
  ...
  </servlet>
  <!-- Action Servlet Mapping -->
  <servlet-mapping>
  ...
  </servlet-mapping>

  <!-- The Welcome File List -->
  <welcome-file-list>
     <welcome-file>index.jsp</welcome-file>
  </welcome-file-list>
```

```
<!-- Application Tag Library Descriptor -->
<taglib>
  <taglib-uri>/WEB-INF/app.tld</taglib-uri>
  <taglib-location>/WEB-INF/app.tld</taglib-location>
</taglib>

<!-- Struts Tag Library Descriptors -->
<taglib>
  <taglib-uri>/WEB-INF/struts-bean.tld</taglib-uri>
  <taglib-location>/WEB-INF/struts-bean.tld</taglib-location>
</taglib>

<taglib>
  <taglib-uri>/WEB-INF/struts-html.tld</taglib-uri>
  <taglib-location>/WEB-INF/struts-html.tld</taglib-location>
</taglib>

<taglib>
  <taglib-uri>/WEB-INF/struts-logic.tld</taglib-uri>
  <taglib-location>/WEB-INF/struts-logic.tld</taglib-location>
</taglib>
</web-app>
```

Struts provides a number of Java tag libraries designed to emulate and replace standard HTML directives. This allows JSP pages to be more easily integrated within the Struts framework without requiring extensive use of embedded Java code. In Chapter 9, you will create a custom Java tag to enhance the functionality of your SAP Web application. For now, you will use the Struts Java tags to become familiar with implementing Java tag libraries.

Building a Basic Struts XML Configuration

The final step in the Struts installation involves creating a very basic XML configuration file that will eventually house the screen flow mapping information. Create a file called struts-config.xml in the webapps/sap/WEB-INF directory and add the following lines to it:

```
<?xml version="1.0" encoding="ISO-8859-1" ?>
<!DOCTYPE struts-config PUBLIC
          "-//Apache Software Foundation//DTD Struts Configuration 1.0//EN"
          "http://jakarta.apache.org/struts/dtds/struts-config_1_0.dtd">
<struts-config>
```

```xml
<!-- ========== Form Bean Definitions ==================================== -->
  <form-beans>
  </form-beans>
<!-- ========== Global Forward Definitions =============================== -->
  <global-forwards>
  </global-forwards>
<!-- ========== Action Mapping Definitions =============================== -->
  <action-mappings>
  </action-mappings>
</struts-config>
```

This represents a skeleton version of the `struts-config.xml`, which contains three commented lines that indicate what type of configuration is maintained in this file. Throughout the development effort, you will need to add or change lines in this file according to the screen and workflow requirements of your application.

Developing a Login Application with Struts

Most application development in Struts follows the same formula, which closely matches the components outlined in the MVC design pattern. Your first Struts application reuses some of the components from the login application you developed in Chapter 6.

Roughly speaking, objects within your application development fall into one of these three categories:

Model components: For the SAP application, the model objects consist of the BAPI interfaces and the `InterfaceCaller` class that you developed in previous chapters. You need to add new BAPI calls to this class as you continue to develop. However, the existing class maintains a `checkPassword()` method that can be used in the Struts login application. In addition, you will create an `ActionForm` class to model the input forms from the login Web page.

View components: You have already developed two JSP pages that can be reused as the view objects in the new application. This layer also includes a properties file that maintains static HTML display data such as the user name and password prompt.

Controller components: These objects deal with mapping between the model and view components. You will use the `struts-config.xml` file to maintain these mappings and to create an `Action` class that you can use to transcribe HTTP-based into class method calls to the `InterfaceCaller` class.

Modeling a Web-Based Form in Struts

Typically, applications developed in Struts use a Java bean to model input data from HTML forms. This allows the Struts framework to easily transcribe data sent via HTTP into standard JavaBeans getter and setter methods. Known as ActionForm beans, these classes are declared within the struts-config.xml and can be used both in JSP pages and Action classes to retrieve data sent via a Web form.

The benefit of using ActionForm beans is that Struts automatically provides several important services to the end user:

Field validation: Certain fields may need to be validated before they are sent to the Action class. The simplest way to validate is by checking whether a required field is blank. If that field is blank, Struts redirects the user back to the referring page with a message that indicates the field that must be filled. Field validation can be more complex, but it is usually restricted to basic operations such as date formatting or required field input.

Field repopulation: If a user is redirected back to the referring page, ActionForm beans automatically repopulate the form input values. This allows the user to fix any mistakes to existing field input without having to retype each value.

Unique representation: Each instance of an ActionForm bean is unique to a specific user. Struts uses the user's session ID to determine whether an ActionForm has been created and to whom it belongs. Struts automatically creates a new ActionForm if it does not find one for a given user.

You are not required to implement ActionForm beans for user input in Struts. The alternative would be to pull data directly from the HTTP stream within an Action class. However, this method does not take advantage of any validation or error handling provided by ActionForm beans and increases the load on your Action classes.

An ActionForm bean does not need to be tied to a single HTML input form. You can easily use ActionForm beans to model data across different screens or even transactions. I recommend that you do not use a single ActionForm bean to span multiple functional areas in an application. For instance, the login application contains a discrete unit of application functionality, so it will have an ActionForm bean dedicated solely to it.

Once again, you will be deploying classes in the /webapp/sap/WEB-INF/classes/com/apress/ejsap directory that contains your previous Web application development. Create a new file called LoginForm.java and add the following code to it:

Developing Web Applications with Struts

```
package com.apress.ejsap;

import org.apache.struts.action.ActionError;
import org.apache.struts.action.ActionErrors;
import org.apache.struts.action.ActionForm;
import org.apache.struts.action.ActionMapping;
import javax.servlet.http.*;

public final class LoginForm extends ActionForm {
}
```

Notice that the class `LoginForm` extends the Struts `ActionForm` class. This is what gives your `ActionForm` bean access to all of the methods for adding new fields as well as validating and resetting their values. You can choose to use certain features of the `ActionForm` bean in the application by overriding appropriate methods in this class. For example, if you wanted to handle validation strictly through the JSP page, you would not want to implement the `validate()` method within your `ActionForm` class. However, this chapter explores the most commonly used facets of the Struts framework, so the `LoginForm` bean utilizes several popular methods available in the `ActionForm` class.

The first step you must take to create an `ActionForm` bean is to identify any form fields that need input from the user. The login application needs only two input fields, the user name and the password. These must be defined as class level variables and are typically declared `private`. Because a bean uses `get()` and `set()` methods to retrieve and modify field values, class-level variables should not be directly accessible outside of the bean, hence their declaration as `private`.

```
public final class LoginForm extends ActionForm {
  private String password = null;
  private String username = null;
}
```

In order to access these variables from the outside world, the `LoginForm` bean must implement `get()` and `set()` methods for each. These method names are part of the JavaBeans specification and allow a class to be used as a modular component within different types of application development.

```
public final class LoginForm extends ActionForm {
  private String password = null;
  private String username = null;
```

197

```java
    public String getUSERNAME() {
       return (this.username);
    }
    public void setUSERNAME(String USERNAME) {
       this.username = USERNAME;
    }
    public String getPASSWORD() {
       return (this.password);
    }
    public void setPASSWORD(String PASSWORD) {
       this.password = PASSWORD;
    }
}
```

Both get() and set() methods should be declared public so that classes outside of this bean's package can use them. These methods are important because they allow you to control how a field value is set and what should be done in order to retrieve it. The login application does not require any field manipulation at this point, so setting and returning values is fairly straightforward.

> **NOTE** *The naming convention for* get() *and* set() *methods uses each prefix (*get *or* set*) followed by the appropriate property name. In Java, the first word of a method name is typically set in lowercase and any words following have the first letter capitalized. Struts attempts to map field names in a Web page to the method names following a* get *or* set *prefix. As a result, you may find that it helps if you use methods names that Web developers can remember easily. Because a method name like* getusername() *does not follow good Java coding practice, this book uses field names set in all capitals as both method names and Web page field names. The alternative would be to use a method name like* getUsername(), *but that would rely on the Web developer remembering to capitalize only the first letter of each field name of a Web page. However, the latter method name does conform to the JavaBeans specification, whereas the former does not.*

setUSERNAME() takes a String called USERNAME as its sole parameter and assigns the value of this object to the username variable declared at the class level. Remember, the term this is a reserved keyword in Java that refers to variables and methods within the current class. getUSERNAME() requires no parameters but it returns a String object back to the class that has called it. These methods are allowed to act on the privately declared username variable because they are all part of the LoginForm class.

The password variable also requires get() and set() methods similar to those used to access the username variable. However, you may also wish to implement a field manipulation here to ensure that the value of this variable is compliant with SAP standards. Depending on the R/3 system configuration, SAP passwords may be case sensitive. It is common to set all Internet user passwords to uppercase to avoid the confusion caused by mixed-case passwords. Using the setPASSWORD() method, you could force the String PASSWORD to always be set to uppercase. If you did, the body of the setPASSWORD() method would look like this:

```
this.password = PASSWORD.toUpperCase();
```

You could take this one step further by trimming any leading or trailing spaces from the PASSWORD value using the trim() method. The statement would now look like this:

```
this.password = PASSWORD.toUpperCase().trim();
```

From now on, when you use this method to retrieve a password, you are guaranteed that it will be formatted correctly for your R/3 configuration. Moreover, these field requirements are hidden to anyone using the bean and require less SAP-specific understanding by other developers working on the application.

The LoginForm class also supports a reset() method so that all properties in the bean can reset to their default state.

```
  public void reset(ActionMapping mapping,
                    HttpServletRequest request) {
    this.password = null;
    this.username = null;
  }
```

Finally, the LoginForm bean needs to override the optional validate() method in order to perform basic validation on input fields coming from a Web page.

```
  public ActionErrors validate(ActionMapping mapping,
                               HttpServletRequest request) {
    ActionErrors errors = new ActionErrors();
    if ((username == null) || (username.length() < 1)) {
        errors.add("username", new ActionError("error.username.required"));
    }
    if ((password == null) || (password.length() < 1)) {
        errors.add("password", new ActionError("error.password.required"));
    }
    return errors;
  }
```

199

This method performs two major functions within the Struts framework. First, it evaluates the variables that have been set in this bean according to prescribed criteria. In this case, the `LoginForm` checks to see whether the `username` variable is set to `NULL` or whether the length of the variable is less than one. If either condition is met, then the `validate()` method knows that the input value does not meet the basic criteria for being passed on to an `Action` class.

When an error condition occurs, the second major function of the `validate()` method takes effect. Notice that an instance of the `ActionErrors` class had been instantiated at the start of this method. `ActionErrors` is a Struts class that provides an easy way to encapsulate error messages created through the course of application execution. These messages can be retrieved and displayed back to the end user through a Web page.

Using the `add()` method of the `errors` instance, you can specify a property name and new `ActionError` instance to be added to the `ActionErrors` stack. The `ActionError` is instantiated with a `String` key that you can use to look up the specific error message to be displayed back to the end user. These keys are associated with message strings in an external properties file similar to the `sapdata.properties` used in earlier examples. The next section details how to build and use this file.

Your `LoginForm` class should now look something like this:

```
package com.apress.ejsap;

import org.apache.struts.action.ActionError;
import org.apache.struts.action.ActionErrors;
import org.apache.struts.action.ActionForm;
import org.apache.struts.action.ActionMapping;
import javax.servlet.http.*;

public final class LoginForm extends ActionForm {
    private String password = null;
    private String username = null;

    public String getPASSWORD() {
        return (this.password.toUpperCase().trim());
    }
    public void setPASSWORD(String PASSWORD) {
        this.password = PASSWORD;
    }
    public String getUSERNAME() {
        return (this.username);
    }
    public void setUSERNAME(String USERNAME) {
        this.username = USERNAME;
    }
```

```
  public void reset(ActionMapping mapping,
                    HttpServletRequest request) {
    this.password = null;
    this.username = null;
  }
  public ActionErrors validate(ActionMapping mapping,
                               HttpServletRequest request) {
    ActionErrors errors = new ActionErrors();
    if ((username == null) || (username.length() < 1)) {
        errors.add("username", new ActionError("error.username.required"));
    }
    if ((password == null) || (password.length() < 1)) {
        errors.add("password", new ActionError("error.password.required"));
    }
    return errors;
  }
}
```

This may seem like a lot of work just to deal with two input form fields from a Web page. Consider, however, that this class not only encapsulates these fields but also provides validation and error messaging to indicate possible problems to the end user. Struts uses the values set in the `LoginForm` bean to automatically repopulate input form values if the user is redirected back to the login page to update or fix a field.

Using the ApplicationResources File

You have already used Java properties files to provide a simple configuration file for SAP system variables. Although this allowed anyone who basically understood SAP to modify and update the functionality of your application, it still meant that a developer had to actually implement Java code to retrieve this information. Struts provides a series of Java wrappers and tag library directives that simplify access to static data maintained in a Java properties file.

In the `LoginForm` class, the `validate()` method creates a new instance of the `ActionError` class using the following statement:

```
errors.add("username", new ActionError("error.username.required"));
```

This `ActionError` instance is added to the `errors` stack by the Struts framework and returned to `ActionServlet`. The `ActionError` instance encapsulates an error message based on the text string passed to it as a parameter. So where does this text string get mapped to a user-friendly error message? In the Struts framework, you can optionally deploy a Java properties file to not only deal with error messages, but to provide simple access to static text strings anywhere within your Web application.

By default, this properties file is called `ApplicationResources.properties`. It can be renamed, as long as it keeps the file extension `.properties`. You have already configured the Struts framework to use `ApplicationResources.properties` in the `web.xml` file:

```
<init-param>
  <param-name>application</param-name>
  <param-value>com.apress.ejsap.ApplicationResources</param-value>
</init-param>
```

As detailed in this configuration, you must save the `ApplicationResources.properties` file in `com/apress/ejsap/` under the current Web application deployment directory. You can relocate and rename this properties file, but you must configure `web.xml` so that Struts will be able to find the correct file.

Create a new text file called `ApplicationResources.properties` in the `/webapps/sap/WEB-INF/com/apress/ejsap/` directory. Throughout the course of this development, you will need to add more entries to this file, so you might want to keep it open.

TIP *You can make changes to the* `ApplicationResources.properties` *file while the Tomcat application server is running. However, Tomcat can take up to five minutes to refresh its cache and grab new or modified entries from the properties file. If you need to immediately test changes to* `ApplicationResources.properties`, *stop and restart the Tomcat server. Any changes made to this file take effect when Tomcat redeploys the Web application.*

For now, you need to have two entries in this properties file to deal with `LoginForm`—one for the username error and another for the password error:

```
error.username.required=<li>Username is required
error.password.required=<li>Password is required
```

Notice the use of the `<li>` HTML tag at the start of each message. Because these text messages are displayed in a Web browser, you can use HTML to enhance the message formatting. Struts also provides some default properties tags that offer additional formatting.

```
errors.header=<h3><font color="red">Application Error</font></h3>You must
  correct the following error(s) before proceeding:<ul>
errors.footer=</ul><hr>
```

This creates a bulleted list that contains any error messages that come out of the Struts framework.

Designing the Login View

Similar to the JSP pages created in the previous chapter, the login view consists of a login request and login response page. The view is responsible for collecting user name and password information from the end user, forwarding it to the controller, and displaying the appropriate response. Actually, the login view might consist of three JSP pages: a request page, response page, and an error page. You could use the error page to indicate that a problem occurred in authentication and to request that the user to try again. Because the goal is to streamline the Web application, you will be building a request page with built-in error display to tell the end user to try again.

Create a new JSP page called `saplogin.jsp` in the `/webapps/sap` directory. Notice that you are not using the same `login.jsp` from the previous chapter. This means that both the Struts and non-Struts version of the login application will be deployed in the Tomcat server, so it will be easier to compare differences between the two.

The first step in developing a JSP page in the Struts framework is to import the Struts tag libraries:

```
<%@ page language="java" %>
<%@ taglib uri="/WEB-INF/lib/struts.tld" prefix="struts" %>
<%@ taglib uri="/WEB-INF/lib/struts-bean.tld" prefix="bean" %>
<%@ taglib uri="/WEB-INF/lib/struts-html.tld" prefix="html" %>
```

Like other JSP import statements, `<%@taglib...%>` tells the Java Virtual Machine (JVM) that this page requires access to an external library. The `taglib` directive declares a tag library, followed by the `uri` attribute, which indicates the location of that tag library. Recall that you already copied all of the Struts tag libraries into the `/webapps/sap/WEB-INF/lib/` directory when you installed the Struts toolkit. In order to access these Java tags from within the JSP page, you need to assign the library with a unique identifier or `prefix`. You set this `prefix` to an arbitrary text string that is used to reference a unique library in the JSP page.

All tag libraries must have the file extension `.tld`, which stand for "Tag Library Descriptor." A TLD is an XML document that describes each individual tag as well as the tag library. You will see how this works in Chapter 9, when you develop and deploy your own tag library.

Once the tag libraries have been declared, you can replace the standard HTML directives with new "Struts-aware" Java tags. These look very similar to their HTML counterparts; however, they provide a much-enhanced level of transparent functionality to your users.

```
<%@ page language="java" %>
<%@ taglib uri="/WEB-INF/lib/struts.tld" prefix="struts" %>
<%@ taglib uri="/WEB-INF/lib/struts-bean.tld" prefix="bean" %>
<%@ taglib uri="/WEB-INF/lib/struts-html.tld" prefix="html" %>
<html:html>
  <HEAD>
    <TITLE>SAP Login</TITLE>
    <html:base/>
  </HEAD>
  <BODY>
    ...
  </BODY>
</html:html>
```

To format a Java tag directive, simply use the declared prefix for that tag library followed by the name of the tag, and separated them with a semicolon. In the previous example, notice the several different Struts tags combined with standard HTML tags. Struts provides replacements for HTML tags that need to be tightly integrated with the runtime framework. Here, the standard <HTML> tag has been replaced with <html:html> in order to allow the JSP page to extract any locale- or language-specific information for the user, if it exists.

The <html:base/> tag renders a reference to the absolute location of its page. Because Web applications such as Struts use servlet redirects, the file returned to the browser can often be completely different from the one you requested. Always use this tag in your Struts-based Web application and place it in the <HEAD> section of the page.

> **NOTE** The <html:html> tag requires a closing tag, </html:html>, whereas <html:base/> does not. As in standard HTML, some tag directives, such as line breaks (<BR>) do not need to indicate where display formatting should end. These tags have a self-defining end and are not considered to brace or bracket any data. The <htm:base/> tag displays a line of text and is not applied across multiple lines in the Web page. Because the Java tab library specification requires XML-compliant HTML, you must always terminate single tags with a trailing slash.

Recall that the LoginForm bean might return errors to the requesting JSP page. Struts provides a tag directive to display these errors from anywhere within the Web page. In the following login page, these errors are displayed at the top of the form, before the user name and password fields:

```
<BODY>
  <html:errors/>
  ...
</BODY>
```

This additional flexibility lets you determine where (if at all) errors messages display on a given page. If you were to omit this tag, users would simply be redirected back to the login page without any error messages.

Finally, you need to implement the actual login form. Again, with the help of Struts tags, you can easily integrate the login form into the application framework. First, describe the form attributes:

```
<html:form action="saplogin.do" method="post" name="login"
           type="com.apress.ejsap.LoginForm">
```

`<html:form ... >` uses the `form` tag from the Struts HTML tag library. The `action` attribute is set to the HTTP request submitted by this form. Your SAP Web application is currently configured to pass all HTTP requests with the `.do` file extension to the `ActionServlet` controller. `ActionServlet` then attempts to map the filename, `saplogin`, to an `Action` class that processes authentication through JCo. The `name` attribute specifies an identifier for the form. The `type` attribute indicates the `ActionForm` class with appropriate `get()` and `set()` methods for the fields in this form. This example looks for the `LoginForm` class found at `/com/apress/ejsap/`.

Now you need to add prompts for the user name and password.

```
<bean:message key="prompt.username"/>
...
<bean:message key="prompt.password"/>
...
```

Instead of entering text prompts for the user name and password directly into the JSP page, this page uses the `ApplicationResources` properties file to display static data. Here your application uses the `<bean:message ... >` tag to look up text strings in the `ApplicationResources` file deployed through `web.xml`. The `key` attribute specifies the retrieval key that maps to the requested text message.

You will need to add two new entries in the `ApplicationResources.properties` file:

```
prompt.username=Username:
prompt.password=Password:
```

Next you need to create the form fields that allow the user to input his user name and password:

```
<bean:message key="prompt.username"/>
<BR>
<html:text property="USERNAME" size="25"/>
<BR>
<bean:message key="prompt.password"/>
<BR>
<html:password property="PASSWORD" size="25"/>
```

Again, these tags are based on Struts tags; they replace their standard HTML `<input type=...>` counterparts. `<html:text...>` creates a normal text field and `<html:password...>` creates a masked password field. The `property` attribute must map to a setter method in the `LoginForm` so that this field can be validated and processed within the `Action` class.

> **NOTE** *If you ever need to internationalize your application, all you need is a translated version of the* `ApplicationResources` *file. The language displayed in your application is based on locale information stored in the HTTP header, similar to the internationalized application you created using properties files in Chapter 5.*

Last, but not least, this JSP page implements a Struts Submit button:

```
<html:submit property="submit" value="Submit"/>
```

`<html:submit...>` renders an HTML Form button. The `value` attribute provides the text string to be displayed on the button face, and the `property` attribute indicates the name of this button.

Your `saplogin.jsp` page should now look something like this:

```
<%@ page language="java" %>
<%@ taglib uri="/WEB-INF/lib/struts.tld" prefix="struts" %>
<%@ taglib uri="/WEB-INF/lib/struts-bean.tld" prefix="bean" %>
<%@ taglib uri="/WEB-INF/lib/struts-html.tld" prefix="html" %>
<html:html>
  <HEAD>
    <TITLE>SAP Login</TITLE>
```

```
        <html:base/>
      </HEAD>
      <BODY>
        <html:errors/>
        <H1>SAP Login</H1>
        Please enter your SAP Internet username and password:
        <P>
        <html:form action="saplogin.do" method="post" name="login"
                   type="com.apress.ejsap.LoginForm">
          <bean:message key="prompt.username"/>
          <BR>
          <html:text property="USERNAME" size="25"/>
          <BR>
          <bean:message key="prompt.password"/>
          <BR>
          <html:password property="PASSWORD" size="25"/>
          <P>
          <html:submit property="submit" value="Submit"/>
        </html:form>
      </BODY>
    </html:html>
```

Figure 7-8 shows the Web page that the `saplogin` JSP page renders.

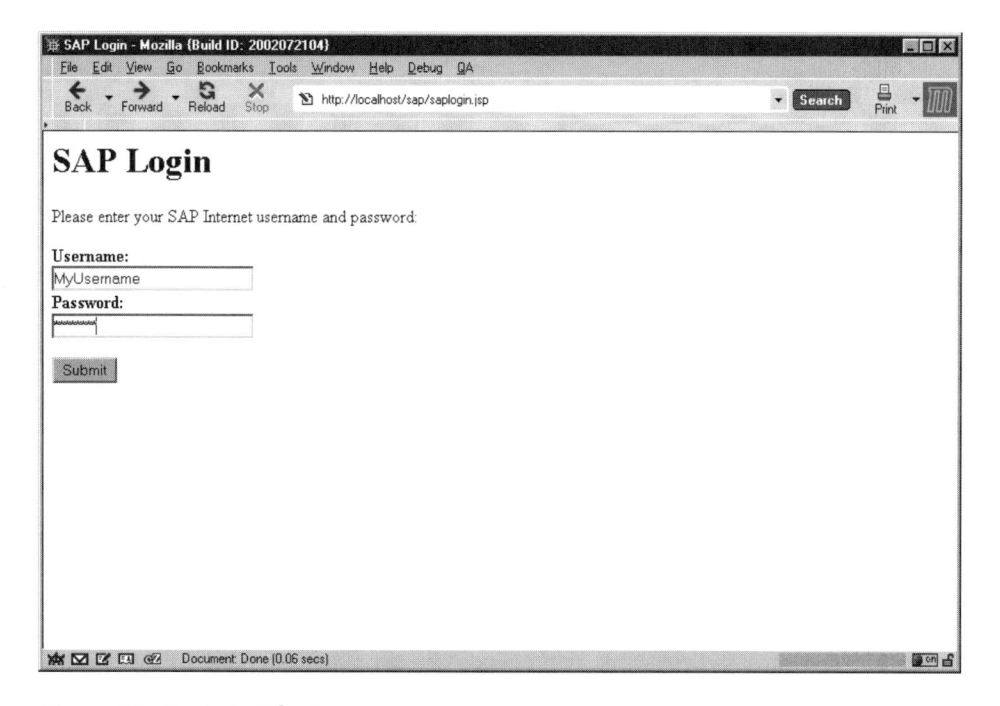

Figure 7-8. Basic SAP login screen

Chapter 7

The login result page is far simpler, at least for the moment. It displays if the user is successfully authenticated in the SAP system. For now, it retrieves the user name value the Action class stored in the HTTP session and displays it back to the end user:

```
<%@ page language="java" %>
<%@ taglib uri="/WEB-INF/lib/struts.tld" prefix="struts" %>
<%@ taglib uri="/WEB-INF/lib/struts-bean.tld" prefix="bean" %>
<%@ taglib uri="/WEB-INF/lib/struts-html.tld" prefix="html" %>
<html:html>
  <HEAD>
    <TITLE>SAP Login</TITLE>
    <html:base/>
  </HEAD>
  <BODY>
  <H1>SAP Login</H1>
  <P>
    <H3>Welcome, <%= session.getAttribute("USERNAME") %>.</H3>
    You have been successfully authenticated in SAP.
  </BODY>
</html:html>
```

Figure 7-9 shows a successful login result rendered in a Web browser.

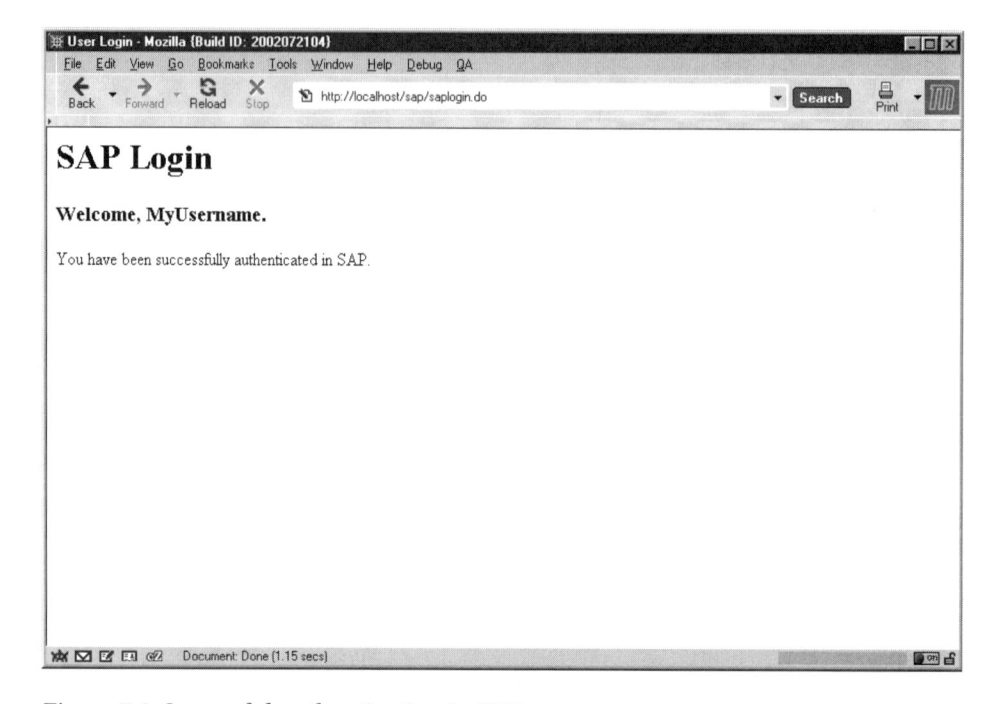

Figure 7-9. Successful authentication in SAP

The next section details an Action class that processes the values sent through the login form and calls JCo to authenticate the end user in SAP.

Building the Login Action Class

Struts provides a fairly comprehensive set of Java libraries you can use to develop Action classes that can directly interact with information coming in over the Web. Action classes provide three major functions within your Struts Web application:

- Process incoming HTTP data

- Call JCo connector classes

- Translate JCo responses into Web-legible data

You can also use Action classes to check whether a user has been successfully logged into the application and to provide additional validation of data fields. By using ActionForward mappings, you can easily redirect the user to the appropriate page based on her need for authentication or additional information.

First, create a new Java class called LoginAction.java and save it in the /webapps/sap/WEB-INF/classes/com/apress/ejsap directory.

> **NOTE** *As a somewhat unofficial naming convention, this book uses the suffix* Action *to indicate a Struts* Action *class. The class name prefix points to the functionality encapsulated in that class. You can use any naming convention in your Struts Web application. The important point is that you are consistent in your class names so that you do not confuse yourself and others.*

In order to use the Struts application libraries, you must first import those classes into your Java class. Instead of importing every class in the Struts package, this Action class imports only those specific Struts libraries the application requires. In addition to lowering memory overhead in the JVM, this strategy allows you to individually review each Struts class this application utilizes.

```
package com.apress.ejsap;

import java.io.IOException;
import java.util.*;
import javax.servlet.*;
import javax.servlet.http.*;
```

Chapter 7

```
import org.apache.struts.action.Action;
import org.apache.struts.action.ActionForm;
import org.apache.struts.action.ActionForward;
import org.apache.struts.action.ActionMapping;
import org.apache.struts.action.ActionServlet;
import org.apache.struts.action.ActionErrors;
import org.apache.struts.action.ActionError;
import com.apress.ejsap.*;

public final class LoginAction extends Action {
   ...
}
```

As you can see, the `LoginAction` class extends the `Action` class in its declaration statement. As you saw earlier, this allows the Java class to implement methods in the `Action` class as if they were native methods. The Struts `Action` class provides two key methods as a way to integrate within the application framework. Both methods are called `perform()` and they differ only by the type of servlet environment in which they are executed. Because this is a Web-based application, you will be using the `perform()` method that passes HTTP data to the `Action` class and requires the response to be formatted accordingly.

```
public final class LoginAction extends Action {
   public ActionForward perform(ActionMapping mapping,
                                ActionForm form,
                                HttpServletRequest request,
                                HttpServletResponse response)
      throws IOException, ServletException
   {
      ...
   }
}
```

The `perform()` method implemented here takes the following four objects as parameters. Within the Struts framework, the `ActionServlet` is the only component that directly calls this `perform()` method. As a result, it is up to the `ActionServlet` to pass the appropriate objects, without any intervention from the developer, so that the `Action` class can communicate with a Web browser.

ActionMapping: Provides a reference to the information passed from the user request to the `ActionServlet`. This class also lets you create `ActionForward` instances in order to forward the user to the appropriate page based on logic in the `Action` class.

Developing Web Applications with Struts

ActionForm: Provides a reference to the form associated with a given request. For the login application, `ActionForm` is an instance of the `LoginForm` bean we developed in the section "Modeling a Web-Based Form in Struts." However, because `perform()` does not explicitly specify the `LoginForm` class as a parameter, you need to subclass this object when it is instantiated in the `LoginAction` class.

HttpServletRequest and **HttpServletResponse**: Provide communication to and from the Web browser over the HTTP data stream. These objects maintain an individual's session as well as information about the Web browser and user attributes.

Once the `LoginAction` class has access to those key object instances, it can process and convert Web data into a JCo-compatible call. Actually, this class uses the `InterfaceCaller` instance that was deployed when the Tomcat server was started (see Chapter 6). Because this class strictly encapsulates your JCo calls, it is easier to think of `InterfaceCaller` as part of the JCo development. In reality, both `InterfaceCaller` and the JCo libraries comprise the model components of your Struts application design, with `LoginAction` functioning as part of the control layer.

The `LoginAction` classes need to grab the `username` and `password` fields from the Web browser input. These values are automatically stored in the `LoginForm` bean and validated in the `ActionServlet`. In order to retrieve the `LoginForm`, you must subclass the `ActionForm` instance passed as a parameter in the `perform()` method:

```
LoginForm loginForm = (LoginForm) form;
String username = loginForm.getUSERNAME();
String password = loginForm.getPASSWORD();
```

This code creates a new instance of `LoginForm` that equals an explicitly classed instance of the `ActionForm` form object. Having created this instance, you can use the `get()` methods provided in the bean to access form field values. An easier and more concise way to retrieve these values is simply to class the `form` instance when the `username` and `password` instances are created.

```
String username = ((LoginForm) form).getUSERNAME();
String password = ((LoginForm) form).getPASSWORD();
```

Now that the field values have been translated from HTTP data to Java `String` objects, the `LoginAction` class can call the `checkPassword()` method from the `InterfaceCaller` class. But first, you need to retrieve the shared instance of this class from the `ServletContext` object:

211

```
ActionServlet actServ = getServlet();
ServletContext servContext = actServ.getServletContext();
InterfaceCaller infCaller =
        (InterfaceCaller)servContext.getAttribute("ifaceCaller");
```

ActionServlet maintains the servlet context, so first you need to retrieve an instance of the ActionServlet, called actServ. You can use the getServletContext() method on actServ to provide the shared ServletContext instance, called servContext, and you can retrieve an instance of the InterfaceCaller class from servContext using its getAttribute() method. Recall, that the InterfaceServlet loaded at startup stores this instance in the ServletContext using the text string "ifaceCaller".

The LoginAction class can now call the checkPassword() method on infCaller in order to authenticate the user against an R/3 system:

```
Hashtable result = infCaller.checkPassword(username, password);
```

Using the Hashtable result returned from this call, LoginAction checks the RETURN.TYPE field to ensure that the user was authenticated in SAP. If the authentication failed, this class adds an ActionError instance to an instance of ActionErrors, called errors:

```
ActionErrors errors = new ActionErrors();
if ("E".equals((String)result.get("RETURN.TYPE"))) {
   errors.add(ActionErrors.GLOBAL_ERROR,
              new ActionError("error.authentication.fail"));
}
```

Normally, you use the ActionErrors class to deal with the error messages returned by the validate() method of an ActionForm class like LoginForm. However, this class can be effectively used to report any error message back to the requesting JSP page, regardless of its source. The previous code snippet demonstrates how the ActionErrors class can be used to direct the user back to the requesting JSP page with the additional error message being displayed. Rather than developing a new JSP with its own entry in the Struts screen flow configuration, the login application reuses an existing JSP, saplogin.jsp, and simply displays the error message that has been retrieved from the ApplicationResources file.

In order to add a new error message to ActionErrors, the LoginAction class must call the add() method and pass in a property name and an ActionError instance that represents the error message. The property name value indicates the name of the form field that cannot be validated (see the earlier section entitled "Modeling a Web-Based Form in Struts" for more details). Because the

Developing Web Applications with Struts

authentication error does not relate to a specific field, you must use the GLOBAL_ERROR property marker to indicate that a general or system-level error has occurred.

Likewise, you need to add a new entry to the ApplicationResources file:

```
error.authentication.fail=
                <li>You have not been authenticated by SAP. Please try again.
```

If any error messages exist, the application must return a valid ActionForward instance to the ActionServlet and stop execution:

```
if (!errors.empty()) {
  this.saveErrors(request, errors);
  return (new ActionForward(mapping.getInput()));
}
```

Based on your application logic, you could add multiple errors entries to the errors instance. Each of these messages would be added to this instance and returned to the requesting JSP page for display. This code checks whether or not the errors instance is empty (remember, an exclamation point or bang in Java is equivalent to the NOT operator). If that condition is met, the code calls the saveErrors() method that is part of the current class by extending Action. saveErrors() requires two parameters: the HttpSerlvetRequest instance passed in by ActionServlet, and the ActionErrors instance that encapsulates any error messages reported by LoginAction. The final statement in this if block returns a new ActionForward object, which you can instantiate using one of that class's default constructors. In this case, the constructor takes a text string that indicates the URL path to which the user should be redirected. The ActionServlet sends an instance of the ActionMapping class to LoginAction. By using the getInput() method on this ActionMapping instance, the LoginAction class can redirect the user to the requesting JSP page, saplogin.jsp.

> **NOTE** *A* return *statement in Java immediately ends execution of the current class and returns control to the calling application or class. You determine the type of class this statement must return when you declare the current method. In this case, the* perform() *method must return an* ActionForward *instance anytime a* return *directive is issued.*

After you ensure that no error conditions are met, you can use LoginAction to return an ActionForward indicating that the user has been successfully authenticated in SAP. However, before doing so, you may want to set certain field values in the user's session object to provide additional information for the view layer to display.

213

```
HttpSession session = request.getSession();
session.setAttribute("USERNAME", username);
```

This code retrieves an instance of the `HttpSession` object from `request` using the `getSession()` method; then it sets the attribute name "USERNAME" equal to the value of `username`. You may wish to set additional session attributes to provide dynamic content through subsequent JSP pages. In this limited Web application, the login application simply requires the user name to display a customized greeting once the user has logged in.

The final `return` statement creates an `ActionForward` instance based on a mapping in the Struts configuration file:

```
return (mapping.findForward("success"));
```

This statement creates an `ActionForward` instance based on the URL path associated with the "success" mapping in the `struts-config.xml` file. The next section demonstrates how you can configure this file based on the various application components that you have already developed.

Before we move on, let's look at what the `LoginAction` class should now look like:

```
package com.apress.ejsap;

import java.io.IOException;
import java.util.*;
import javax.servlet.*;
import javax.servlet.http.*;
import org.apache.struts.action.Action;
import org.apache.struts.action.ActionForm;
import org.apache.struts.action.ActionForward;
import org.apache.struts.action.ActionMapping;
import org.apache.struts.action.ActionServlet;
import org.apache.struts.action.ActionErrors;
import org.apache.struts.action.ActionError;

import com.apress.ejsap.*;

public final class LoginAction extends Action {
  public ActionForward perform(ActionMapping mapping,
                               ActionForm form,
                               HttpServletRequest request,
                               HttpServletResponse response)
    throws IOException, ServletException
```

```
{
   String username = ((LoginForm) form).getUSERNAME();
   String password = ((LoginForm) form).getPASSWORD();

   ActionServlet actServ = getServlet();
   ServletContext servContext = actServ.getServletContext();
   InterfaceCaller infCaller =
                  (InterfaceCaller)servContext.getAttribute("ifaceCaller");

   Hashtable result = infCaller.checkPassword(username, password);
   ActionErrors errors = new ActionErrors();
   if ("E".equals((String)result.get("RETURN.TYPE"))) {
     errors.add(ActionErrors.GLOBAL_ERROR,
              new ActionError("error.authentication.fail"));
   }
   if (!errors.empty()) {
     this.saveErrors(request, errors);
     return (new ActionForward(mapping.getInput()));
   }
   HttpSession session = request.getSession();
   session.setAttribute("USERNAME", username);
   return (mapping.findForward("success"));
   }
}
```

Configuring the Struts Login Application

With all of your Struts application components developed, the final step involves configuring the screen flow using `struts-config.xml`. You saw a skeleton version of this file earlier that described its three major sections:

```
<?xml version="1.0" encoding="ISO-8859-1" ?>
<!DOCTYPE struts-config PUBLIC
         "-//Apache Software Foundation//DTD Struts Configuration 1.0//EN"
         "http://jakarta.apache.org/struts/dtds/struts-config_1_0.dtd">
<struts-config>
<!-- ========== Form Bean Definitions ===================================== -->
<!-- ========== Global Forward Definitions ================================ -->
<!-- ========== Action Mapping Definitions ================================ -->
</struts-config>
```

The first, Form Bean Definitions, describes any `ActionForm` beans that should be deployed by the Struts framework. At this point, you only need to deploy the `LoginForm` bean to handle incoming login form fields.

```
<!-- ========== Form Bean Definitions ==================================== -->
<form-beans>
  <!-- Loginform bean -->
  <form-bean      name="login"
                  type="com.apress.ejsap.LoginForm"/>
</form-beans>
```

The XML document type definition (DTD) for `struts-config` requires all form beans to be enclosed in the `<form-beans>...</form-beans>` tag directive. As you develop new forms, you will add additional form bean descriptions within these tags. You define the individual form bean using a single `<form-bean .../>` tag that does not require an end tag. You need to give it a `name` attribute to specify a unique identifier in order to reference it through action mappings, and a `type` attribute that points to the fully qualified Java class name of the form bean. In this case, the `LoginForm` bean has been deployed in the `com.apress.ejsap` package and is assigned the unique identifier "login".

Next, `struts-config.xml` describes any default or global forwards that your application needs:

```
<!-- ========== Global Forward Definitions ============================ -->
  <global-forwards>
    <forward    name="login"                    path="/saplogin.jsp"/>
  </global-forwards>
```

Although the `LoginAction` does not use this forward, you should understand its function in a larger application. Recall that the `perform()` method of an `Action` class must return an `ActionForward` object to tell the `ActionServlet` where to direct the user. The global forward provides a mechanism that sends users to a default page when an `ActionForward` created with this text string is sent to `ActionServlet`. The benefit of a global forward is that any `Action` class deployed within the Struts Web application can use it. It can also be overridden by an individual action mapping without affecting how other `Action` classes use it.

The last section in struts-config.xml describes the specific action mappings that make up the bulk of your applications screen flow:

```
<!-- ========== Action Mapping Definitions ============================ -->
<action-mappings>

<!-- Process a user login -->
   <action     path="/saplogin"
               type="com.apress.ejsap.LoginAction"
               name="login"
               scope="session"
               input="/saplogin.jsp">
      <forward name="success" path="/saploginResult.jsp"/>
   </action>

</action-mappings>
```

Each action mapping must be enclosed in <action>...</action> tags. The <action> tag has a number of required attributes that describe how this mapping should be used:

path: The inbound URL request that should be matched to select this action mapping.

type: Fully qualified Java class name of the Action class used by this mapping.

name: The name of the form bean that was defined in this file to be used by this action.

scope: Either "request" or "session"; used to indicate the scope in which the form bean should be created.

input: URL path to which the user should be returned if a validation error occurs in the form bean.

You must also define a <forward> tag for each unique ActionForward returned by the Action class. These forwards make up the actual screen flow control of your application by directing the user to specific pages based on returns from the Action class. The name attribute is the text string that is used by an Action class to select a given forward. The path attribute is the URL path to which the user should be redirected if this forward has been selected.

Notice the strong decoupling between the Action class and the Web browser interface. The Action class has no knowledge of the actual URL path, which has been abstracted into an arbitrary text string. If you need to point the response from an Action class to a different JSP page, simply modify the path attribute to reflect this new configuration. You do not need to update any Java code and anyone with a little understanding of HTML can make this change.

Your `struts-config.xml` should now look like this:

```xml
<?xml version="1.0" encoding="ISO-8859-1" ?>

<!DOCTYPE struts-config PUBLIC
          "-//Apache Software Foundation//DTD Struts Configuration 1.0//EN"
          "http://jakarta.apache.org/struts/dtds/struts-config_1_0.dtd">
<struts-config>
<!-- ========== Form Bean Definitions =================================== -->
   <form-beans>
     <!-- Login form bean -->
     <form-bean       name="login"
                      type="com.apress.ejsap.LoginForm"/>
   </form-beans>
<!-- ========== Global Forward Definitions ============================== -->
   <global-forwards>
     <forward    name="login"                    path="/saplogin.jsp"/>
   </global-forwards>
<!-- ========== Action Mapping Definitions ============================== -->
   <action-mappings>
<!-- Process a user login -->
     <action     path="/saplogin"
                 type="com.apress.ejsap.LoginAction"
                 name="login"
                 scope="session"
                 input="/saplogin.jsp">
        <forward name="success" path="/saploginResult.jsp"/>
     </action>
   </action-mappings>
</struts-config>
```

The last step is to start (or restart) your Tomcat server and test the new login application. Point your Web browser to `http://localhost/sap` and enter your SAP Internet user name and password.

The next section expands on your login application by adding material search and detail functionalities.

More Struts Development

Although login functionality is certainly essential to any Web application, it does not offer a great deal of end-user functionality. The remainder of this chapter illustrates additional functional development using the Struts framework. Rather than explain each piece of individual code, I used this section to highlight any new techniques I used in the application development.

Since you have already developed material list functionality in the previous chapters, it makes sense to reuse that development in your current effort. When you have completed this chapter, your Struts application will

- Authenticate a user in the SAP system.

- Retrieve a list of materials based on a material search key.

- Select and retrieve a material detail from a list of materials.

To implement the material search functionality, this application uses two additional R/3 BAPIs: BAPI_MATERIAL_GETLIST and BAPI_MATERIAL_GETDETAIL. Currently, your InterfaceCaller class provides a method that retrieves a list of materials from SAP and it can be easily reused in your Struts application. However, you will need to add a new method that retrieves the details of a material based on a single material key.

Calling the Material Detail BAPI

Based on your previous development of the InterfaceCaller class, you shouldn't find adding a new method to be too difficult. Implement the getMaterialDetail() method in the InterfaceCaller class using the following code:

```
package com.apress.ejsap;

import com.sap.mw.jco.*;
import java.util.Hashtable;
import java.util.ResourceBundle;
import java.io.*;
public class InterfaceCaller {
  ...
  public Hashtable getMaterialDetail(String material) {
    JCO.Function function = getFunction("BAPI_MATERIAL_GET_DETAIL");
    JCO.ParameterList listParams = function.getImportParameterList();
    listParams.setValue(material, "MATERIAL");
    aConnection.execute(function);

    JCO.ParameterList resultParams = function.getExportParameterList();
    JCO.Structure fieldList = resultParams.getStructure("MATERIAL_GENERAL_DATA");
```

```
      Hashtable returnHash = new Hashtable();
      if (fieldList.getFieldCount() > 0) {
        for (JCO.FieldIterator fI = fieldList.fields(); fI.hasMoreElements();)
        {
          JCO.Field tabField = fI.nextField();
          returnHash.put(tabField.getName(), tabField.getString());
        }
      }
      return returnHash;
    }
```

This method takes a `String` object as its sole parameter. The major difference between this and the other material method is the SAP structure it uses to return the material detail data. Based on information provided through SAP's Function Builder, the structure is called `MATERIAL_GENERAL_DATA` and it returns a standard `JCO.Structure` instance. The `getMaterialDetail()` method populates and returns a Java `Hashtable`, which contains key/values pairs that mirror SAP field name/value relationships.

Now that `InterfaceCaller` has been updated with this new BAPI call, you are ready to begin customizing your Struts application.

Customizing the Struts Application

This example follows the same steps you took to build the login application. In order to add this new material search functionality, you need to follow these steps:

1. Create forms beans to represent any new Web page fields.

2. Build new JSP pages to take input and display search results.

3. Develop new `Action` classes to call BAPI functionality.

4. Add new `ActionMappings` in the Struts configuration.

First, you need to add a new `ActionForm` bean to deal with the material search parameter.

Building a Material Form Bean

This is perhaps the simplest step; the material search form bean only needs to deal with a single field. Because this application allows the user to search for a material based on the SAP material identifier, the form bean is even more basic than LoginForm.

Create a new class under webapps/sap/WEB-INF/classes/com/apress/ejsap called MaterialForm.java and add the following code:

```
package com.apress.ejsap;

import org.apache.struts.action.ActionError;
import org.apache.struts.action.ActionErrors;
import org.apache.struts.action.ActionForm;
import org.apache.struts.action.ActionMapping;
import javax.servlet.http.*;

public final class MaterialForm extends ActionForm {
  private String material = null;

  public String getMATERIAL() {
    return (this.material);
  }
  public void setMATERIAL(String MATERIAL) {
    this.material = MATERIAL.toUpperCase().trim();
  }
  public void reset(ActionMapping mapping,
                    HttpServletRequest request) {
    this.material = null;
  }
  public ActionErrors validate(ActionMapping mapping,
                               HttpServletRequest request) {
    ActionErrors errors = new ActionErrors();
    if ((material == null) || (material.length() < 1)) {
        errors.add("material", new ActionError("error.material.required"));
    }
    return errors;
  }
}
```

This bean uses the same field manipulation and validation found in the LoginForm class. You will also need a new error message in the ApplicationResources file:

```
error.material.required=<li>Please enter material to search
```

Chapter 7

Creating Material Search JSP Pages

Since you have already modified the `InterfaceCaller` class, you know that the `Action` classes will ultimately return two different `Hashtable` instances. The first `Hashtable` displays a list of materials, and the second displays detailed data based on the material selected from the first list.

You need to add a link from the `saploginResult.jsp` to the new material search functionality:

```
<%@ page language="java" %>

<%@ taglib uri="/WEB-INF/lib/struts.tld" prefix="struts" %>
<%@ taglib uri="/WEB-INF/lib/struts-bean.tld" prefix="bean" %>
<%@ taglib uri="/WEB-INF/lib/struts-html.tld" prefix="html" %>

<html:html>
   <HEAD>
      <TITLE>SAP Login</TITLE>
<html:base/>
   </HEAD>
   <BODY>
<html:errors/>
   <H1>SAP Login</H1>
   <P>
      <H3>Welcome, <%= session.getAttribute("USERNAME") %>.</H3>
      You have been successfully authenticated in SAP.
      <P>
<A HREF="/sap/materialsearch.jsp">Material Search</A>
   </BODY>
</html:html>
```

This link takes the user to the material search Web page that contains a single field and a Submit button:

```
<%@ page language="java" %>

<%@ taglib uri="/WEB-INF/lib/struts.tld" prefix="struts" %>
<%@ taglib uri="/WEB-INF/lib/struts-bean.tld" prefix="bean" %>
<%@ taglib uri="/WEB-INF/lib/struts-html.tld" prefix="html" %>

<html:html>
   <HEAD>
      <TITLE>Material Search</TITLE>
<html:base/>
   </HEAD>
```

```
<BODY>
  <html:errors/>
  <H1>Material Search</H1>
  <P>
  Enter a full or partial material number to search for:
  <P>
  <html:form action="materialsearch.do" method="post"  name="material"
        type="com.apress.ejsap.MaterialForm">
    <bean:message key="prompt.material"/>
    <html:text property="MATERIAL" size="25"/>
    <P>
    <html:submit property="submit" value="Submit"/>
  </html:form>
</BODY>
</html:html>
```

Notice that this form needs another text string in the `ApplicationResources` file:

```
prompt.material=<B>Material:</B>
```

The form described in this page uses the `MaterialForm` bean developed earlier and relies on an action mapping called "materialsearch".

Figure 7-10 shows the single entry material search screen.

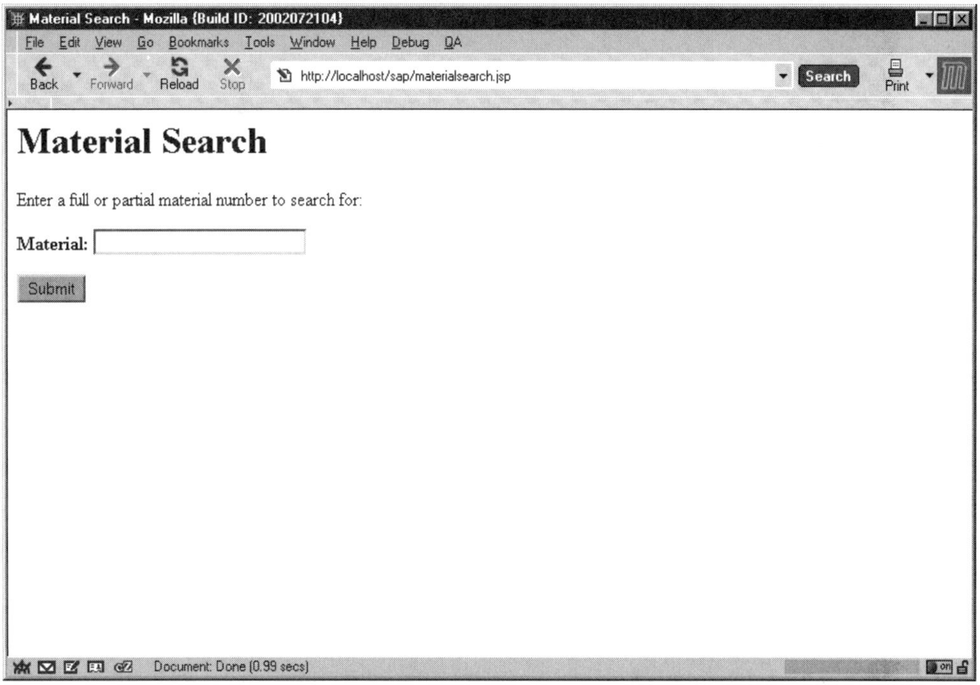

Figure 7-10. Material search Web page

Chapter 7

As mentioned earlier, the material search returns a `Hashtable` instance. The material search result page loops through the `Hashtable` and displays a list of materials matching the search parameter:

```jsp
<%@ page language="java" %>
<%@ page import="java.util.*" %>
<%@ taglib uri="/WEB-INF/lib/struts.tld" prefix="struts" %>
<%@ taglib uri="/WEB-INF/lib/struts-bean.tld" prefix="bean" %>
<%@ taglib uri="/WEB-INF/lib/struts-html.tld" prefix="html" %>

<html:html>
  <HEAD>
    <TITLE>Material Search Results</TITLE>
<html:base/>
  </HEAD>
  <BODY>
<html:errors/>
  <H1>Material Search Results</H1>
  Select a material from the list for more information:
  <TABLE BORDER=1>
  <TR><TD><B>Material</B></TD><TD><B>Description</B></TD></TR>
<%
  Hashtable resultHash = (Hashtable)session.getAttribute("MATERIALS");
  Hashtable tempRow;
  for (Enumeration e = resultHash.elements(); e.hasMoreElements();) {
    tempRow = (Hashtable)e.nextElement();
%>
  <TR>
    <TD><A HREF="/sap/materialdetail.do?MATERIAL=<%=
                (String)tempRow.get("MATERIAL") %>">
    <%= (String)tempRow.get("MATERIAL") %></A>
    </TD>
    <TD><%= (String)tempRow.get("MATL_DESC") %></TD>
  </TR>
<P>
<%
  }
%>
</TABLE>
</BODY>
</html:html>
```

Rather than using a form to take input from the user, this JSP page displays a list of materials as hyperlinks to the next page. When you click one of these links, the browser calls `materialdetail.do`, which passes the selected material identifier to an `Action` class configured in `struts-config.xml`. With this link, you can pass a name/value pair directly through the URL instead of entering the data using the Web page. Once Struts has processed that link, it looks like this in the Web browser:

```
http://localhost/sap/materialdetail.do?MATERIAL=SAMPLE_MATERIAL
```

The question mark (?) following `materialdetail.do` indicates that a query string follows. An equals sign (=) separates name/value pairs and a semicolon (;) delimits these pairs. The material identifier will be stored in the `request` object mapped to the `MATERIAL` key.

Figure 7-11 shows what the display results of an SAP material search look like in a Web browser.

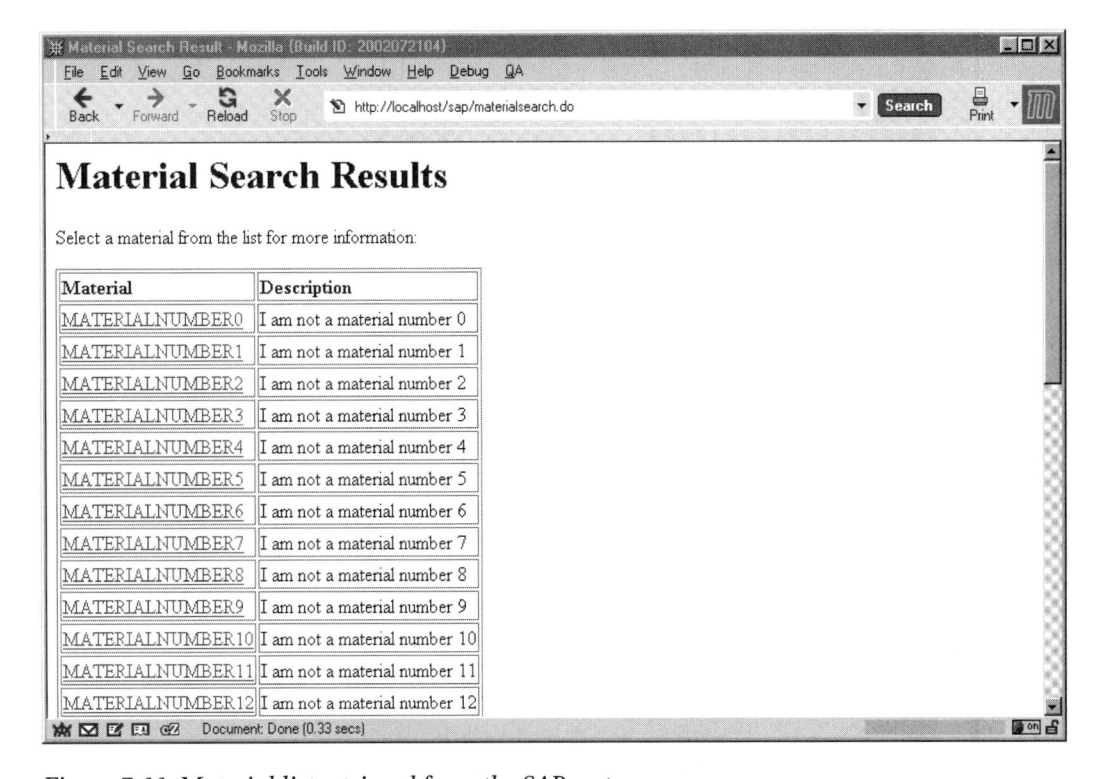

Figure 7-11. Material list retrieved from the SAP system

Finally, the material detail results are displayed in this JSP page:

```jsp
<%@ page language="java" %>
<%@ page import="java.util.*" %>
<%@ taglib uri="/WEB-INF/lib/struts.tld" prefix="struts" %>
<%@ taglib uri="/WEB-INF/lib/struts-bean.tld" prefix="bean" %>
<%@ taglib uri="/WEB-INF/lib/struts-html.tld" prefix="html" %>

<html:html>
  <HEAD>
    <TITLE>Material Detail Result</TITLE>
<html:base/>
  </HEAD>
  <BODY>
<html:errors/>
<H1>Material Detail</H1>
The following material record has been retrieved from SAP.
<P>
<B>Material: <%= request.getParameter("MATERIAL") %> </B>
<TABLE BORDER=1>
  <TR><TD><B>Field</B></TD><TD><B>Value</B></TD></TR>
<%
  Hashtable resultHash = (Hashtable)session.getAttribute("MATERIALDETAIL");
  String field;
  for (Enumeration e = resultHash.keys(); e.hasMoreElements();) {
    field = (String)e.nextElement();
%>
  <TR>
    <TD><%= field %></TD>
    <TD><%= (String)resultHash.get(field) %></TD>
  </TR>
<%
  }
%>
</TABLE>
</BODY>
</html:html>
```

Figure 7-12 shows what the material detail looks like in a Web browser.

Developing Web Applications with Struts

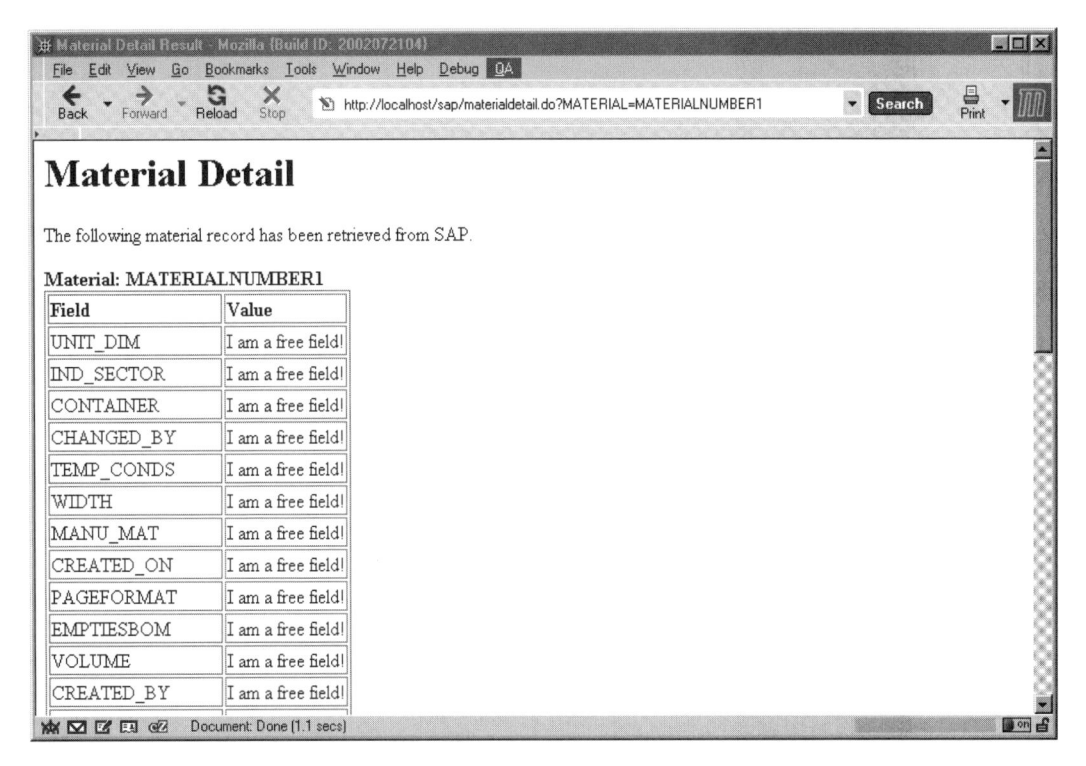

Figure 7-12. Material detail results screen

Chapter 8 looks at some advanced techniques for organizing these results and making it easier for a Web designer to display only the required fields.

Developing Material Action Classes

The next step is to encapsulate calls to the `InterfaceCaller` class in two different `Action` classes. The first class, `MaterialAction`, calls the `getMaterialList()` method and stores the `Hashtable` result in the user's Web session.

Create a class called `MaterialAction.java` in the `/webapps/sap/WEB-INF/classes/com/apress/ejsap` directory and add the following code:

```
package com.apress.ejsap;

import java.io.IOException;
import java.util.*;
import javax.servlet.*;
import javax.servlet.http.*;
```

227

```java
import org.apache.struts.action.Action;
import org.apache.struts.action.ActionForm;
import org.apache.struts.action.ActionForward;
import org.apache.struts.action.ActionMapping;
import org.apache.struts.action.ActionServlet;
import org.apache.struts.action.ActionErrors;
import org.apache.struts.action.ActionError;

import com.apress.ejsap.*;

public final class MaterialAction extends Action {
  public ActionForward perform(ActionMapping mapping,
                               ActionForm form,
                               HttpServletRequest request,
                               HttpServletResponse response)
    throws IOException, ServletException
  {
    String material = ((MaterialForm) form).getMATERIAL();

    ActionServlet actServ = getServlet();
    ServletContext servContext = actServ.getServletContext();
    InterfaceCaller infCaller =
       (InterfaceCaller)servContext.getAttribute("ifaceCaller");
    Hashtable result = infCaller.getMaterialList(material);

    ActionErrors errors = new ActionErrors();
    if (result.size() < 1) {
      errors.add(ActionErrors.GLOBAL_ERROR,
                 new ActionError("error.material.noreturn"));
    }
    if (!errors.empty()) {
      this.saveErrors(request, errors);
      return (new ActionForward(mapping.getInput()));
    }
    HttpSession session = request.getSession();
    session.setAttribute("MATERIALS", result);
    return (mapping.findForward("success"));
    }
}
```

You also need to add a new entry in `ApplicationResources.properties`:

```
error.material.noreturn=<li>No materials found in search
```

Developing Web Applications with Struts

Similar to the `LoginAction` class, `MaterialAction` returns the user to the originating form page with an error message if it doesn't find any materials. You could add a new JSP page and `ActionMapping` to deal with the error condition; however, reusing the search form page cuts down on some redundant development.

Create a class called `MaterialDetailAction.java` and add the following code to it:

```
package com.apress.ejsap;

import java.io.IOException;
import java.util.*;
import javax.servlet.*;
import javax.servlet.http.*;
import org.apache.struts.action.Action;
import org.apache.struts.action.ActionForm;
import org.apache.struts.action.ActionForward;
import org.apache.struts.action.ActionMapping;
import org.apache.struts.action.ActionServlet;
import org.apache.struts.action.ActionErrors;
import org.apache.struts.action.ActionError;

import com.apress.ejsap.*;

public final class MaterialDetailAction extends Action {
  public ActionForward perform(ActionMapping mapping,
                               ActionForm form,
                               HttpServletRequest request,
                               HttpServletResponse response)
    throws IOException, ServletException
  {
    String material = request.getParameter("MATERIAL");

    ActionServlet actServ = getServlet();
    ServletContext servContext = actServ.getServletContext();
    InterfaceCaller infCaller =
 (InterfaceCaller)servContext.getAttribute("ifaceCaller");

    Hashtable result = infCaller.getMaterialDetail(material);
    ActionErrors errors = new ActionErrors();
    if (result.size() < 1) {
      errors.add(ActionErrors.GLOBAL_ERROR,
                 new ActionError("error.material.nodetail"));
```

```
      }
      if (!errors.empty()) {
        this.saveErrors(request, errors);
        return (new ActionForward(mapping.getInput()));
      }
      HttpSession session = request.getSession();
      session.setAttribute("MATERIALDETAIL", result);
      return (mapping.findForward("success"));
      }
}
```

You will need to add this entry to `ApplicationResources`:

```
error.material.nodetail=<li>No material detail could be found
```

Notice that this `Action` class does not use an `ActionForm` to retrieve the material identifier. Because the material number has been passed through the URL, you can retrieve this value directly from the `request` object.

Configuring the Action Mappings

Last, but not least, you need to configure `struts-config.xml` with new action mappings for the material search and detail functionality.

Add the following mappings to this file:

```
  <action-mappings>
<!-- Execute material search -->
     <action     path="/materialsearch"
                 type="com.apress.ejsap.MaterialAction"
                 name="material"
                 scope="session"
                 input="/materialsearch.jsp">
   <forward name="success" path="/materialsearchResult.jsp"/>
     </action>

<!-- Retrieve material detail -->
     <action     path="/materialdetail"
                 type="com.apress.ejsap.MaterialDetailAction"
                 name="material"
                 scope="session"
                 input="/materialsearchResult.jsp">
   <forward name="success" path="/materialdetailResult.jsp"/>
     </action>
```

And add this entry to deploy your new form bean:

```
<form-beans>
  <!-- Material form bean -->
  <form-bean     name="material"
                 type="com.apress.ejsap.MaterialForm"/>
</form-beans>
```

Remember to add these entries between the existing `<form-beans>...</form-beans>` and `<action-mappings>...</action-mappings>` tag directives, rather than creating new tags.

Summary

That's it! Restart your Tomcat server and test the new material search functionality. Although much of this development can be expanded, this tutorial provides a functional skeleton for Web-based SAP applications.

To review, in this chapter, you looked at the following topics:

- Understanding and implementing the Model-View-Control design pattern

- Implementing an open source MVC called Struts

- Building a complete application with the Struts framework

You should now be able to build your own Struts applications that use SAP's RFCs and BAPIs. Depending on the specific requirement, a variety of developers can use Struts to easily maintain these applications. As part of your development infrastructure, Struts simplifies the development of new Web applications and allows you to delegate responsibility to the appropriate personnel (Web designer, Java programmer, and so on).

The next chapter explores some advanced techniques for building applications that use both SAP and non-SAP databases. You will also discover some new ways to move Java code out of your JSP pages and into custom Java tags.

CHAPTER 8

Crossing the Chasm: Bridging SAP and an External Database

THE PHRASE "NO MAN IS AN ISLAND" can be applied equally well to an SAP R/3 system. In many instances, an SAP system alone is not able to support every critical business application your company requires. The Java 2 Platform, Enterprise Edition (J2EE) offers a comprehensive set of infrastructure tools to integrate your company's existing SAP implementation with external applications and datastores.

At this point, the Enterprise Java development in this book has centered exclusively on the R/3 database. However, because of a variety of factors, your company likely has one or more systems outside of SAP supporting key business applications, and you need to look beyond strict SAP application development. Because you have the ability to link SAP and non-SAP systems, your company can maximize existing technology investments and you can quickly roll out new functionality, both inside and outside of SAP.

This chapter takes a close look at augmenting existing SAP business applications with information stored in an external, customized database.

Specifically, this chapter looks at the following:

- Overviewing Java Database Connectivity (JDBC)

- Deploying the Hypersonic SQL database

- Building a material catalog application

The first section deals with relational database access via Java.

Java Database Connectivity

Perhaps the most common data storage mechanism today is that of the relational database. Whether you are running commercial applications such as SAP or developing homegrown systems, this type of database allows you to model and store complex relationships among different types of information. Through the JDBC API, you can build Java applications that communicate directly with a relational database, using standard Structured Query Language (SQL) statements.

SQL Statements

SQL provides an American National Standards Institute (ANSI) standard language for accessing database systems. As a high-level database language, SQL can be programmed using human readable statements and syntax. The combination of an English-like command structure and complex database functionality makes SQL a powerful tool in any developer's kit.

> **TIP** Although this section is not an exhaustive review of SQL, it should help you understand some key concepts. For a good tutorial on SQL, check out the JDBC short course called SQL Primer at http://java.sun.com.

Every SQL statement begins with a verb that indicates the action to be performed. Some of the most frequently used are those that provide a certain level of database manipulation: UPDATE, INSERT, SELECT, and DELETE. These functional verbs are typically followed by a clause or a series of strings that indicate where the statement is operating. These clauses may contain one or more keywords that denote field names, table names, expressions, and other statements. As you will see in later examples, a single SQL statement can contain many clauses.

Reading and adding data to tables form the basis for most of your interaction with a relational database. The SELECT statement is used to retrieve table data based on a prescribed matching query:

```
SELECT genre, album FROM artist_catalog WHERE artist = 'Jon Spencer'
```

The functional verb SELECT instructs the application to retrieve table rows that match the criteria specified in the remaining query clause. Immediately following SELECT, the keywords genre and album indicate the table columns from which data should be retrieved. If an asterisk * had been used instead, the SELECT statement would retrieve data from every column in the table. The FROM keyword names the table against which this query should be run—in this case, the artist_catalog table. Finally, the WHERE clause specifies any requisite matching criteria. This is a very basic example that simply matches the query to any table row where the artist column equals "Jon Spencer". Ultimately, this SELECT statement would return album and genre information from Jon Spencer's extensive music catalog.

This second example demonstrates adding new rows to an existing database table:

```
INSERT INTO artist_catalog VALUES('Boss Hog','Defender','Indie','Win Coma')
```

The leading verb in this statement, INSERT, tells the application to create a new row in the table artist_catalog. VALUES encapsulates the data to be inserted based on an existing column structure. In this example, artist_catalog has four columns: artist, album, genre, and songtitle. The data must be input in the order denoted by the column organization. This SQL statement creates a new table row in artist_catalog containing the artist information specified for "Boss Hog".

As you can see, SQL is not an overly difficult language to learn, but don't let its apparent simplicity fool you. Using SQL, you can develop database applications using advanced techniques such as multitable joins and nested SELECT statements. Table 8-1 illustrates some of the most common SQL directives and their respective descriptions.

Table 8-1. Common SQL Directives

SQL SYNTAX	DESCRIPTION
SELECT	Retrieves information from one or more tables in the database
INSERT INTO	Adds new rows of data into an existing table
UPDATE	Modifies existing table data in the database
DELETE FROM	Removes rows in a database table
CREATE TABLE	Creates a new table in the database with the column characteristics specified
ALTER TABLE	Modifies existing table definition
COMMIT	Commits a transaction to the database and ends its session
ROLLBACK	Removes any changes since the last COMMIT or ROLLBACK

In essence, SQL allows you to manipulate the contents of a database through its declarative structure. Rather than defining programmatic procedures for how the data is stored, SQL defines what information should be processed and lets the database implementation handle the rest.

So how does SQL fit into Java? With a JDBC, your application can use SQL statements to act on any compliant, relational database.

JDBC Overview

Ultimately, the goal of ANSI SQL is to provide an industry-wide database language that exists largely outside of proprietary database implementations. Of course, many companies have added non–ANSI SQL extensions to augment existing SQL functionality, but these additions follow closely to standard SQL syntax. SQL has become an essential tool for building databases because of its ubiquity in the industry, and because it has very much simplified life for the average database programmer and consultant. Unfortunately, the situation for individual database connectors is not quite so simple.

> **NOTE** *Commercial databases that offer support for SQL-based database access include, but are certainly not limited to, Oracle, IBM's DB2, and Microsoft's SQL Server.*

Historically, database companies have provided proprietary, platform-dependent database connectors so that application developers could utilize their systems. Although SQL was the language of choice for most companies, no such standard existed for the actual database connector. Moreover, depending on the company, the multiplatform support for a given connector may be limited or nonexistent. This forced developers to refactor applications for each specific database connector as functionality changed, systems were upgraded, and so on.

To counter this redundancy in connectors and development, the Java 2 platform introduced the JDBC API. Employing the platform independence of Java 2, JDBC provides an API that can directly interface with a number of different proprietary database connectors. Instead of building applications using connectors based on native language support, JDBC allows you to develop for different database systems without coding for a different connector each time.

Nonetheless, JDBC must still interact with the native database connector, regardless of how the developer uses the JDBC API. You have already seen examples of abstracted or middle tier layers such as Java Servlets that adapt Web browser requests into Java code directives. JDBC provides another type of middleware layer, designed to translate Java-based calls to the connector APIs provided by the database vendor. Commonly known as the JDBC driver, this layer comes in several different flavors, depending on the type of database driver the vendor provides.

Figure 8-1 illustrates the various components of a typical JDBC connector that allow a Java application to interact with a database.

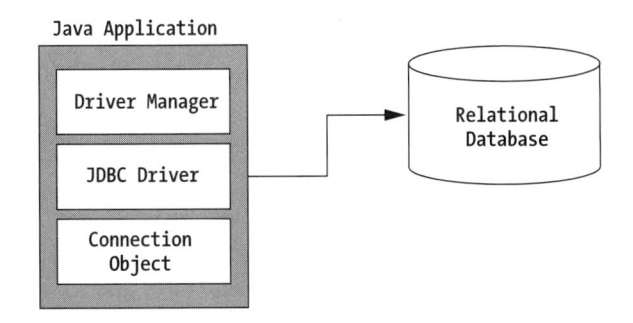

Figure 8-1. Diagram of the JDBC architecture

JDBC Drivers

Although you will only be using one of the four major driver types, you should understand the alternatives. This chapter was written in the rarefied air of a truly pure Java application that includes a pure Java database. The real world often doesn't work out so cleanly, so you are very likely to encounter systems that require a different approach to communicating with a database. (A good resource for JDBC drivers can be found at http://industry.java.sun.com/products/jdbc/drivers.)

The first of these driver types, the JDBC-ODBC bridge, comes in handy if you have to do any development on an older Microsoft platform.

Type 1: The JDBC-ODBC Bridge

Open Database Connectivity (ODBC) refers to a specification originally designed as an API to execute standard SQL calls on the Microsoft platform. The Type 1 JDBC driver provides a bridge between the JDBC API and the ODBC API. This driver translates JDBC calls into the appropriate ODBC calls, which sends them to an ODBC source via ODBC libraries.

The high number of interactions between the various APIs means that each client application must fully support the JDBC-ODBC bridge, the ODBC driver, and the JDBC API. These interactions make the bridge a somewhat inefficient connector for Java-based database applications. The JDBC-ODBC bridge does not scale effectively when you use it in high traffic applications and provides only limited ODBC functionality through the JDBC API. You may want to experiment with this connector if you need to connect to a local Microsoft Access database, but I do not recommend it for enterprise application development.

Type 2: Half and Half

Like your favorite serving-size creamer, the Type 2 driver offers doses of both a Java API and the native vendor connector. This driver translates JDBC calls directly into the vendor-defined API calls. Similar to the Type 1 driver, Type 2 relies partially on a native connector API so that each application client must still maintain some platform-dependent code.

Unlike the Type 1 driver, Type 2 is more efficient and offers complete access to the API the database vendor provides. These drivers were more common several years ago before many large-scale database providers started offering pure Java JDBC drivers.

Type 3: Database Connector Server

An interesting approach to high-traffic database application servers, the Type 3 driver is actually a connector server that maintains a gateway to multiple database systems. The JDBC driver connects to an intermediate server, which completes the request using one of the other three database drivers (most likely a Type 2).

This type of driver is very dependent on the middleware server vendor, in terms of included APIs, protocols, and so on. However, the Type 3 driver has the advantage of even further abstracting the connections to a database server (or servers) running on the backend. You gain some additional flexibility in that the database connector types can change without affecting the client applications using them.

Type 4: Pure Java Driver

Perhaps the most common of JDBC drivers, the Type 4, converts JDBC calls into network calls based on protocols defined by the database vendor. This means that you are making direct socket calls to the database, thereby offering much better performance than either Type 1 or Type 2 drivers. Every major database vendor provides Type 4 JDBC drivers, and you can even find third-party drivers for enhanced performance and special requirements.

The tutorial application demonstrates how to use a Type 4 driver. Anything else is pretty much outside the scope of this book (however much I would love to show you the power of a Type 3).

JDBC Packages

All of the development in this chapter is based on the JDBC 3.0 API, which is included in the J2SDK1.4 installation. One of the major differences in this release of the API is the inclusion of all JDBC APIs including the Optional Package API. Previously, this had been maintained as a separate download, but now it is integrated into the Java 2 1.4 development kit.

The JDBC 3.0 API includes two major packages:

> `java.sql`: This package provides many of the basic client-server classes for accessing and manipulating data stored in a relational database. A major function of this API is a driver framework through which Java applications can dynamically access data from different sources. Much of this package is devoted to passing SQL statements to a database and translating SQL data types to Java.

`javax.sql`: As a supplement to `java.sql`, this package provides the server-side database components for the JDBC API. Introduced to support the Enterprise Java platform, `javax.sql` deals with key distributed computing concepts such as connection pooling and transactional connectivity. This package simplifies database application development by hiding some of the driver-level details and further abstracting changes to the data source or database driver from the client application.

The examples in this chapter take you through two distinct types of JDBC application development based on these packages. The phase `java.sql` represents deals with the more traditional database development geared towards desktop applications. This tutorial builds on the client application created in Chapter 5 and illustrates a client/server application.

Enterprise application development is more appropriately handled by the `javax.sql` package. Note that you will not be developing to the exclusion of the `java.sql` classes; rather you will be augmenting the client/server architecture with a stronger emphasis on the server side. This development builds on the Struts application created in Chapter 7.

However, a prerequisite to any database development is the database itself. The next section details the installation of an open source database, called Hypersonic SQL.

Deploying the Hypersonic SQL Database

The Hypersonic SQL Database (hsqldb) engine is a relational database written entirely in Java. The hsqldb offers a very small footprint (100KB) database system that runs on almost every Java-compliant platform. hsqldb offers both disk-based and in-memory database tables, as well as a small Web server and a GUI-based database manager. Although it is a great tool for quick prototyping and lightweight database development, I do not recommend hsqldb as part of a production implementation. It is an open source project that does not offer any form of commercial support, which is a must-have in any mission critical, business application environment.

As daunting as this may sound, the developers of Hypersonic SQL (hsql) have made it very simple to deploy this lightweight, pure Java database. You can find the installation archive at `http://sourceforge.net/projects/hsqldb`; to ensure compatibility with the code in this chapter, download the 1.7.1 package on the Files page.

Deploying hsql is fairly straightforward. Unzip the installation download into a temporary directory and navigate to the `lib` directory. Then copy the `hsqldb.jar` file into your `<JAVA_HOME>/jre/lib/ext` directory so that it will be available through the Java Virtual Machine (JVM).

To test the installation, bring up a command prompt and execute the following statement:

Crossing the Chasm: Bridging SAP and an External Database

```
start java org.hsqldb.Server -database ejsapdb
```

This should open a new console window and load the hsqldb as a standalone server. Figure 8-2 shows a typical start-up screen for the hsqldb standalone server.

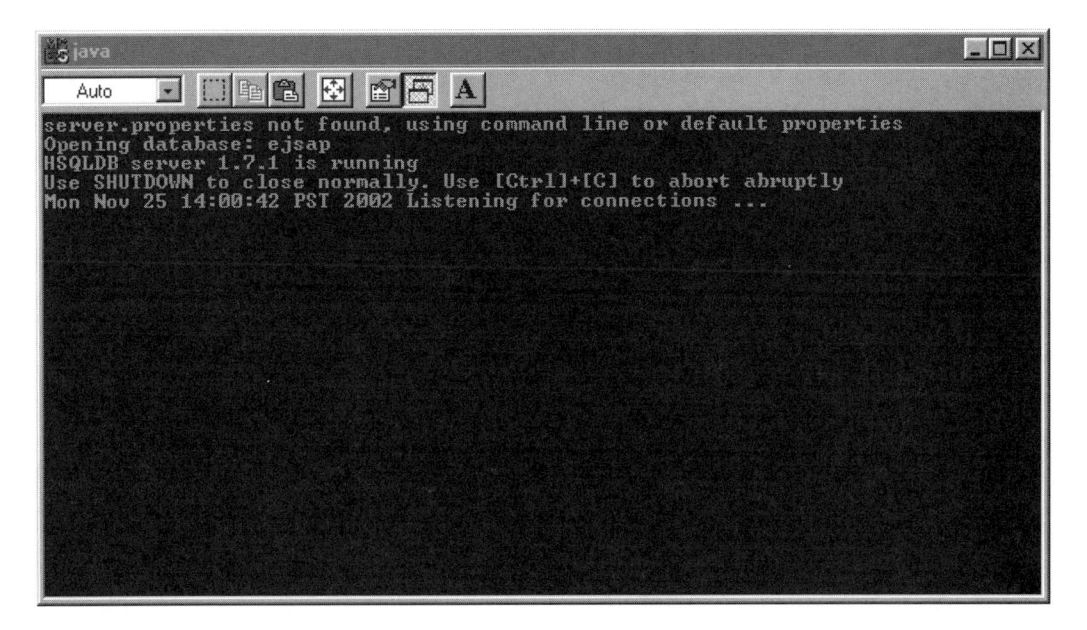

Figure 8-2. hsqldb start-up console

You can connect to this database using the hsqldb database manager, executable through this command statement:

```
java org.hsqldb.util.DatabaseManager
```

This loads a Java GUI that initially requests the type of database engine with which you wish to connect. Figure 8-3 depicts the Connect screen for the hsqldb database manager.

Select HSQL Database Engine Server from the Type drop-down list. When you select this option, the Driver and URL fields change. These fields contain the driver and location names for the database server that you will later use in the application development. You also have the option of entering a user name and password to access this database. Because you have not added user identities to the database, leave these fields with their default settings.

You are now logged into the database server and can manipulate it using standard SQL statements. Figure 8-4 illustrates the Database Manager GUI.

Chapter 8

Figure 8-3. Connect screen for `DatabaseManager` *class*

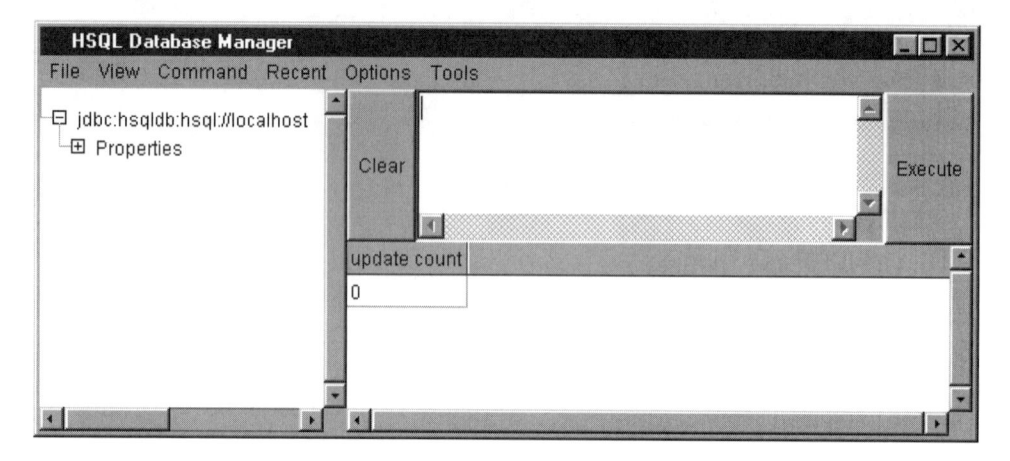

Figure 8-4. hsqldb Database Manager GUI

This utility provides you with the opportunity to play with some SQL statements and test statements that could be used in your Java application. In the SQL execute window (sandwiched between the Clear and Execute buttons), enter the following statement and hit the Execute button:

```
CREATE TABLE mytable (firstname VARCHAR(30), lastname VARCHAR(30))
```

This creates a new table in the database called MYTABLE with two columns labeled FIRSTNAME and LASTNAME. Refresh the Database Manager from the View menu or by pressing Ctrl-R on the keyboard and open the tree structure in the left windowpane. The screen should now look similar to Figure 8-5.

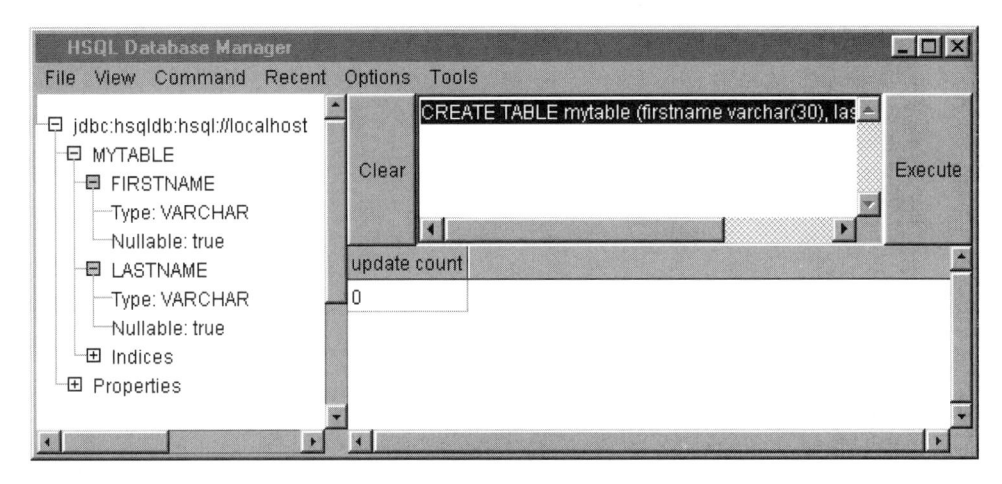

Figure 8-5. Database table tree structure

Next, you need to add some data into this newly created table, using the SQL INSERT function. The following statement adds a new row into MYTABLE:

```
INSERT INTO MYTABLE (FIRSTNAME, LASTNAME) VALUES ('Ejsap', 'Guru')
```

Now, add another row:

```
INSERT INTO MYTABLE (FIRSTNAME, LASTNAME) VALUES ('Sap', 'Expert')
```

And finally:

```
INSERT INTO MYTABLE (FIRSTNAME, LASTNAME) VALUES ('J2EE', 'Master')
```

With some row data in your table, use the SELECT statement to retrieve and display those values:

```
SELECT * FROM MYTABLE
```

Figure 8-6 shows the results from this database query.

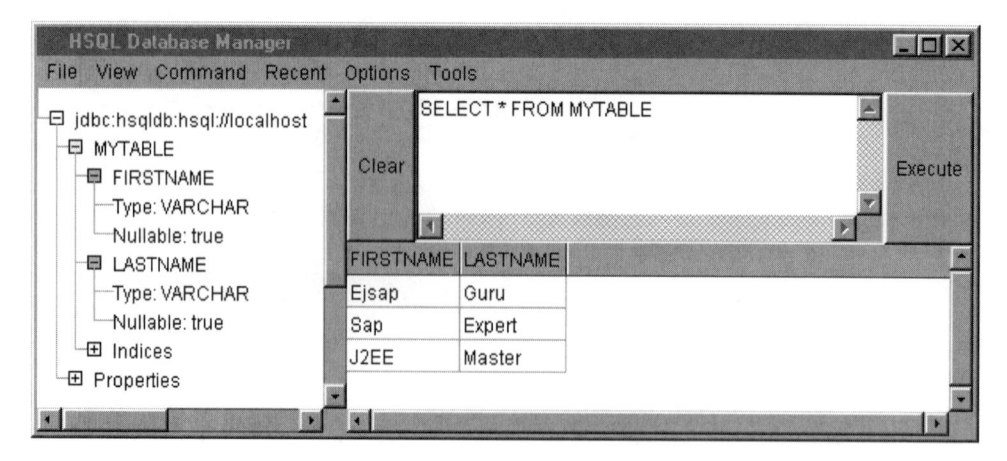

Figure 8-6. Database query results

The Database Manager provides a limited GUI environment in which you can create and maintain database tables. You could use this tool to load a new database or modify existing tables, but this would do little to further your Java application programming education. The next section kicks off some real application development and demonstrates how to load up the database from a custom Java class.

Building Database Tables

This section deals with two approaches to populating a database with record sets. The first approach, using standard SQL calls and JDBC connectivity, outlines a generic application that can be used with almost any relational database management system (RDBMS). The second relies on several proprietary SQL extensions that are part of the hsqldb API. Because you will likely be using a preexisting database system, the focus of this section is not on building complex database architecture. Rather, the purpose is to populate a test database that can be tied to an R/3 system via your Struts application. Should you choose to use a different database for tutorial and test applications, the first approach provides code that is connector independent. However, hsqldb contains features that make creating a new database from existing records fairly simple, which makes it a great choice for prototype or proof-of-concept applications.

Populating a Generic Database

As mentioned earlier, SQL provides a fairly straightforward language set for building and querying database records. Using the `java.sql` API, you can readily build Java applications that generically access and modify most commercial and open source database systems.

Application Overview

In the following exercise, you will build a standalone Java class that can

- Create a new table in the database.

- Add records (rows) to this table.

- Retrieve and display these records.

- Delete the table from the database.

Because this is a fairly basic example, you will execute the class from a command line, passing string parameters to indicate the desired function to be called. Although not as elegant as a GUI-based application, this class will become the foundation for populating the hsql database with records directly from SAP.

Connecting to the Database

The first step in building a database-aware Java application is creating a connection object based on a vendor defined JDBC driver.

> **TIP** *You can find the code for this chapter in the Downloads section of the Apress Website* (http://www.apress.com).

```
import java.sql.*;

public class MaterialTableAction {
  static String dbDriver = "org.hsqldb.jdbcDriver";
  static String dbURL = "jdbc:hsqldb:hsql://localhost";
  static Connection conn = null;
  static Statement stat = null;
}
```

This code describes a class called MaterialTableAction and defines several class-level variables that will be used throughout the application. The dbDriver string is the fully qualified class name for the JDBC connector provided by the database vendor. Because you are using the hsql database, your application must use the driver located at `org.hsqldb.jdbcDriver`.

The second string variable, `dbURL`, defines a location for the database server to be accessed by this application. For your development, this code is running against a local database instance, so using the `localhost` qualifier is appropriate. However, if this application must be deployed across a network environment, you would replace `localhost` with an IP address or fully qualified domain name (`192.168.2.1` or `www.mydomain.com`, respectively). As you can see, you can modify either of these strings to reflect a different database driver or server location and you could externalize them by using a properties configuration file.

The last two variables instantiated are `Connection` and `Statement` objects that will be used later in the application. They are created at the class level so that subsequent class methods can have equal access to them.

In order to call a database, the class must first create a database connection:

```java
import java.sql.*;

public class MaterialTableAction {
...
  public MaterialTableAction() {
    try {
     Class.forName(dbDriver);
     conn = DriverManager.getConnection(dbURL, "sa", "");
     stat = conn.createStatement();
    } catch (SQLException e) {
       System.out.println("SQL exception");
       e.printStackTrace();
    } catch (ClassNotFoundException cEx) {
       System.out.println("Class not found exception");
       e.printStackTrace();
    }
  }
}
```

A default constructor, `MaterialTableAction()`, automatically attempts to create a database connection based on the values defined as class-level variables. The following statement

```java
Class.forName(dbDriver);
```

dynamically creates a new instance of the database driver class. Using this instance, the application calls the `getConnection()` method of the `DriverManager` class to get a new `Connection` object, called `conn`. Notice that `getConnection()`

takes three String parameters. The first is the URL location of the database server, the second is a username, and the third is a password. Recall that the hsql database comes with a default user, "sa", that does not require a password. Although this suffices for a demo application, you will need to define database users with the appropriate privileges using configuration software provided by the database vendor.

Once a database connection has been made, the code creates a new Statement instance using the createStatement() method. The Statement class allows you to pass SQL commands directly to the database and retrieve any results or messages from the database.

Finally, this application catches the two possible exceptions, SQLException and ClassNotFoundException, and prints an error message out to the console when either of these exceptions is thrown.

Adding Command Line Execution

At this point, your application consists of a default constructor that creates a database connection and a set of class-level variables to access that connection. Because this application needs to run from a command console, the next step is to add a main() method that will be called by the JVM.

```
public static void main(String[] args) {
  String action = args[0];
  MaterialTableAction createTab = new MaterialTableAction ();

}
```

In order to control access to the database, your main() method retrieves variables set at the command line using the String array passed in as a parameter. The variable action is set to the first element of this array and will be used to determine the type of database functionality to execute.

The last statement creates a new instance of your MaterialTableAction class by calling this class's default constructor. Remember that this constructor creates a new database connection and provides a Statement object you can use to access the database system.

Creating the Database Table

Relying on a series of else if statements, the remainder of your application will execute various database calls, depending on the specific command line argument.

```
    if (action.equals("create")) {
       stat.executeUpdate(
                  "CREATE TABLE MATERIALS"
                  + "(MATERIAL VARCHAR(30), "
                  + "DESCRIP VARCHAR(256))");
    }
```

If the argument is set to create the application attempts to create a new database table called MATERIALS. To do so, this application calls the executeUpdate() method on the stat object. This method takes a single String parameter that is comprised of an SQL statement. The SQL command to create a new table looks like this:

```
CREATE TABLE MATERIALS (MATERIAL VARCHAR(30),DESCRIP VARCHAR(256))
```

CREATE TABLE is the SQL command, MATERIALS is the table name, and the values in parentheses describe column names and field types for this table. This application uses the VARCHAR field type to store data as strings of different lengths.

Deleting the Database Table

The next else if block deletes a table based on the command line argument delete:

```
else if (action.equals("delete")) {
    stat.executeUpdate("DROP TABLE MATERIALS");
}
```

The SQL statement DROP TABLE MATERIALS tells the database to delete the MATERIALS table along with any stored records.

Adding Records to the Table

In order to add new records to the database, the following block takes two additional command line arguments to fill the MATERIAL and DESCRIP fields of the MATERIALS table.

```
else if (action.equals("add")) {
    stat.executeUpdate(
      "INSERT INTO MATERIALS VALUES('" + args[1] + "','" + args[2] + "')");
}
```

The SQL statement `INSERT INTO MATERIALS VALUES('VALUE1','VALUE2')` creates a new record in the `MATERIALS` table by populating the two columns in this table with the second and third elements of the `args` array.

Retrieving Records from the Table

The last `else if` block retrieves all of the values stored in the `MATERIALS` table and prints its values to the command console.

```
else if (action.equals("select")) {
    ResultSet rs = stat.executeQuery("SELECT * FROM MATERIALS");
    System.out.println("Select table results:");
    System.out.println("----------------------------------------");
    while (rs.next()) {
      System.out.println("Material:    " + rs.getString("MATERIAL"));
      System.out.println("Description: " + rs.getString("DESCRIP"));
      System.out.println ("----------------------------------------");
    }
}
```

This code introduces a new `java.sql` class called `ResultSet`. In previous examples, you used the `executeUpdate()` method to modify the database. To retrieve records, you must use a different method, called `executeQuery()`. This method also relies on standard SQL statements to, as implied by the method name, query a given database or table. However, unlike the `executeUpdate()` method, `executeQuery()` returns a `ResultSet` object that contains any data retrieved from the database.

The SQL statement `SELECT * FROM MATERIALS` instructs the database to return all records from the `MATERIALS` table. An instance of the `ResultSet` class is returned by this method call and stored as the variable `rs`. A `while` statement loops through every entry in `rs` using its `next()` method, and the values for each field are retrieved using the `getString()` method.

Catching Exceptions and Closing the Connection

You have probably noticed that the code detailed so far has not included any type of exception handling. Recall from Chapter 4 that Java exceptions allow you to implement clean error handling within your application. You can wrap the entire `if...elseif` block in a single `try` block because your application only needs to catch one type of exception.

The following code demonstrates a `try...catch` block that catches and prints a stack trace for an instance of `SQLException`:

249

```
try {
// Insert if...elseif block here
} catch (SQLException e) {
  e.printStackTrace();
}
```

Because Java database connections require additional memory overhead in the JVM, your application should provide a mechanism to release used system resources. You could normally code this release mechanism using standard close() methods provided by the `java.sql.Connection` and `java.sql.Statement` objects. In this case, the code would look something like this:

```
try {
// Insert if...elseif block here
} catch (SQLException e) {
  e.printStackTrace();
}
try { conn.close(); }
catch (Exception e) {}
try { stat.close(); }
catch (Exception e) {}
```

However, should an error occur and an exception get thrown, the database connection might not get closed properly. In order to ensure that these connections are closed, your application must implement a finally clause in the try...catch block. The finally clause allows you to explicitly execute code before releasing control to the remainder of the application.

```
try {
// Insert if...elseif block here
} catch (SQLException e) {
  e.printStackTrace();
}
finally
{
  try { stat.close(); }
  catch (Exception e) { e.printStackTrace(); }
  try { conn.close(); }
  catch (Exception e) { e.printStackTrace(); }
}
```

Your MaterialTableAction class should now look like this:

Crossing the Chasm: Bridging SAP and an External Database

```java
import java.sql.*;

public class MaterialTableAction {
 static String dbDriver = "org.hsqldb.jdbcDriver";
 static String dbURL = "jdbc:hsqldb:hsql://localhost";
 static Connection conn = null;
 static Statement stat = null;

 public MaterialTableAction() {
  try {
   Class.forName(dbDriver);
   conn = DriverManager.getConnection(dbURL, "sa", "");
   stat = conn.createStatement();
  } catch (SQLException e) {
     System.out.println(SQL Exception);
     e.printStackTrace();
  }
    catch (ClassNotFoundException cEx) {
     System.out.println("Class not found exception);
     cEx.printStackTrace();
  }
 }
 public static void main(String[] args) {
  String action = args[0];
  MaterialTableAction createTab = new MaterialTableAction();
  try {
   if (action.equals("create")) {
    stat.executeUpdate(
      "CREATE TABLE MATERIALS"
       + "(MATERIAL VARCHAR(30), "
       + "DESCRIP VARCHAR(256))");
   } else if (action.equals("delete")) {
    stat.executeUpdate("DROP TABLE MATERIALS");
   } else if (action.equals("add")) {
    stat.executeUpdate(
      "INSERT INTO MATERIALS VALUES('" + args[1] + "','" + args[2] + "')");
   } else if (action.equals("select")) {
    ResultSet rs = stat.executeQuery("SELECT * FROM MATERIALS");
    System.out.println("Select table results:");
    System.out.println("----------------------------------------");
    while (rs.next()) {
     System.out.println("Material:    " + rs.getString("MATERIAL"));
     System.out.println("Description: " + rs.getString("DESCRIP"));
     System.out.println("----------------------------------------");
    }
```

```
    }
  } catch (SQLException e) {
     e.printStackTrace();
  }
  finally
  {
   try { stat.close(); }
   catch (Exception e) { e.printStackTrace(); }
   try { conn.close(); }
   catch (Exception e) { e.printStackTrace(); }
  }
 }
}
```

Executing the Database Class

If the hsql database isn't already running, start it with this command line statement:

```
start java org.hsqldb.Server -database ejsapdb
```

Next, execute the `MaterialTableAction` class to create the `MATERIALS` table:

```
java MaterialTableAction create
```

To add new records to the table use the "add" string followed by the material name and description:

```
java MaterialTableAction add material1 description1
```

After adding several records to the `MATERIALS` table, retrieve all entries using the "select" string:

```
java MaterialTableAction select
```

Finally, delete the table and all of its material records using the "delete" string:

```
java MaterialTableAction delete
```

Obviously, this is a very basic example of how to use a JDBC connector to create and populate a database table and records. However, the advantage of this class is that you can use it with almost any commercial database by simply swapping out the JDBC connector. Of course, there are far simpler mechanisms for building and maintaining a database, including the use of proprietary SQL extensions. The next section takes a quick look at an extension the hsql database provides that allows you to quickly populate a database using a plain text file as the source.

Using hsql to Build a Database Quickly

Normally, database tables are stored in file structures that are specific to a given database. This allows database vendors to optimize for different file systems and differentiate between competing products. On the other hand, there are times when performance is less of a factor than timeliness, and the ability to quickly create database tables from existing files becomes paramount. The hsql database can use plain text files, with a common delimiter, to store and update table records.

One major advantage to using a text file as a database table is that of legibility. Plain text files can be read and modified using a standard text editor, and then they can be reimported into the database system. Another advantage is portability. These files can be transferred easily between systems with minimal integration. Is this an optimal solution for a production or mission critical system? No, the use of this capability is mainly recommended when you are building prototypes or you want to use it as a testing support for your development team. For the purpose of this chapter, the main benefit of using text file database tables is to show the use of an SQL extension provided by a specific database vendor.

Building the Table from a Text File

To add plain text table functionality to the `MaterialTableAction` class, you simply need to change the `if` block that deals with the `create` clause:

```
if (action.equals("create")) {
   stat.executeUpdate("CREATE TEXT TABLE MATERIALS"
         + "(MATERIAL VARCHAR(30), "
         + "DESCRIP VARCHAR(256))");
   stat.executeUpdate("SET TABLE MATERIALS SOURCE \"materials.csv\"");
}
```

Notice that the CREATE command is now followed by the TEXT indicator. This tells the hsql database to create a read-only table that will use a plain text file to store table records. Because you still need to tell the database the number of columns and field types in this table, everything else in the SQL statement remains the same.

In order to add and modify records in this new table, you must specify the text file to be used as the database table. The SET TABLE statement is followed by the name of the table created in the previous SQL command, and the SOURCE attribute specifies the plain text file.

> **NOTE** *SQL statements require that double quotes be used to indicate a string value. However, the double quote character is reserved in Java syntax; this means you need an escape character anytime the application must pass the double quote character as a string value. In this case,* SOURCE "materials.csv" *must be replaced with* SOURCE \"materials.csv\" *so that Java will pass the double quote character to the hsql database as part of the SQL statement.*

Creating the Plain Text File

The hsql database will now attempt to use the file materials.csv as the MATERIALS table. To use a preexisting text file, save it as materials.csv in the same directory that the MaterialTableAction class is being executed. If no such file exists, when the create clause is called, hsql will create an empty file called materials.csv.

Your plain text file should look something like this:

```
material1,description1
material2,description2
material3,description3
material4,description4
material5,description5
material6,description6
material7,description7
material8,description8
```

Notice that the material and description fields are delimited using a comma. The default behavior of the SET TABLE SOURCE statement is to determine fields based on the position and number of commas in each line. However, you could use any single character delimiter in the text file as long as that character is specified in the SQL statement.

```
SET TABLE MATERIALS SOURCE "materials.csv;fs=~"
```

In this case, the tilde (~) is the field separator, which is set using the fs attribute in the file source string.

Updating the Text File Table

In addition to using a delimited text file as a table source, you can also programmatically update this file through the database. To do so, you need to perform a fairly simple modification to the add clause in MaterialTableAction.

```
else if (action.equals("add")) {
  stat.executeUpdate(
    "INSERT INTO MATERIALS VALUES('" + args[1] + "','" + args[2] + "')");
  stat.executeUpdate("CHECKPOINT");
}
```

The CHECKPOINT command forces an update against any open data files as well as flushing these files to disk.

Your MaterialTableAction class can now read in records from the materials.csv file as well as write new entries into this file. Add some new records using the command line interface, then open materials.csv in a text editor to ensure that these changes took effect. Remember, you will need to delete the existing MATERIALS table and rerun the create command to import your plain text file.

Now that you have had some experience with basic SQL and JDBC connectivity, you are ready to tie an hsql database into a live SAP system. The next section shows you how to tweak the MaterialTableAction class to load the hsql database with records directly from SAP.

Loading the Database from SAP

Perhaps the simplest way to build your hsql database is to load records directly from SAP. You have already developed the Java class that can retrieve a list of materials from SAP, so the next logical step is to add that list as records in an hsql table.

In order to reuse this database in the final application, you need to add a new column to the hsql database. This column will maintain the physical file location for an image associated with a given material number. Recall that the ultimate material catalog Web application will pass this file location to the Web server in order to display images in a browser.

Here is the code for this new class:

```
import java.sql.*;
import java.util.Hashtable;
import java.util.Enumeration;
```

Chapter 8

```java
public class SapMaterialAction {
 static String dbDriver = "org.hsqldb.jdbcDriver";
 static String dbURL = "jdbc:hsqldb:hsql://localhost";
 static Connection conn = null;
 static Statement stat = null;
 public SapMaterialAction() {
  try {
   Class.forName(dbDriver);
   conn = DriverManager.getConnection(dbURL, "sa", "");
   stat = conn.createStatement();
  } catch (SQLException e) {
     System.out.println("SQL Exception");
     e.printStackTrace();
  }
    catch (ClassNotFoundException cEx) {
     System.out.println("Class not found exception");
     cEx.printStackTrace();
  }
 }
 public static void main(String[] args) {
  String action = args[0];
  SapMaterialAction createTab = new SapMaterialAction();
  try {
   if (action.equals("create")) {
    InterfaceCaller ifCaller = new InterfaceCaller();
      stat.executeUpdate("CREATE TABLE SAPMATERIALS"
           + "(MATERIAL VARCHAR(30), "
           + "DESCRIP VARCHAR(256), "
           + "IMAGE VARCHAR(256))");
      Hashtable returnHash = ifCaller.getMaterialList(args[1]);
      Hashtable rowHash;
      for (Enumeration e = returnHash.elements(); e.hasMoreElements();) {
       rowHash = (Hashtable)e.nextElement();
       stat.executeUpdate(
         "INSERT INTO SAPMATERIALS VALUES('"
            + (String)rowHash.get("MATERIAL")
            + "','" + (String)rowHash.get("MATL_DESC")
            + "','images//default.gif')");
      }
    } else if (action.equals("delete"))
      stat.executeUpdate("DROP TABLE SAPMATERIALS");
```

```
      else if (action.equals("add"))
        stat.executeUpdate("INSERT INTO MATERIALS VALUES('"
                           + args[1] + "','"
                           + args[2] + "','"
                           + args[3] + "')");
      else if (action.equals("select")) {
        ResultSet rs = stat.executeQuery("SELECT * FROM SAPMATERIALS");
        System.out.println("Select table results:");
        System.out.println("--------------------------------------");
        while (rs.next()) {
          System.out.println("Material:    " + rs.getString("MATERIAL"));
          System.out.println("Description: " + rs.getString("DESCRIP"));
          System.out.println("Image:       " + rs.getString("IMAGE"));
          System.out.println("--------------------------------------");
        }
      }
      else if (action.equals("update")) {
        stat.executeUpdate("UPDATE SAPMATERIALS SET IMAGE = '"
                    + args[2] + "' WHERE MATERIAL = '"
                    + args[1] + "'");
      }
    } catch (SQLException e) { e.printStackTrace(); }
    finally
    {
      try { stat.close(); }
      catch (Exception e) { e.printStackTrace(); }
      try { conn.close(); }
      catch (Exception e) { e.printStackTrace(); }
    }
  }
}
```

Although this class is similar to `MaterialTableAction`, it has been implemented as `SapMaterialAction`. Make sure that the file name and the class name match before you try to compile it.

`SapMaterialAction` is almost identical to `MaterialTableAction`, except that the create clause instantiates the `InterfaceCaller` class and uses its `getMaterialList()` method to retrieve materials from SAP. This block creates a new table, called SAPMATERIALS, and loads that table from a `Hashtable` returned by `InterfaceCaller`. The SAPMATERIALS table is created with a new column, called `IMAGE`. When `SapMaterialAction` creates and loads this table for the first time, a default value of `images/default.gif` is stored in the `IMAGE` field. This is the file location for the default image to be used by the Web server, if a specific image for that material does not exist.

This class also has a new `else if` block to allow you to update the IMAGE field in a given record. The UPDATE SQL command specifies the table and column to be modified and a conditional expression to match a record or set of records.

```
UPDATE SAPMATERIALS SET IMAGE = 'images/newimage.gif' WHERE
  MATERIAL='somematerial'
```

The WHERE clause in this statement is optional. In this application, it narrows the field update to only those records that match a specified material number. As with previous command line arguments, the material number and image location are entered at runtime.

Here is a quick rundown of the command line options in this application and how to use them:

`java SapMaterialAction create <search criteria>`: Creates a database table called SAPMATERIALS and loads it with material records retrieved from SAP. The "search criteria" string limits the number of records retrieved from SAP based on the material number. Entering an asterisk (*) as the search criteria instructs the SapMaterialAction class to retrieve all material records from SAP and load them into the hsql database.

`java SapMaterialAction delete`: Deletes the SAPMATERIALS table from the hsql database.

`java SapMaterialAction add <material> <description> <image location>`: Adds a new record to SAPMATERIALS. Note the additional image location field required in this add.

`java SapMaterialAction select`: Displays all entries in the SAPMATERIALS table.

`java SapMaterialAction update <material number> <image location>`: Changes the image location for the material number specified in the command line. Any materials that require an individual image should be updated with this command.

Run the `select` clause after you create the table and update some of the records with material images. The output should look something like this:

```
----------------------------------------
Material:     MATERIAL1
Description:  First material description
Image:        images/default.gif
----------------------------------------
Material:     MATERIAL2
Description:  Second material description
Image:        images/material2.gif
----------------------------------------
Material:     MATERIAL3
Description:  Third material description
Image:        images/material3.gif
----------------------------------------
Material:     MATERIAL4
Description:  Fourth material description
Image:        images/default.gif
----------------------------------------
Material:     MATERIAL5
Description:  Fifth material description
Image:        images/material5.gif
----------------------------------------
```

Notice that the records whose IMAGE field has not been updated are using the default value of images/default.gif. This simple expedient allows you to update the material database with image files as they become available, rather than requiring a complete catalog when the database is initially created.

> **NOTE** *The file location of the default image is specified as* images/default.gif. *This is a relative file path that tells the Web server to retrieve the image from a directory called* images *that resides underneath the current directory. Currently, your Struts application is deployed in* tomcat/webapps/sap. *To provide Web access to the* default.gif *file, you need to create a new directory called* images *in* tomcat/webapps/sap. *This will be the default directory for all material images required in this application.*

Now that the materials database has been populated and you have created a few images for specific materials, it's time to build the actual Web application. The last section in this chapter deals with tying your existing Struts Web application to the hsql database and displaying results from table queries alongside data from SAP.

Chapter 8

Bringing It Together with Struts

At this point, you should be fairly comfortable with basic JDBC and SQL syntax. Of course, this chapter has barely even scratched the surface of database programming, a subject that takes up entire books, sometimes even spanning multiple volumes. A good source for more information can be found in *Beginning Java Databases: JDBC, SQL, J2EE, EJB, JSP, XML,* by Kevin Mukhar, Todd Lauinger, and John Carnell (Wrox Press, 2001).

However, armed with the basics, you can easily create and maintain external databases to supplement an existing R/3 system. Why would you ever want to do this? Obviously, SAP provides tools to manage outside content and even binary data types such as images and formatted documents. If your company has implemented SAP Knowledge Management functionality, you are likely already familiar with one version of content management. Likewise, in SAP's Web Application Server, you can store and retrieve binary content via an HTTP interface that emulates a standard URL call.

On the other hand, there are times when storing and retrieving binary data as database record types can cause an inordinate amount of overhead on the application server. In this case, the bottleneck is the R/3 application server, which is responsible for translating information from database tables into their binary counterparts. By migrating some of this responsibility to an external database or file system, you can greatly increase the performance of an SAP instance without sacrificing application functionality.

In the previous application, you designated a column as IMAGE and stored the relative file path and file name for representative material images. The goal was to provide additional content for use solely in a Web application, rather than customize or extend existing SAP tables or BAPIs. Because these images are only to be used in this Web application, it makes sense to externalize that information without risking changes to current applications or interfaces within SAP. Finally, instead of storing the actual binary image file, your application uses the file system as a repository for images, and relies on the hsql database to simply describe where those files can be found.

Figure 8-7 illustrates the lookup and rendering mechanism from the perspective of a Web server. Notice that the actual image binary never passes through the database system. This greatly reduces the overhead on the database and enhances overall response time throughout the architecture.

Now that you have a database populated with material numbers from SAP and the directory paths for the images of these materials, it's time to integrate a call to this database in the Struts application.

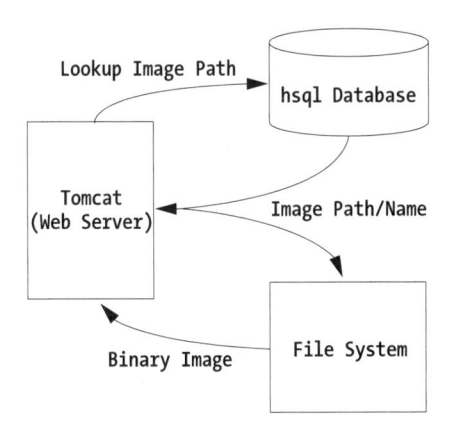

Figure 8-7. Image lookup and rendering through a Web server

Approaching the Basic Application Design

Recall that the Action class layer in Struts maintains the interface to your database model or data interface layer. Currently, the Action classes rely on InterfaceCaller for all communication back to the SAP application server. Just as you have encapsulated these JCo calls into a single Java class, you should also bundle the JDBC into an external Java class.

You are not required to maintain JDBC outside of the Action classes and could just as easily modify an existing Action class to directly call the hsql database. However, this approach has many disadvantages, including a lack of flexibility should anything in the database interface need to change (JDBC driver, table structure, and so on). In fact, it is not uncommon to break down the database interface layer into several different classes, such as a database connection class and multiple SQL classes that are responsible for queries, updates, and creates. For the tutorial application, you will use one class to maintain the connection and SQL SELECT statement. Chapter 9 looks at connection pooling using the JCo connector database.

> **CAUTION** *When you build database applications that might experience high-level traffic, you must ensure performance at the JVM level. Because Java is an object-oriented language, it is easy to inadvertently create redundant instances of the same class; these can overload the JVM. Database connections are generally expensive to maintain from a system resource perspective, so I recommend that you use pooling or factory manager design patterns to maintain consistent performance and access to your applications.*

Chapter 8

In order to add hsql database functionality into the Struts application, you will take the following steps:

1. Develop a new Java class to maintain database connectivity and SQL queries.

2. Call this new class in the `MaterialDetailAction` class based on a material number selected through the Web application.

3. Modify `materialdetailResult.jsp` to display the appropriate image from the file path stored in the database.

The following section details the Java class that is responsible for a database connection and performs the specific database lookup required based on the material number passed to it.

Building the Standalone Database Class

The first step in encapsulating hsql database connectivity is to create a new Java class called `MaterialDb.java`. This class should be created in the `tomcat/webapps/sap/WEB-INF/classes/com/apress/ejsap` directory so that it can be part of the same Java package you used for your other Struts application classes.

Here is the code for this new class:

```
package com.apress.ejsap;

import java.sql.*;
import java.util.Hashtable;

public class MaterialDb {
  static String dbDriver = "org.hsqldb.jdbcDriver";
  static String dbURL = "jdbc:hsqldb:hsql://localhost";
  static Connection conn = null;
  static Statement stat = null;
  public MaterialDb() {
    try {
    Class.forName(dbDriver);
    conn = DriverManager.getConnection(dbURL, "sa", "");
    stat = conn.createStatement();
    } catch (SQLException e) {
       System.out.println("SQL Exception");
       e.printStackTrace();
    }
```

```
    catch (ClassNotFoundException cEx) {
      System.out.println("Class not found exception");
      cEx.printStackTrace();
  }
}
public Hashtable getMaterial(String material) {
    Hashtable returnHash = new Hashtable();
    try {
      ResultSet rs = stat.executeQuery("SELECT *"
                    + " FROM SAPMATERIALS"
                    + " WHERE MATERIAL = '"
                    + material + "'");
      rs.next();
      returnHash.put("MATERIAL", rs.getString("MATERIAL"));
      returnHash.put("DESCRIPTION", rs.getString("DESCRIP"));
      returnHash.put("IMAGE", rs.getString("IMAGE"));
    } catch (SQLException e) {
        System.out.println(material + e.getMessage());
        returnHash.put("ERROR", e.getMessage());
    }
    finally
    {
      try { stat.close(); }
      catch (Exception e) { e.printStackTrace(); }
      try { conn.close(); }
      catch (Exception e) { e.printStackTrace(); }
    }
    return returnHash;
  }
}
```

Much of this code should look familiar to you because it was taken directly from the SapMaterialAction class. Note that the default constructor is still responsible for creating both the Connection and Statement instances so that these are available to any methods within the class. The major difference is the removal of a main method and the addition of a getMaterial() method. This method takes a single String parameter and returns a Hashtable instance to the calling class.

The getMaterial() method has two purposes, to execute a query against the database and to return the results formatted as a Hashtable object. This allows you to completely abstract the database call and the JDBC API from the Action class, reducing the interdependency between the model and controller layer in your application. Notice that your application consistently uses the Hashtable class to transport results, whether from a call to SAP via JCo or to the hsql database via a JDBC connector. Although not the most efficient mechanism for storing and retrieving data, the `Hashtable` offers a consistent interface that relies on simple name/value pairs. This means that, at any given layer in the application, a developer can expect to use a standard Java 2 class, rather than being forced to have knowledge of a specific API.

Likewise, you will notice that the SQL `SELECT` statement uses the optional `WHERE` clause to reduce the number of results returned in the database query. Because you have populated the `SAPMATERIALS` table directly from the R/3 system, it is safe to assume that there will be only one record for a given material number. However, you can add additional, redundant material records using the `ADD` clause of your `SapMaterialAction` class. By calling `rs`'s `next()` method only once, this class sets the pointer at the first record of the `ResultSet` instance. Be aware that if your database contains multiple records keyed to the same material number, this code will only use the first record returned to populate the `Hashtable`.

The `MaterialDb` class will be available for you to use in your `Action` classes after you compile it in the `webapps/sap/WEB-INF/classes/com/apress/ejsap` directory.

Advanced SQL Select Queries

The `SELECT` statement is perhaps one of the most powerful and complex standard SQL commands available. It provides you with a great deal of flexibility when you are dealing with multiple records that may span several database tables, and it offers a high level of granularity for specific queries.

In addition to the `WHERE` clause, `SELECT` offers `AND` and `OR` to join two or more conditions:

```
SELECT * FROM SAPMATERIALS WHERE MATERIAL='MATERIAL1'
            OR IMAGE='images/material1.gif'
```

The `BETWEEN` clause forces the query to only select from the range specified:

```
SELECT * FROM SAPMATERIALS WHERE MATERIAL
            BETWEEN 'MATERIAL1' AND 'MATERIAL10'
```

By using `ORDER BY`, you can control and sort the table rows by column:

```
SELECT * FROM SAPMATERIALS ORDER BY MATERIAL, IMAGE
```

Crossing the Chasm: Bridging SAP and an External Database

You can retrieve data from multiple tables by keying to primary fields:

```
SELECT * FROM SAPMATERIALS, SAPINVENTORY
            WHERE SAPMATERIALS.MATERIAL=SAPINVENTORY.MATERIAL
```

Lastly, `SELECT` can use different join types to further refine queries:

```
SELECT * FROM SAPMATERIALS INNER JOIN SAPINVENTORY
            ON SAPMATERIALS.MATERIAL=SAPINVENTORY.MATERIAL
```

Obviously, there is a great deal more to using `SELECT` and the entire SQL command set than I can present in this book. Simply be aware that, should you need to build or access more complex RDBMSs, SQL provides a flexible language for modeling complex interactions with a database in your applications.

Adding the Database Call to an Action Class

As described earlier, your Web application will use the external material database to support an extended description of a given material. Based on this usage, the most logical class in which to maintain your database logic is `MaterialDetailAction`. Recall that this `Action` class retrieves a detailed material record from SAP based on a user's selection and returns that record as a `Hashtable` to the Web front end.

Similar to the `InterfaceCaller` class, `MaterialDb` can be used directly within your `Action` class. With the additional call added to the class, `MaterialDetailAction` should now look like this:

```
package com.apress.ejsap;

import java.io.IOException;
import java.util.*;
import javax.servlet.*;
import javax.servlet.http.*;
import org.apache.struts.action.Action;
import org.apache.struts.action.ActionForm;
import org.apache.struts.action.ActionForward;
import org.apache.struts.action.ActionMapping;
import org.apache.struts.action.ActionServlet;
import org.apache.struts.action.ActionErrors;
import org.apache.struts.action.ActionError;
```

Chapter 8

```java
public final class MaterialDetailAction extends Action {
  public ActionForward perform(ActionMapping mapping,
                               ActionForm form,
                               HttpServletRequest request,
                               HttpServletResponse response)
    throws IOException, ServletException
  {
    String material = request.getParameter("MATERIAL");
    ActionServlet actServ = getServlet();
    ServletContext servContext = actServ.getServletContext();
    InterfaceCaller infCaller =
       (InterfaceCaller)servContext.getAttribute("ifaceCaller");
    Hashtable result = infCaller.getMaterialDetail(material);
    ActionErrors errors = new ActionErrors();
    if (result.size() < 1) {
      errors.add(ActionErrors.GLOBAL_ERROR,
                 new ActionError("error.material.nodetail"));
    }
    if (!errors.empty()) {
      this.saveErrors(request, errors);
      return (new ActionForward(mapping.getInput()));
    }
//New code added to support external database
    MaterialDb materialDb = new MaterialDb();
    Hashtable dbHash = materialDb.getMaterial(material);
    if ((String) dbHash.get("ERROR") == null) {
      result.put("IMAGE", dbHash.get("IMAGE"));
    }
    else {
      result.put("IMAGE", "images/default.gif");
    }
    HttpSession session = request.getSession();
    session.setAttribute("MATERIALDETAIL", result);

    return (mapping.findForward("success"));
    }
}
```

This new code simply instantiates an instance of the `MaterialDb` class and calls the `getMaterial()` method, passing in the material number retrieved from the `request` instance earlier in the class. If a key set to "ERROR" is found in the returned `Hashtable`, the code sets the "IMAGE" key in the `result` `Hashtable` to the default image and file path location (`images/default.gif`). Otherwise, the "IMAGE" key is set to the value returned in `dbHash` using a key of the same name.

As before, the `result` Hashtable is stored in the user's session, with the additional "IMAGE" key available to the front end. In the next section, you will retrieve the value of this key in a JavaServer Pages (JSP) page, and use it to display the image, if any, associated with a material record.

Displaying the Material Image in a JSP Page

At this point, the remainder of your application development should seem pretty straightforward. In order to test this application, make sure that you have an `images` directory underneath the `webapps/sap` directory and some saved image files keyed to the file names in your hsql database.

Utilizing standard Web server architecture, your JSP page will retrieve the image file path and file name and then format it as an HTML image tag. When the Web server renders this tag, it will automatically pick up an image from the file system and render it to the user's Web browser.

```
<IMG SRC="images/myimage.gif">
```

The SRC attribute of this tag requires either a relative path or a fully qualified URL to the location of the image to be displayed. A fully qualified URL would have the following format:

```
http://www.somedomain.com/images/myimage.gif
```

Because this Web application is being deployed in the same root directory as the `images` directory, this file path can be relative to the root path shared by JSP pages, HTML pages, and images.

```
<%@ page language="java" %>
<%@ page import="java.util.*" %>
<%@ taglib uri="/WEB-INF/lib/struts.tld" prefix="struts" %>
<%@ taglib uri="/WEB-INF/lib/struts-bean.tld" prefix="bean" %>
<%@ taglib uri="/WEB-INF/lib/struts-html.tld" prefix="html" %>

<html:html>
  <HEAD>
    <TITLE>Material Detail Result</TITLE>
<html:base/>
  </HEAD>
```

Chapter 8

```
      <BODY>
<html:errors/>
<H1>Material Detail</H1>
The following material record has been retrieved from SAP.
<P>
<B>Material: <%= request.getParameter("MATERIAL") %> </B>
<TABLE BORDER=1>
   <TR><TD><B>Field</B></TD><TD><B>Value</B></TD></TR>
<%
Hashtable resultHash = (Hashtable)session.getAttribute("MATERIALDETAIL");
%>
<!-- New code to display the material image -->
<TR><TD>MATERIAL IMAGE</TD>
<TD><IMG SRC="<%= resultHash.get("IMAGE") %>"></TD></TR>
<%
String field;
for (Enumeration e = resultHash.keys(); e.hasMoreElements();) {
  field = (String)e.nextElement();
%>
   <TR>
     <TD><%= field %></TD>
     <TD><%= (String)resultHash.get(field) %></TD>
   </TR>
<%
  }
%>
</TABLE>
</BODY>
</html:html>
```

The addition of a new row at the top of the material record table displays the image associated with a material (or a default if there is no image).

```
<IMG SRC="<%= resultHash.get("IMAGE") %>">
```

This is the HTML statement that sets the SRC attribute of an image tag to the value keyed to "IMAGE" from the resultHash instance. As shown in Figure 8-8, the material detail results screen of your Web application should now have an image row associated with each material record.

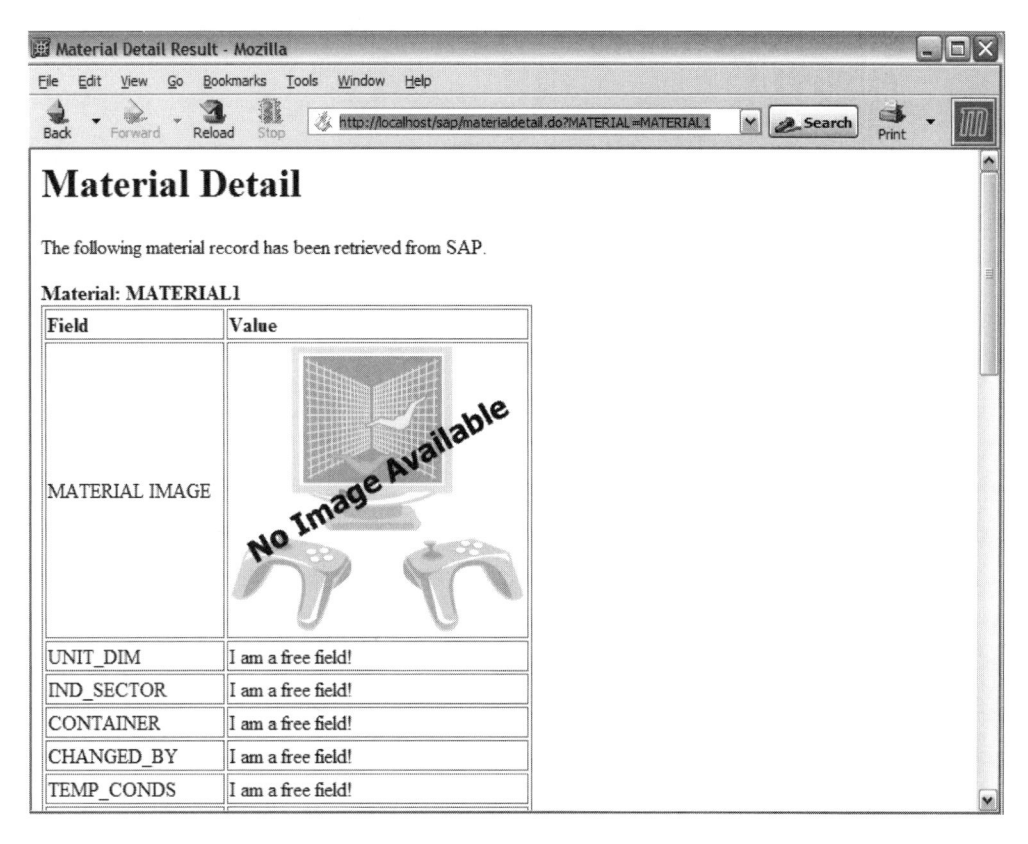

Figure 8-8. Material detail display with default image

Summary

Although by no means exhaustive, this chapter should have familiarized you with some of the basic working concepts that surround JDBC. By now, you should be comfortable with the essential SQL command set, and you should be able to build, modify, and query database tables using it.

You will find the ability to quickly create external databases for both prototype and production environments invaluable. When tied to an SAP system, you gain a great deal of presentation flexibility for building Web applications whose data requirements may not wholly reside in R/3. In addition, learning the SQL language is a good way to supplement your understanding of database systems, in general. Of course, as an R/3 developer, you are likely familiar with SAP's SQL-style implementation and can apply that knowledge outside of the ABAP Workbench through Java database applications.

Coupled with Struts, the hsql database offers a powerful framework for deploying advanced Web applications. Even without SAP, you can offer users a complete application solution that combines rich data content via the database with standardized interfaces through a Web browser.

CHAPTER 9
Advanced Java Programming in SAP

THE FINAL CHAPTER IN THIS BOOK is devoted to advanced Java and JCo programming techniques that enhance existing applications and offer new functionality in the SAP environment. Although the JCo API can be used strictly for basic connectivity into the SAP system, it also offers extensive optimization and framework tools.

This chapter looks at the following:

- Optimizing with native JCo connection pools

- Building a JCo server

- Developing custom Java tags

Connection pooling in JCo is based on a standard design pattern that you would normally implement by hand. The first section details how you can add JCo's easy-to-use pooling mechanism into your existing application development. JCo also provides a server interface API that provides outbound connectivity from within the SAP system. In the second section, I detail this technique using a combined Java/ABAP tutorial. You have already used the JavaServer Page Standard Tag Library (JSTL) to simplify Web page development and to hide complex Java logic and are likely interested in building you own custom tags. The last section demonstrates a custom tag that provides default behavior in the material catalog JSP.

Introducing JCo Connection Pools

Chapter 6 demonstrated how you could use a shared context to let users access a common instance of the InterfaceCaller class. Limiting the number of InterfaceCaller instances created by the Java Virtual Machine (JVM) allowed you to optimize usage of Java server resources during times of peak traffic. Web applications that connect to SAP via JCo pose a similar threat when you do not restrain the number of JCO.Client instances used by these applications to an acceptable limit. Fortunately, the JCo API provides a connection pooling mechanism that allows your Java applications to better manage connections to the SAP application server.

If you plan to provide generic access to certain functions in SAP, using connection pools is an excellent way to increase performance. Each unique or named user connection your JCo application creates uses up resources in the R/3 system. Both foreground or SAP GUI users and background users such as those accessing the system via RFC share these resources. Allowing an unrestricted number of named user connections via JCo can have a negative impact on SAP GUI users who are simultaneously accessing the system. A connection pool allows you to optimize this resource usage by relying on a single generic user connection shared by multiple instances of your JCo application.

Advanced Java Programming in SAP

When you implement a connection pool in your application, you will follow steps similar to these:

1. Check to see if a connection pool already exists; if you do not find one, create a new connection pool.

2. Retrieve a connection from the pool.

3. Execute BAPI/RFC calls using this connection.

4. Release the connection back into pool.

Figure 9-1 outlines the connection pooling mechanism used by a Java application.

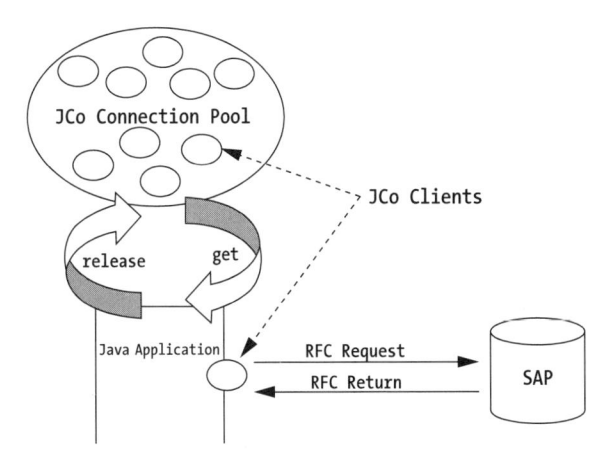

Figure 9-1. Connection pool diagram

The connection pool functions by allowing you to specify a limited number of SAP connections at runtime. Your application can then manage these connections through the JCO.PoolManager to optimize the use of valuable system resources. In this case, your application only creates the connections in the pool once and then reuses them throughout the lifecycle of the pool. Currently, the InterfaceCaller class must create a new JCO.Client instance every time it connects to the SAP system. In a real-world application, this action could quickly overload the Java application server with extraneous connections, or it could impact performance on the SAP application server by allowing too many simultaneous logons.

However, the connections in a JCo pool are always authenticated with the same user name. This means that your application cannot readily use named SAP accounts to ensure the correct privileges and authorizations for Web-based users. The material catalog scenario I outlined in previous tutorials does not require specific authorizations to browse the online catalog. Rather, its purpose is to present a store-style product catalog that can be viewed by anyone with an SAP Internet user account. Should the user need to create a sales order or commit some other type of transaction in SAP, your application would need to reconnect as a named SAP user to guarantee the integrity of that process.

When a JCo pool is created, you must assign it a unique identifier so that subsequent classes can retrieve connections from this pool. A pool identifier is global across the Java Virtual Machine (JVM), ensuring that the connection pool, with a given name, cannot have multiple instances within the application server. You can create multiple pools, but each must have its own unique identifier within the JVM.

The first steps to implementing a connection pool are to define a pool name and to check whether that pool already exists in the JVM:

```
private final String JCO_POOL = "myPool";
JCO.Pool connPool = JCO.getClientPoolManager().getPool(JCO_POOL);
```

This code defines a global, private variable called JCO_POOL and assigns it the value of the connection pool name. By declaring the variable as private final, it effectively becomes a global constant that cannot be modified by any subsequent code. By finalizing this variable, you restrict your application to the creation of a single, named connection pool and prevent the inadvertent instantiation of unwanted pools. The JCO.getClientPoolManager() method accesses the global JCo PoolManger in order to retrieve a JCO.Pool instance.

When no JCO.Pool is stored as "myPool", the method call returns a null value. If a null is returned, your class should then create a connection pool:

```
if (connPool == null) {
   JCO.addClientPool(JCO_POOL,
                     5,
                     sapData);
}
```

You can specify the parameters sent in the addClientPool() method in several different ways. JCO_POOL is a String value that indicates the name of the pool to be created. The second parameter is an integer value that designates the number of connections that should be created and maintained in the pool. The last parameter is an instance of the Properties class; you can use it to set the SAP logon values.

In the current development, your applications pass each logon value as individual parameters to the createClient() method. However, you can pass these parameters more easily by assigning addClientPool() a Java Properties object that specifies your system logon properties.

Fortunately, you can reuse sapdata.properties by reading that file into this class using the FileInputStream class:

```
Properties sapData = new Properties();
try {
  FileInputStream in = new FileInputStream("sapdata.properties");
  sapData.load(in);
  in.close();
} catch (Exception ex) {
  ex.printStackTrace();
}
```

This code creates a new Properties instance, called sapData, and loads the name/value pairs specified in sapdata.properties from a FileInputStream. If you used the naming conventions specified earlier in this book for the properties file, the addClientPool() method should have no problem parsing the logon values.

> **NOTE** *Loading data into the JVM from a file system can be a bit tricky, depending on your operating system. If you are using the Windows OS without setting any additional environment variables, you should store the* sapdata.properties *file in the* tomcat/bin *directory. Recall that the* ResourceBundle *class only needed the properties file stored somewhere in the Java classpath. You may need to move or copy the* sapdata.properties *file to the new directory in order to allow* FileInputStream *to read its values into your class.*

You can now substitute the direct connections currently used in your application with a connection retrieved from the pool. The first spot to try this out would be in your call to retrieve JCO.Repository from SAP:

```
try {
  aConnection = JCO.getClient(JCO_POOL);
  aRepository = new JCO.Repository("SAPRep", aConnection);
}
catch (Exception ex) {
  System.out.println("Failed to retrieve SAP repository");
}
JCO.releaseClient(aConnection);
```

Rather than using the createClient() method, this code calls JCO.getClient(), passing the same global constant it used to create the connection pool. Notice that you no longer need to execute the connect() method on the aConnection instance because the connection to the R/3 system is maintained in the pool.

As before, you create a new JCO.Repository by passing in a String value for the repository name and a JCO.Client instance. However, once your application has created the repository and it no longer requires further connection to SAP, your code should release the connection back to the pool. By passing aConnection to the JCO.releaseClient() method, your application allows this connection to be quickly reused by another method or class.

> **TIP** *You can find the code for this chapter in the Downloads section of the Apress Website* (http://www.apress.com).

With this new knowledge of connection pooling, you should be able to readily modify the existing InterfaceCaller class.

```
package com.apress.ejsap;
import com.sap.mw.jco.*;
import java.util.Hashtable;
import java.util.ResourceBundle;
import java.util.Properties;
import java.io.*;
public class InterfaceCaller {
  private JCO.Client aConnection;
  private IRepository aRepository;
  private final String JCO_POOL = "myPool";
  public InterfaceCaller() {
// New method to create connection pool
    createConnectionPool();
    retrieveRepository();
  }
  public Hashtable getMaterialDetail(String material) {
    JCO.Function function = getFunction("BAPI_MATERIAL_GET_DETAIL");
    JCO.ParameterList listParams = function.getImportParameterList();
    listParams.setValue(material, "MATERIAL");
    aConnection = JCO.getClient(JCO_POOL);
    aConnection.execute(function);
    JCO.releaseClient(aConnection);
    JCO.ParameterList resultParams = function.getExportParameterList();
    JCO.Structure fieldList = resultParams.getStructure("MATERIAL_GENERAL_DATA");
    Hashtable returnHash = new Hashtable();
    if (fieldList.getFieldCount() > 0) {
      for (JCO.FieldIterator fI = fieldList.fields(); fI.hasMoreElements();)
```

```java
        {
          JCO.Field tabField = fI.nextField();
          returnHash.put(tabField.getName(), tabField.getString());
        }
    }
    return returnHash;
}
public Hashtable getMaterialList(String searchParam) {
    JCO.Function function = getFunction("BAPI_MATERIAL_GETLIST");
    JCO.ParameterList tabParams = function.getTableParameterList();
    JCO.Table materials = tabParams.getTable("MATNRSELECTION");
    materials.appendRow();
    materials.setRow(0);
    materials.setValue("I", "SIGN");
    materials.setValue("CP", "OPTION");
    materials.setValue(searchParam, "MATNR_LOW");
    aConnection = JCO.getClient(JCO_POOL);
    aConnection.execute(function);
    JCO.releaseClient(aConnection);
    JCO.ParameterList resultParams = function.getExportParameterList();
    JCO.Table materialList =
        function.getTableParameterList().getTable("MATNRLIST");
    Hashtable returnHash = new Hashtable();
    Hashtable rowHash = new Hashtable();
    int i = 0;
    if (materialList.getNumRows() > 0) {
        do {
            for (JCO.FieldIterator fI = materialList.fields();
                 fI.hasMoreElements();)
              {
                JCO.Field tabField = fI.nextField();
                rowHash.put(tabField.getName(),tabField.getString());
              }
        }
            returnHash.put("line" + i, rowHash);
            rowHash = new Hashtable();
            i++;
          }
          while(materialList.nextRow() == true);
    }
    else {
        System.out.println("Sorry, couldn't find any materials");
    }
    return returnHash;
}
```

```java
public Hashtable checkPassword(String username, String password) {
  JCO.Function function = getFunction("BAPI_CUSTOMER_CHECKPASSWORD");
  JCO.ParameterList listParams = function.getImportParameterList();
  listParams.setValue(username, "CUSTOMERNO");
  listParams.setValue(password, "PASSWORD");
   aConnection = JCO.getClient(JCO_POOL);
  aConnection.execute(function);
  JCO.releaseClient(aConnection);
  JCO.ParameterList resultParams = function.getExportParameterList();
  Hashtable returnHash = new Hashtable();
  returnHash.put("RETURN.TYPE",extractField("RETURN","TYPE",resultParams));
  returnHash.put("RETURN.CODE",extractField("RETURN","CODE",resultParams));
  returnHash.put("RETURN.MESSAGE",
                 extractField("RETURN","MESSAGE",resultParams));
  return returnHash;
   }
 public String extractField(String structure,String field,
                                    JCO.ParameterList parameterList)
{
    return ((JCO.Structure)parameterList.getValue(structure)).getString(field);
}
 public JCO.Function getFunction(String name) {
   try {
       return
aRepository.getFunctionTemplate(name.toUpperCase()).getFunction();
   }
   catch (Exception ex) {}
     return null;
   }
 private void createConnectionPool() {
   Properties sapData = new Properties();
   try {
     FileInputStream in = new FileInputStream("sapdata.properties");
     sapData.load(in);
     in.close();
   } catch (Exception ex) {
     ex.printStackTrace();
   }
   JCO.Pool connPool = JCO.getClientPoolManager().getPool(JCO_POOL);
   if (connPool == null) {
     JCO.addClientPool(JCO_POOL,
                       5,
                       sapData);
   }
 }
```

```
  private void retrieveRepository() {
    try {
      aConnection = JCO.getClient(JCO_POOL);
      aRepository = new JCO.Repository("SAPRep", aConnection);
     }
    catch (Exception ex) {
      System.out.println("Failed to retrieve SAP repository");
    }
    JCO.releaseClient(aConnection);
  }
}
```

Notice that I have removed the `ResourceBundle`, along with its associated `String` variables, because the class now loads logon values directly from the physical properties file. Likewise, it should be fairly obvious why I removed the call to `createConnection()` and replaced it with `createConnectionPool()`.

Now that you have updated the application to use connection pooling, you need to stop and restart the Tomcat application server for those changes to take effect. `InterfaceCaller` should load automatically on startup and you can test the JCo connection pool by executing the material catalog application. If you want to test the effectiveness of a connection pool, try removing the `JCO.releaseClient()` statements from the `InterfaceCaller.checkPassword()` method. Recompile and restart the Tomcat server.

You should be able to execute a login through the Web application five times (enter a user name and password, hit the Submit button, then hit the Back button and try again). On the sixth attempt, the application should throw an exception with the group set to

`JCO.Exception.JCO_ERROR_RESOURCE`

This message, which should be visible in the Tomcat command console, indicates that you have exceeded the maximum number of connections available in the pool. Eventually the unused connections will timeout and you will be able to login again. However, this should give you a feel for how connections should be used and released by your applications.

The next section introduces the `JCO.Server` interface and shows you how to build a standalone Java server that can be called from within SAP.

Calling Java Objects from Within SAP

Throughout the course of this book, you have focused on communicating with SAP interfaces via different types of Java applications. SAP sees this as inbound communication, where an outside program makes a call into the R/3 system. However, the JCo API provides for bidirectional access. This means that, in addition to inbound connectivity, an SAP application can also make outbound calls to an external system, utilizing standard RFC destinations.

The JCo API supplies a class-level server that you can implement within a Java application to provide RFC-style services to an SAP application. On startup, the JCO.Server registers itself with a specified program ID in the target SAP host. You must configure this program in an RFC destination in order to allow access via an ABAP program. Figure 9-2 illustrates the communication between SAP and an external Java object using the JCo server.

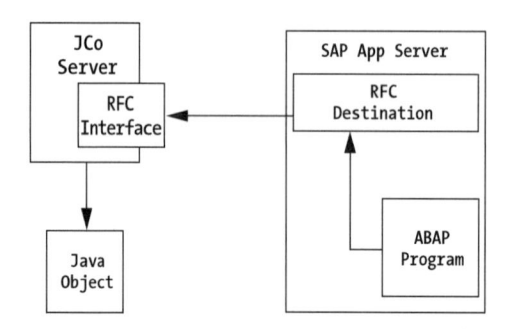

Figure 9-2. JCo server communication diagram

To use the JCo server, you must first define the interface that the SAP application will call via an RFC destination. There are two ways to do this: you can build a custom JCO.Repository with the required interface, or you can deploy the interface in SAP and retrieve it via an SAP-generated JCO.Repository. Although both methods are valid, this section details the use of the latter. The former requires that interface definitions be externalized from the SAP system, which leads to a greater degree of decentralized administration overhead. By utilizing SAP's existing Function Builder, you can take advantage of the more centralized development and deployment capabilities of the R/3 system. For more information on building your own JCO.Repository, check out the documentation and examples supplied in the JCo zip file you downloaded from the SAP Web site. This documentation can be found in the directory where you installed JCo (<JCO_INSTALL>/docs/jco).

Defining the RFC Interface in SAP

Before you can build the RFC interface, you must define the appropriate structures through SAP's Data Dictionary. Because this example returns a table to the ABAP program, you must create a structure to hold its field definitions. Depending on the SAP system release, you will need to use either the ABAP

Dictionary transaction (SE11) or the Object Navigator. Either way, you must create a structure called ZJCO_STRUCT and define the three fields specified in Table 9-1.

Table 9-1. Field Definition for Structure ZJCO_STRUCT

COMPONENT	COMPONENT TYPE
IDENT	CHAR10
SHORT_TEXT	CHAR_35
LONG_TEXT	CHAR_132

Be sure to enter a description in the Short Text figure, and then save and activate your new structure. If the structure activated successfully, you should end up with a screen similar to Figure 9-3. When you are asked for a transport request, save it as a local object for the purposes of this tutorial.

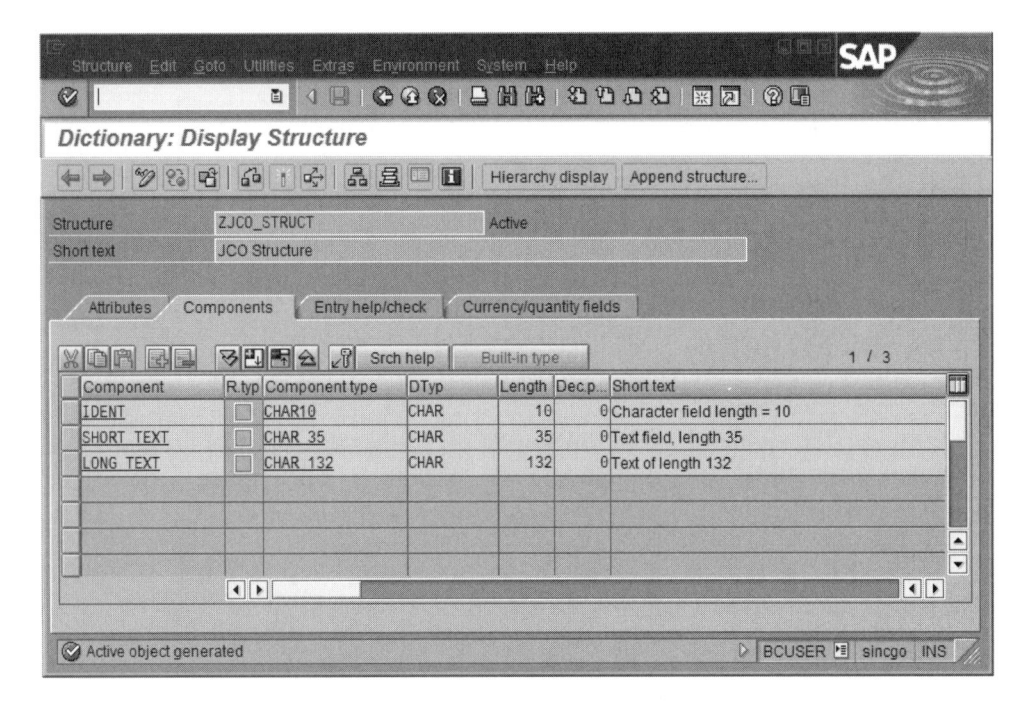

Figure 9-3. ZJCO_STRUCT *structure*

Now that the structure has been defined, you can load the Function Builder (SE37) and build the RFC interface. After you have finished loading and building, create a new RFC called Z_RFC_JCO_INTERFACE. In the Attributes tab, set Processing Type to Remote-Enabled Module as depicted in Figure 9-4.

Chapter 9

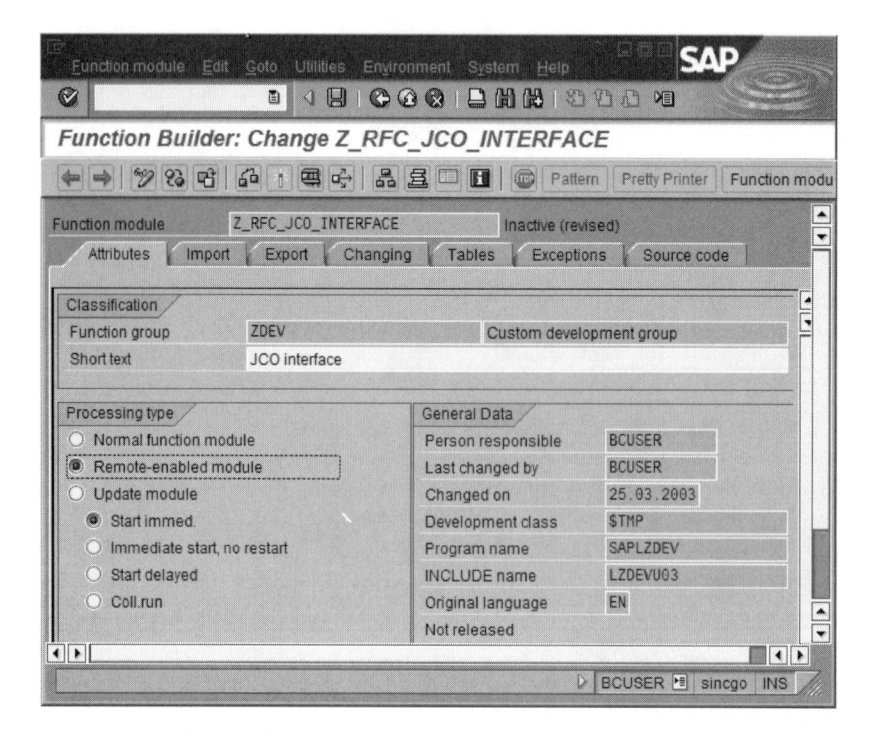

Figure 9-4. The Attributes tab in Function Builder

Now navigate to the Import tag and create a parameter entry field called **IDENT** with a Type Spec of **LIKE** and a Reference Type of **ZJCO_STRUCT**. Be sure to check the Pass Value flag to set this as a value parameter rather than as a reference parameter. Figure 9-5 depicts these parameter settings.

In the Export tab, create a new parameter entry called **EX_IDENT**, setting the field values equal to those used in the Import tab. Finally, in the Tables tab, create a parameter entry called **TAB_IDTEXT**, using a Type Spec of **LIKE** and a Reference Type of **ZJCO_STRUCT**. Now you can save and activate the RFC; once you have done so, you are ready to build your JCo server.

Advanced Java Programming in SAP

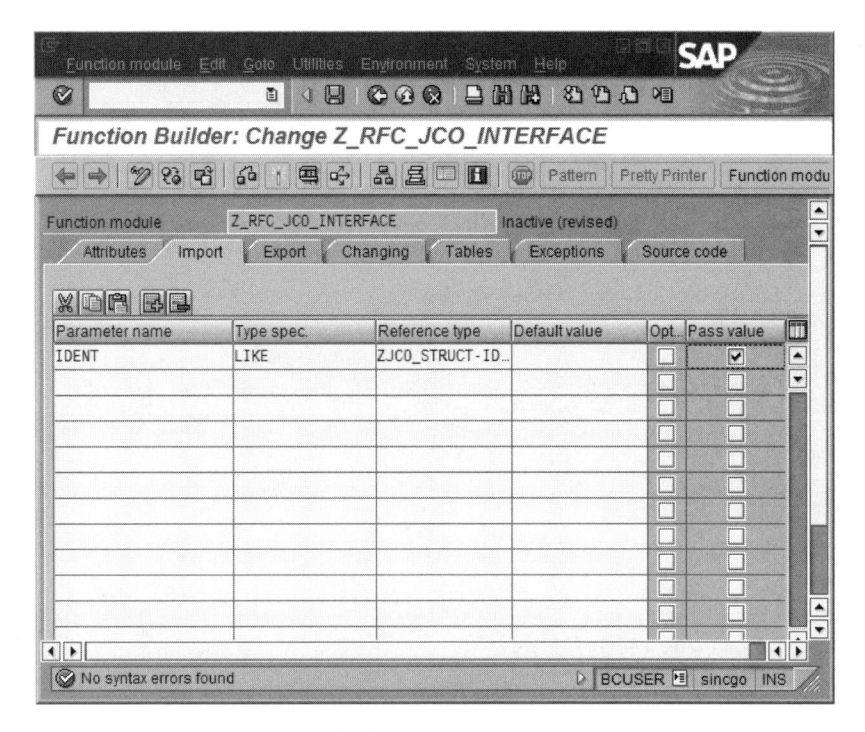

Figure 9-5. The Import tab in Function Builder

Building the JCo Server

The Java application that will become your JCo server must extend the
JCO.Server class that comes with the JCo API. By extending this class, your Java
application inherits all of the functionality available in JCO.Server.

```
import com.sap.mw.jco.*;
public class SampleServer extends JCO.Server {
  public SampleServer(String gwhost, String gwserv, String progid, IRepository repository)
  {
  super(gwhost,gwserv,progid,repository);
  System.out.println("JCO Server has been started");
  }
...
}
```

The default constructor of SampleServer requires four parameters: three String objects and a JCO.IRepository instance. Notice that this constructor simply passes these objects to one of the constructors in the JCO.Server superclass.

Once this constructor has been called by an outside method, the application prints a string to the command console indicating that the server is running. Make sure that the print line follows the super() statement because the compiler will throw an error if your code attempts to execute any statement before it calls the JCO.Server constructor.

> **NOTE** When a class extends another class, the former is known as the subclass and the latter as a superclass. The subclass can directly utilize constructors, methods, and class-level variables in the superclass by way of the reserved keyword super. You can see an example of this usage in the previous code snippet, where super() calls the constructor specified by the parameter signature. You can also specify a method in the superclass using the format super.aSuperClassMethod().

Using the handRequest() Method

In order to extend JCO.Server, you must override this class's handleRequest() method. You can override other methods, but this is the only one required to implement a JCo server.

```
protected void handleRequest(JCO.Function function)
{
  JCO.ParameterList paramsIn  = function.getImportParameterList();
  JCO.ParameterList paramsOut = function.getExportParameterList();
  JCO.ParameterList tables    = function.getTableParameterList();
  System.out.println("Calling service: " + function.getName ());
  ...
}
```

Here, handleRequest() takes a JCO.Function instance as its sole parameter. As you might recall from previous use, the Function class contains the interface definition for a given RFC or BAPI. As before, you must use this object to retrieve the import/export parameters, the structures, and the tables in order to populate a call to the interface. The last statement prints a line to the command console that indicates the name of the RFC/BAPI interface contained in the JCO.Function instance passed to this method.

At this point, SampleServer has a functional representation of the data passed to it by an SAP application. The JCO.Server calls the handleRequest() behind the scenes and allows your application to build a programmatic response.

Advanced Java Programming in SAP

For this example, SampleServer retrieves the value specified as IDENT and attempts to match it to a predefined string in an if...else if block.

```
if (function.getName().equals("Z_RFC_JCO_INTERFACE")) {
  String ident = paramsIn.getString("IDENT");
  JCO.Table idTable = tables.getTable("TAB_IDTEXT");
  idTable.appendRows(2);
  if (ident.equals("BEYE")) {
    idTable.setRow(0);
    idTable.setValue("BEYE", "IDENT");
    idTable.setValue("Blind eye", "SHORT_TEXT");
    idTable.setValue("A blind eye sees only truth", "LONG_TEXT");
    idTable.setRow(1);
    idTable.setValue("BEYE", "IDENT");
    idTable.setValue("Blinded eyes", "SHORT_TEXT");
    idTable.setValue("Your eyes may be blinded, but you are truly free",
                    "LONG_TEXT");
  }
  else if (ident.equals("MIGHT")) {
    idTable.setRow(0);
    idTable.setValue("MIGHT", "IDENT");
    idTable.setValue("Always mighty", "SHORT_TEXT");
    idTable.setValue("Always the mighty are first to fall", "LONG_TEXT");
    idTable.setRow(1);
    idTable.setValue("MIGHT", "IDENT");
    idTable.setValue("Might and maybe", "SHORT_TEXT");
    idTable.setValue("Might and maybe are the musings of the mumbler",
                    "LONG_TEXT");
  }
  paramsOut.setValue(ident,"EX_IDENT");
  tables.setValue(idTable, "TAB_IDTEXT");
}
```

The first if statement checks whether the interface called by the ABAP program is Z_RFC_JCO_INTERFACE. If it is, the statement attempts to match the value specified in the IDENT field against either BEYE or MIGHT. If one of the cases is met, the code sets the SHORT_TEXT and LONG_TEXT values for two different table rows to some nonsense strings.

Finally, the code sets the JCO.Table idTables to the value TAB_IDTEXT in the tables parameter list. This returns the JCO.Table to whatever SAP application called the JCo server interface.

Executing the JCo Server

Now create a new file called `SampleServer.java` and save the following code in it:

```java
import com.sap.mw.jco.*;

public class SampleServer extends JCO.Server {
  public SampleServer(String gwhost, String gwserv, String progid,
                                       IRepository repository)
  {
    super(gwhost,gwserv,progid,repository);
    System.out.println("JCO Server has been started");
  }
  protected void handleRequest(JCO.Function function)
  {
    JCO.ParameterList paramsIn  = function.getImportParameterList();
    JCO.ParameterList paramsOut = function.getExportParameterList();
    JCO.ParameterList tables = function.getTableParameterList();
    System.out.println("Calling service: " + function.getName());

    if (function.getName().equals("Z_RFC_JCO_INTERFACE")) {
     String ident = paramsIn.getString("IDENT");
     JCO.Table idTable = tables.getTable("TAB_IDTEXT");
     idTable.appendRows(2);
     if (ident.equals("BEYE")) {
      idTable.setRow(0);
      idTable.setValue("BEYE", "IDENT");
      idTable.setValue("Blind eye", "SHORT_TEXT");
      idTable.setValue("A blind eye sees only truth", "LONG_TEXT");

      idTable.setRow(1);
      idTable.setValue("BEYE", "IDENT");
      idTable.setValue("Blinded eyes", "SHORT_TEXT");
      idTable.setValue("Your eyes may be blinded, but you are truly free",
                                "LONG_TEXT");
     }
     else if (ident.equals("MIGHT")) {
      idTable.setRow(0);
      idTable.setValue("MIGHT", "IDENT");
      idTable.setValue("Always mighty", "SHORT_TEXT");
      idTable.setValue("Always the mighty are first to fall", "LONG_TEXT");
```

```
      idTable.setRow(1);
      idTable.setValue("MIGHT", "IDENT");
      idTable.setValue("Might and maybe", "SHORT_TEXT");
      idTable.setValue("Might and maybe are the musings of the mumbler",
                            "LONG_TEXT");
    }
    paramsOut.setValue(ident,"EX_IDENT");
    tables.setValue(idTable, "TAB_IDTEXT");
   }
  }
}
```

In order to load the server, you must call it from a command line Java application in which you pass the four parameters required by the server class's default constructor. Create a new file called ServerTest.java and save the following code to it:

```
import com.sap.mw.jco.*;

public class ServerTest{
 public static void main(String[] argv)
 {
    JCO.Client aConnection =
                    JCO.createClient("client", "username",
                                               "password", "language",
                                               "host", "system number");
    aConnection.connect();
    IRepository repository = new JCO.Repository("serverRep", aConnection);
    aConnection.disconnect();
    JCO.Server myServer   myServer =
          new SampleServer("sincgo","sapgw00","JCOSERVER",repository);
    myServer.start();
 }
}
```

Because the RFC interface was defined in SAP, you can simply retrieve an instance of the repository from SAP and pass it directly to SampleServer. Be sure to replace the text strings specified in the createClient() method with values appropriate to your SAP system. The ServerTest application represents a quick-and-dirty way to load your JCo server and has not been optimized for deployment in a production environment.

In order to access `SampleServer` from SAP, compile and execute the `ServerTest` application. `SampleServer` will register itself as `JCOSERVER` with the SAP host, which enables it to be called from an SAP application.

Calling a JCo Server from Inside SAP

Before an ABAP program can call the JCo server, you must define an RFC destination in SAP. The RFC destination allows an internal, SAP application to access an external resource or program. In order to call a JCo server from within SAP you must take following steps:

1. Create a new RFC destination in SM59.

2. Register the program name specified by `SampleServer` in the RFC destination.

3. Build an ABAP application to call `SampleServer` through this destination.

In SAP, go to RFC Destination transaction (SM59) and create a new RFC destination. Enter **JCOSERVER_DESTINATION** as the RFC Destination, select "T" as the Connection Type, and add a general description. Save the entry and you should see a screen similar to Figure 9-6.

Figure 9-6. Defining an RFC destination

Select the Registered Server Program radio button and enter **JCOSERVER** as the Program ID. Enter the host name of your SAP system and the SAP gateway. The SAP gateway is usually "sapgw" followed by the system number; however, check with your BASIS administrator if you are unsure of these settings. Save this RFC destination and navigate to the ABAP workbench (SE80).

> **NOTE** *If there is any question of network connectivity between your JCo server and the SAP system, you can test the connection using the RFC destination. Start the JCo server using* ServerTest, *and then hit the Test Connection button from the RFC Destination maintenance screen. If SAP returns a series of logon time statistics, the connection was successful. However, if you get any errors back, you will need to check with a network administrator to ensure that communication between the two systems is possible.*

In the ABAP Workbench, create a new application called **ZJCO_CLIENT** and add the following code to it:

```
REPORT ZJCO_CLIENT.
DATA it_idtext TYPE STANDARD TABLE OF ZJCO_STRUCT.
DATA ident TYPE ZJCO_STRUCT-IDENT.
PARAMETERS ident_in(10).
CALL FUNCTION 'Z_RFC_JCO_INTERFACE'
  DESTINATION 'JCOSERVER_DESTINATION'
  EXPORTING
    IDENT     = ident_in
  IMPORTING
    EX_IDENT  = ident
  TABLES
    TAB_IDTEXT = it_idtext.
WRITE: 'Identifier:', ident.
NEW-LINE.
DATA tmp_line LIKE LINE OF it_idtext.
LOOP AT it_idtext INTO tmp_line.
  WRITE: 'Short Text:', TMP_LINE-SHORT_TEXT.
  NEW-LINE.
  WRITE: 'Long Text:', TMP_LINE-LONG_TEXT.
  NEW-LINE.
ENDLOOP.
```

Save, activate, and execute this code. You should be prompted for a string value. Enter either **"BEYE"** or **"MIGHT"** and continue executing. The application will call your JCo server and return a screen that looks like Figure 9-7.

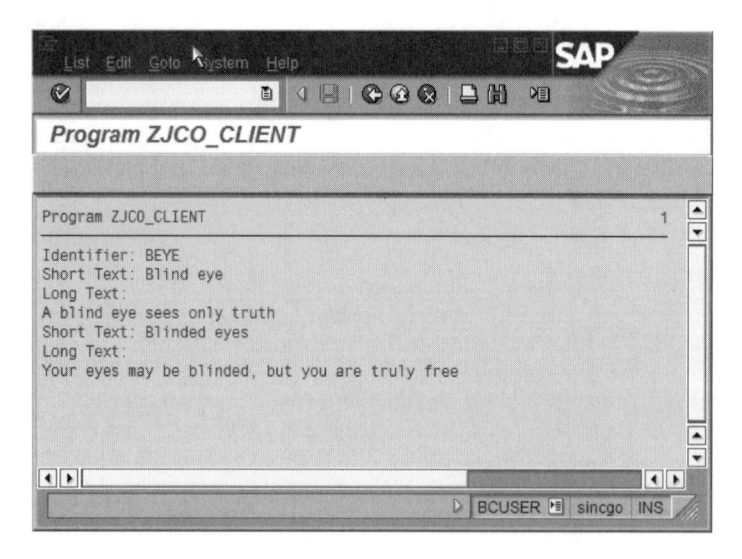

Figure 9-7. Results returned from a JCo server call

This example is designed to roughly introduce the JCo server and how to implement basic, external services for SAP. It is by no means exhaustive; a discussion of the JCo server API and server development could encompass its own book. However, you should have a good idea of what an external server looks like and how to extend ABAP programs beyond the normal boundaries of the SAP application server.

Now I will shift focus somewhat and show you how to build and deploy a custom Java tag. Although the included example does not use JCo, it and other tag libraries provide an invaluable mechanism for tapping the power of Java within an HTML-based user interface.

Building Custom Java Tab Libraries

Chapter 7 introduced the concept of using custom Java tags to simplify the development of JSP within the Struts framework. However, Java tags are certainly not limited to Struts and can be easily developed and deployed as part of any JSP-based Web application. This section demonstrates how to create and use a basic Java tag within your existing application. The included examples assume that you have completed all of the tutorials outlined earlier in the book.

Knowing When to Use a Custom Tag

Implementing Java tags is a great way to reduce the amount of Java embedded in a JSP page, but you should use these tags to support a larger purpose within the application development.

Java tags are useful when you need to address one or more of the following requirements:

Define a consistent and centralized look: By replacing standard HTML with Java tags, you can centralize display details, such as font color, size, bolded, and so on, into a set of external properties files. That way, you can ensure a consistent use of company colors, style guidelines, and standards across the entire site.

Provide default values for dynamic fields: When information is not available from a backend data store, Java tags can act as a mechanism to provide default values. Once again, these defaults can be migrated from the code into an external properties file. This allows you to conduct simple maintenance without making any updates directly to the JSP page.

Hide calls to an external data store: When the display requires a lookup to an external data store (field translation, selection lists, and so on), you can use Java tags to hide the required connection logic. Likewise, these tags can hide complex SQL logic and field manipulation before the information returned by a data store is sent to the JSP page.

This tutorial details the second approach to building a custom Java tag. In Chapter 8, you built a materials database that maintained a file path to an image for each material. However, you may not have had all of the images available when you created the material record, and so you set a default value to the file path for every material. Depending on the size of your SAP material database, the hsql materials table could have a very large number of default image file paths stored as record fields. What happens when you need to change the file path to this default image?

With the current application, you would need to programmatically update each record with the new file path. As an alternative, you could build a custom Java tag that could validate whether an image file path was returned from the hsql database and, if not, could supply a default path to the JSP page. This would allow your HTML programmers to easily redefine the image location for every material that did not have its own image path stored in the hsql database.

The next section details what goes into making such a Java tag and how to implement it within a JSP page.

Creating the Image Path Java Tag

The first step to creating a custom Java tag is to build a tag handler object that can be invoked by the Web container. To do so, the Java object must extend either `TagSupport` or `BodyTagSupport` from the `javax.servlet.jsp.tagext` API.

TagSupport provides single tag support where it does not need to retrieve display content from the Web page:

```
<javatag:mytag />
```

BodyTagSupport allows the tag library to interact with content from the Web page:

```
<javatag:mybodytag>some info to play with</javatag:mybodytag>
```

This Java tag accesses the string data bracketed by the opening and closing tags.

For the purpose of this development, you just need to extend the simpler TagSupport to demonstrate a custom Java tag.

```
package com.apress.ejsap;

import java.io.IOException;
import java.util.Hashtable;
import javax.servlet.jsp.*;
import javax.servlet.jsp.tagext.*;

public class ImageTag extends TagSupport {
...
}
```

TagSupport contains two essential methods that you can override to determine what functionality gets executed at a given time: doStartTag() and doEndTag(). Any code in the doStartTag() method executes immediately when the tag is encountered. As a result, you can complete any required preprocessing before you encounter a body element (if one is included). Because there is no body content in this example, the doStartTag() method simply needs to return the SKIP_BODY directive.

```
  public int doStartTag() throws JspTagException {
    return SKIP_BODY;
  }
```

As implied by the name, the doEndTag() method executes when the JSP page encounters the end of this tag. It is in this method where you will code the image path validation logic. Alternately, you could have moved this logic to the doStartTag() method and only returned an EVAL_PAGE directive to end processing in doEndTag().

```
  public int doEndTag() throws JspTagException {
    Hashtable tabHash = (Hashtable)
        pageContext.getSession().getAttribute("MATERIALDETAIL");
    try {
        if (tabHash.get("IMAGE") != null)
          pageContext.getOut().write((String)tabHash.get("IMAGE"));
        else
          pageContext.getOut().write("images/default.gif");
    } catch (IOException ex) {
      throw new JspTagException
            ("Unable to write ImageTag);
    }
    return EVAL_PAGE;
  }
```

The Java tag API provides access to various HTTP objects via the `PageContext` class. Notice that this method retrieves an instance of the `Hashtable` stored in the `HTTPSession` instance for a user. Recall that the `MaterialDetailAction` class stored this `Hashtable` with all the field results from both SAP and hsql.

This code simply checks for the existence of a key named "IMAGE" in `tabHash` and writes the value associated with it to the `PageContext` JSPWriter. If `tabHash` doesn't have a key with this name, the `doEndTag()` method writes a default file path to the JSP page.

Finally, the method returns an `EVAL_PAGE` directive to indicate that processing has completed and to return control back to the JSP page. Create a new Java file called `ImageTag.java` and add the following code to it:

```
package com.apress.ejsap;

import java.io.IOException;
import java.util.Hashtable;
import javax.servlet.jsp.*;
import javax.servlet.jsp.tagext.*;

public class ImageTag extends TagSupport {
  public int doStartTag() throws JspTagException {
    return SKIP_BODY;
  }
  public int doEndTag() throws JspTagException {
    Hashtable tabHash = (Hashtable)
        pageContext.getSession().getAttribute("MATERIALDETAIL");
```

```
      try {
          if (tabHash.get("IMAGE") != null)
             pageContext.getOut().write((String)tabHash.get("IMAGE"));
          else
             pageContext.getOut().write("images/default.gif");
    } catch (IOException ex) {
      throw new JspTagException
            ("Unable to write ImageTag);
    }
  return EVAL_PAGE;
  }
}
```

Save and compile this class in your `webapps/sap/WEB-INF/classes/com/apress/ejsap` directory. You are now ready to define the custom tag you want to deploy in the Tomcat server.

Deploying a Custom Java Tag

In order to deploy this Java tag in Tomcat, you need to define a Tag Library Descriptor (TLD) and save it in the `webapps/sap/WEB-INF/lib` directory.

To do so, create a new file called `imagetag.tld` and add the following XML to it:

```
<?xml version="1.0" encoding="ISO-8859-1" ?>
<!DOCTYPE taglib
      PUBLIC "-//Sun Microsystems, Inc.//DTD JSP Tag Library 1.1//EN"
      "http://java.sun.com/j2ee/dtds/web-jsptaglibrary_1_1.dtd">
<taglib>
  <tag>
    <name>image</name>
    <tagclass>com.apress.ejsap.ImageTag</tagclass>
    <info>Material image</info>
  </tag>
</taglib>
```

Table 9-2 lists the required XML tags and their individual functions.

Table 9-2. XML Tags in the Java Tag Library

TAG NAME	DESCRIPTION
`<taglib>`	Defines a new Java tag library
`<tag>`	Describes a single Java tag in the library
`<name>`	Defines the name of the tag to be referenced in a JSP page
`<tagclass>`	The fully qualified name of the Java tag class
`<info>`	Brief text description of this tag's purpose

You can now reference the tag library in a JSP page and use the Java tag to validate an image file path.

Using the Custom Tag in a JSP Page

Open `materialdetailResult.jsp` and add a new tag library declaration, like so:

```
<%@ page language="java" %>
<%@ page import="java.util.*" %>
<%@ taglib uri="/WEB-INF/lib/struts.tld" prefix="struts" %>
<%@ taglib uri="/WEB-INF/lib/struts-bean.tld" prefix="bean" %>
<%@ taglib uri="/WEB-INF/lib/struts-html.tld" prefix="html" %>
<%@ taglib uri="/WEB-INF/lib/imagetag.tld" prefix="mytaglib" %>
```

The `prefix` attribute allows you to declare how tags in this library should be referenced in the JSP page.

Modify the existing field image display to call the new Java tag, as shown here:

```
<TR>
<!-- Replace resultHash.get("IMAGE") with tag library -->
        <TD>MATERIAL IMAGE</TD>
        <TD><IMG SRC="<%= mytaglib:image %>"></TD>
</TR>
```

Save this page and restart the Tomcat application server. You may need to add some new material entries to the hsql database that do not have default entries in the `image` field. Of course, you could always tweak `SapMaterialAction` to programmatically match and remove the current default image path entries. Consider it a test of your Java/SQL skills.

Your Web application should now display whatever default image file you specified in the `ImageTag` class. To make it even easier to modify, you could move the string into an external properties file and retrieve it using a `ResourceBundle`. See Chapter 5 for a refresher course.

Summary

This final chapter presented some advanced programming techniques specifically related to Java programming with JCo. At this point, you should be comfortable developing custom Java applications for SAP, using both inbound and outbound programming techniques.

JCo connection pools allow you to provide generic SAP access to a high number of users without fear of overloading the R/3 application server or misusing system resources. Connection pools are a required mechanism in any Web application that is destined for widespread usage across the Internet.

The JCo server API extends the power and flexibility of objects built in Java to new and existing ABAP programs within SAP. JCo servers can be used to provide outbound communication between SAP and non-SAP systems, which is especially critical as your company's system integration needs grow.

Java tag libraries enable you to bridge the gap between Java programmers and Web designers. By offering a simplified set of HTML-style tags to encompass complex Java functionality, you empower your user interface designers with an unprecedented level of interaction with backend systems like SAP.

APPENDIX

Alternate RFC Development in SAP

MUCH OF THE DEVELOPMENT IN this book has focused on several specific SAP BAPIs that are delivered in most standard R/3 implementations. For instance, the customer check password interface comes with the Sales and Distribution (SD) module, and the material BAPIs come with the Materials Management (MM) module. However, there is a chance that your company did not implement these modules as part of its SAP rollout. If that is the case, this appendix will help you define some custom interfaces, internal data structures, and tables to support the example code in this book.

So how can the development outlined in this book apply to custom Remote Function Call (RFC) interfaces? This appendix shows you how to build and extend a custom SAP RFC for use within your JCo applications. Chapter 5 introduced the `InterfaceCaller` class, which allowed you to effectively abstract the native JCo API calls from the rest of the Web application. For this appendix, you will only need to modify this class to support your custom interfaces; the rest of the application will function transparently. Likewise, you can quickly update the command line application outlined in Chapter 4 so that it deals with the custom material list RFC developed in this appendix.

Mapping BAPIs to Custom RFCs

The application in this book uses three different SAP BAPIs:

- BAPI_CUSTOMER_CHECKPASSWORD

- BAPI_MATERIAL_GETLIST

- BAPI_MATERIAL_GETDETAIL

This section details how to build custom RFC equivalents for the material BAPIs and where to find an appropriate alternative for the check password BAPI.

Appendix

Finding an Alternate Check Password BAPI

Because BAPI_CUSTOMER_CHECKPASSWORD relies on SAP for password authentication, you would find it difficult to build a custom replacement. However, regardless of the SAP release or the functional modules implemented by your company, you should be able to find an equivalent to BAPI_CUSTOMER_CHECKPASSWORD. In order to apply SAP Internet user authentication, you must use a BAPI delivered in your R/3 implementation.

In the SAP Function Builder (SE37) look for one of the following BAPIs:

- BAPI_EMPLOYEE_CHECKPASSWORD

- BAPI_DEBTOR_CHECKPASSWORD

- BAPI_CREDITOR_CHECKPASSWORD

- BAPI_VENDOR_CHECKPASSWORD

- BAPI_APPLICANT_CHECKPASSWORD

- BAPI_ATTENDEE_CHECKPASSWORD

If you are starting to sense a trend in the naming convention for this particular BAPI, then you are on the right track. Should you be unable to track down any of these BAPIs, do a search in the Function Builder for the string "BAPI_*_CHECKPASSWORD". Choose from the list and create an appropriate master data record according to the BAPI you selected. For example, in order to use the vendor check password BAPI, you must first create a vendor record in the SAP system.

You will also need an Internet user to authenticate with this BAPI. To obtain one, navigate to the Internet User facility (SU05) or the standard User Maintenance (SU01) for SAP release 6.2 and higher. Enter the ID of the record you created in Chapter 6 and click the Select Options button (F4) next to the Type field. You should see a screen similar to Figure A-1 in which you have the option of choosing between different user types.

Based on the type of partner record you created (customer, vendor, employee, and so on), select the appropriate user type and create an Internet user. Initialize the user and set its password to something that you will remember later on. Because each check password BAPI uses the same interface, you simply need to update InterfaceCaller with the new BAPI name in the checkPassword() method and update the name of the user field.

Alternate RFC Development in SAP

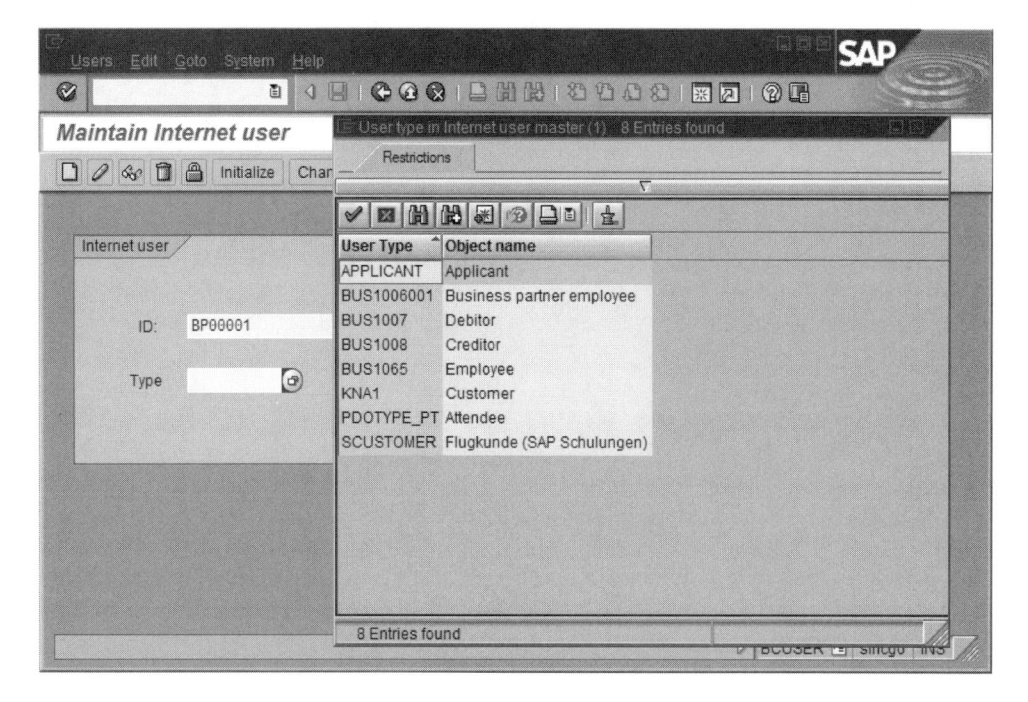

Figure A-1. Selecting a user type for the Internet user

Building a Material List RFC

The first step you need to take to create a material list RFC is to define a custom table in SAP that will act as both a data store and a structure interface. This table needs to contain the following fields:

MATERIAL: A unique material identifier

MATL_DESC: The material description

Because the display requirements in the Web application are fairly basic, defining a table with only these two fields will suffice. You can also extend this table to include additional fields to display in the Web browser, but these are based on the development outlined in previous chapters.

From the ABAP Dictionary (SE11), perform the following steps:

1. Create a new table called **ZMATERIALS.**

2. Select "C" as the Delivery Class.

3. Ensure that full display/maintenance is allowed.

4. Navigate to the Fields tab and add the fields as new entries.

Appendix

Figure A-2 depicts the table maintenance screen with suggested data element values for each field. Be sure to check the Key check box for the MATERIAL field in order to set it to the primary key in this table.

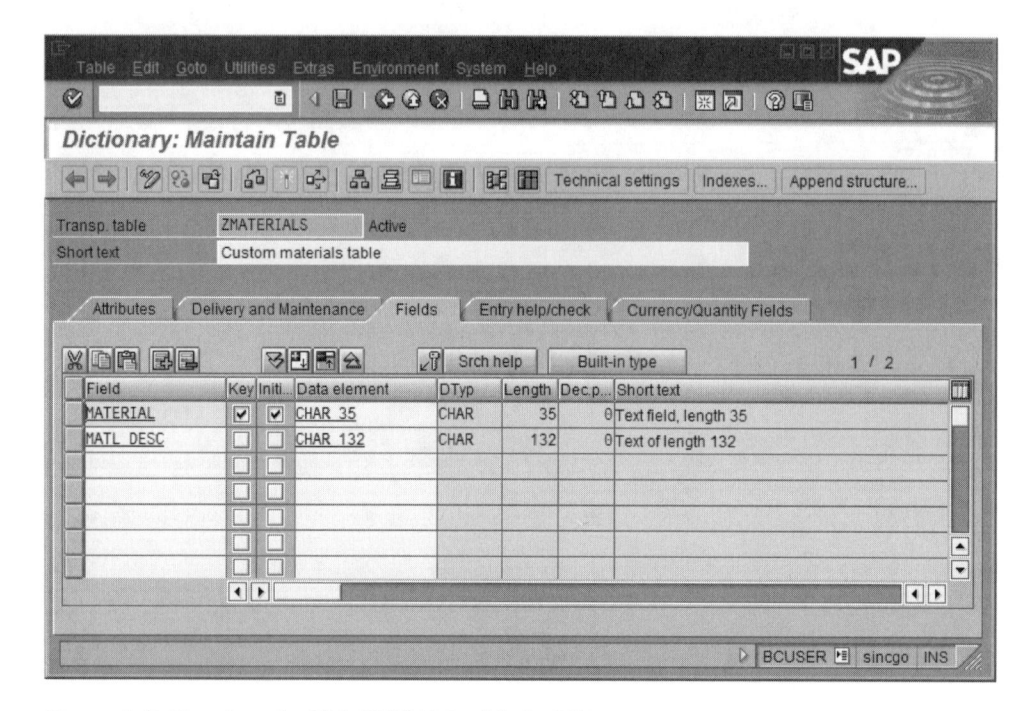

Figure A-2. Creating the ZMATERIALS table in SAP

Click the Technical Settings button, and then enter **USER** as the Data class and **3** as the Size category. Figure A-3 depicts the Technical settings screen.

Save and activate this table; then select Utilities ➤ Table Contents ➤ Create Entries from the SAP file menu. Enter **MATERIAL1** in the MATERIAL field and **MATERIAL1 DESCRIPTION** in the MATL_DESC field (feel free to be more creative in your material names and description), then save the record (Ctrl-S). Repeat this process with at least ten different material numbers so that you have a good selection of materials to display in the Web application.

With the table created and populated, you are ready to build the custom RFC. Navigate to the Function Builder and create a new function called Z_RFC_MATERIAL_GETLIST. In the Attributes tab, select Remote-Enabled Module under Processing type. Click the Import tab; enter **MATERIAL** as the Parameter name, **LIKE** as the Type spec, and **ZMATERIALS-MATERIAL** as the Reference type; and check the Pass Value flag. Click the Tables tab and enter **MATNRLIST** as the Parameter name, **LIKE** as the Type spec, and "**ZMATERIALS**"\ as the Reference type. When you save and activate the RFC, your screen should look like Figure A-4.

300

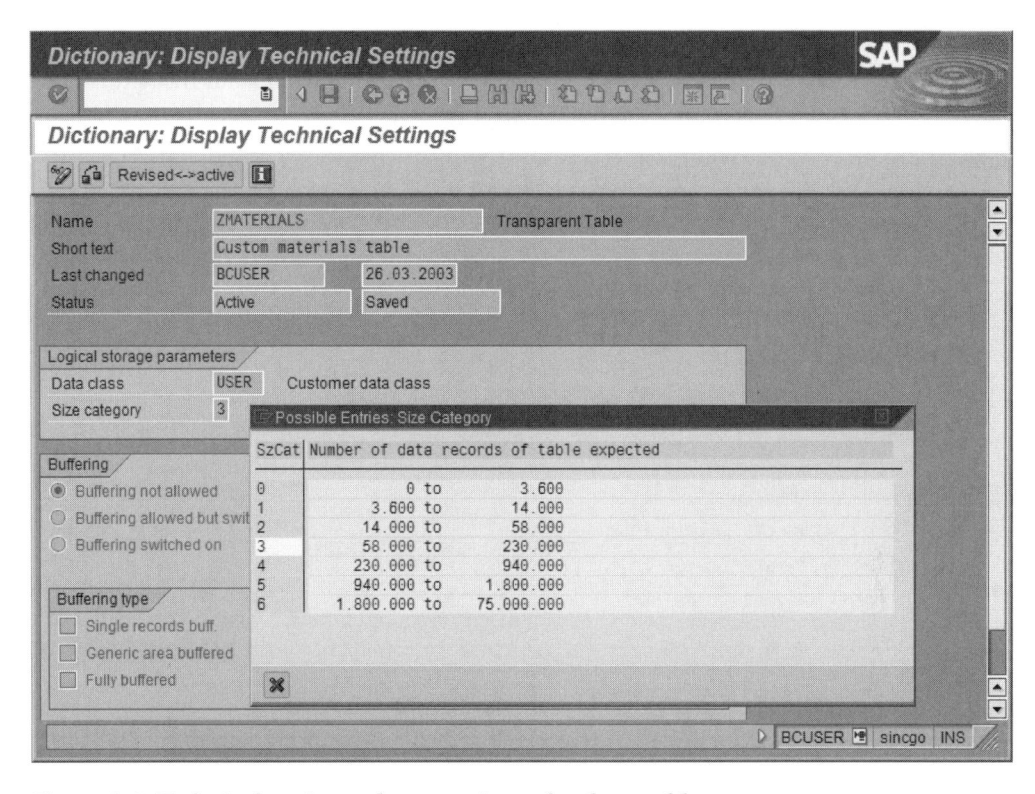

Figure A-3. Technical settings when creating a database table

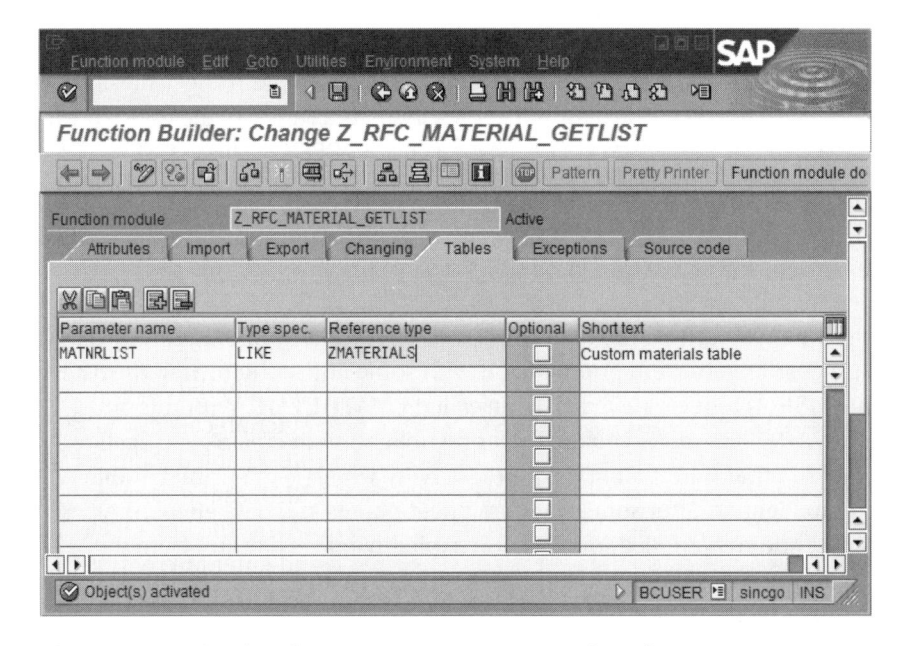

Figure A-4. Activating the Z_RFC_MATERIAL_GETLIST *interface*

301

The last step is to define source code that will return the appropriate table rows based on the value you passed in the MATERIAL field. To do so, click the Source code tab and add the following code:

```
FUNCTION Z_RFC_MATERIAL_GETLIST.
*"----------------------------------------------------------------------
*"*"Local interface:
*"  IMPORTING
*"     VALUE(MATERIAL) LIKE   ZMATERIALS-MATERIAL
*"  TABLES
*"      MATNRLIST STRUCTURE   ZMATERIALS
*"----------------------------------------------------------------------
data wa_zmat like line of MATNRLIST.
refresh matnrlist.
select * from ZMATERIALS into wa_zmat.
  if wa_zmat-material ca MATERIAL.
    append wa_zmat to MATNRLIST.
  endif.
endselect.
ENDFUNCTION.
```

Granted, this is not the prettiest ABAP code ever written, nor by any means is it the most efficient. However, it will serve the purpose at hand—namely to retrieve a list of all table rows that match the given wildcard search parameter. Save and activate the RFC then test it in the Function Builder.

Go to Function Module ➤ Test ➤ Test Function Module and enter a whole or partial material number in the MATERIAL field. Execute the RFC and check the entries in the MATNRLIST table that gets returned. If the table lists a subset of the values previously entered in the ZMATERIALS table, then your custom RFC is a success.

Building a Material Detail RFC

Similar to what you did for the Material List RFC, you start building this RFC by defining a custom table and populating it with some entries. Return to the ABAP Dictionary (SE11) and create a new table called **ZMATDETAIL**. With this table, unlike the ZMATERIALS table, you are under no obligation to create specifically named fields, other than that of the MATERIAL field, which is the primary table key. Refer to Figure A-5 for some suggested field names and data element types.

Because the Web application does not explicitly retrieve values from the Hashtable based on field names, you are free to use whatever naming convention strikes your fancy.

Alternate RFC Development in SAP

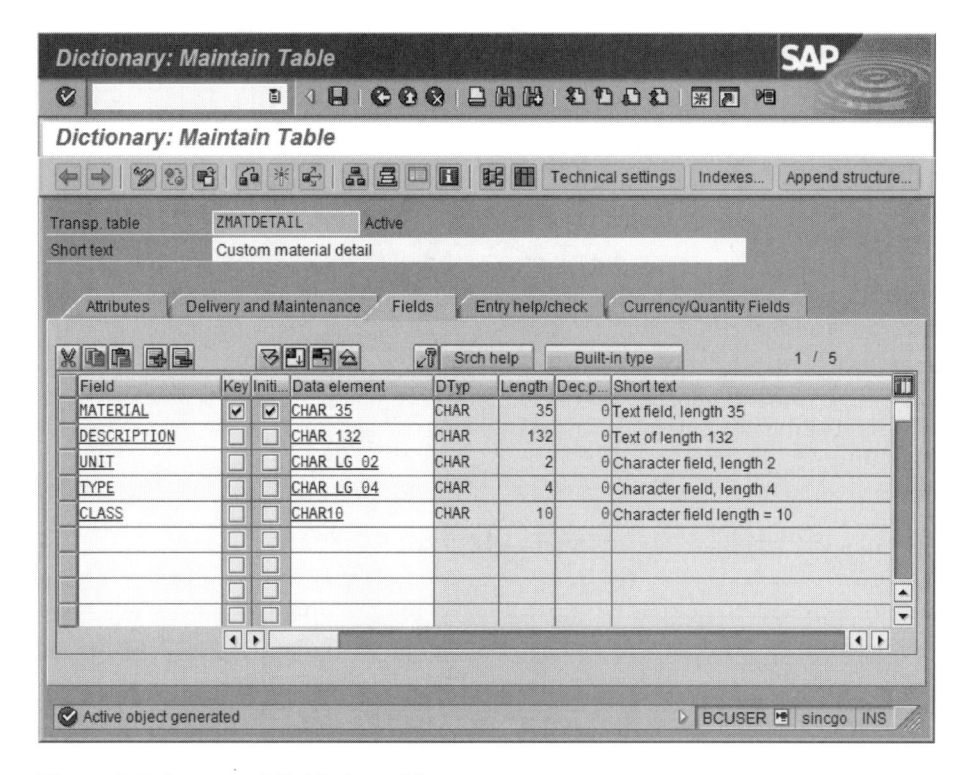

Figure A-5. Suggested fields for table ZMATDETAIL

Enter the same technical settings as you did for the ZMATERIALS table (see Figure A-3). Save and activate this table, and then populate table entries as you did for ZMATERIALS. Make sure that you use the same material names in the MATERIAL field as you used to populate the ZMATERIALS table. Doing so allows your Web application to look up a detail record based on the material selected from the material list lookup.

In the Function Builder, create a new function called **Z_RFC_MATERIAL_ GETDETAIL** and set it to Remotely Enabled in the Attributes tab. In the Import tab, create an entry with **MATERIAL** as Parameter name, **LIKE** as the Type spec, and **ZMATDETAIL-MATERIAL** as the Reference type, and then check the Pass Value field.

Unlike Z_RFC_MATERIAL_GETLIST, this new RFC will return a structure rather than a table. Click the Export tab and define a new entry with **MATERIAL_ GENERAL_DATA** as Parameter name, **LIKE** as the Type spec, and **ZMATDETAIL** as the Reference type, and then check the Pass Value field. Save and activate the function to ensure that the import/export parameters have been set correctly.

Finally, click the Source Code tab and enter the following code:

Appendix

```
FUNCTION Z_RFC_MATERIAL_GETDETAIL.
clear MATERIAL_GENERAL_DATA.
select single * from ZMATDETAIL into MATERIAL_GENERAL_DATA
       where MATERIAL = MATERIAL.
ENDFUNCTION.
```

Once again, this is ugly, but functional, ABAP code. Save and activate this function, then execute it in the Function Builder as you did before. This time, enter a whole material number. The function should return a structure that contains a single record from the ZMATDETAIL table.

The next section details modifications you can make to your InterfaceCaller class so that the Web application will run using these new, custom RFCs.

Updating the InterfaceCaller Class

With one exception, updating InterfaceCaller requires that you merely swap out the BAPI names being used in each method and replace them with the names of your custom RFCs.

> **NOTE** *The following code assumes that you have already added the connection pooling detailed in Chapter 9. If you haven't, simply use the connection methodology outlined in Chapter 5 for the* InterfaceCaller *class.*

Here is the updated InterfaceCaller class:

```
package com.apress.ejsap;

import com.sap.mw.jco.*;
import java.util.Hashtable;
import java.util.Properties;
import java.io.*;
public class InterfaceCaller {
  private JCO.Client aConnection;
  private IRepository aRepository;
  private final String JCO_POOL = "myPool";
  public InterfaceCaller() {
    createConnectionPool();
    retrieveRepository();
  }
```

```java
   public Hashtable getMaterialDetail(String material) {
      aConnection = JCO.getClient(JCO_POOL);
// Changed to reflect new RFC name
      JCO.Function function = getFunction("Z_RFC_MATERIAL_GETDETAIL");
      JCO.ParameterList listParams = function.getImportParameterList();
      listParams.setValue(material, "MATERIAL");
      aConnection.execute(function);
      JCO.releaseClient(aConnection);
      JCO.ParameterList resultParams = function.getExportParameterList();
      JCO.Structure fieldList = resultParams.getStructure("MATERIAL_GENERAL_DATA");
      Hashtable returnHash = new Hashtable();
      if (fieldList.getFieldCount() > 0) {
         for (JCO.FieldIterator fI = fieldList.fields(); fI.hasMoreElements();) {
            JCO.Field tabField = fI.nextField();
            returnHash.put(tabField.getName(), tabField.getString());
         }
      }
      return returnHash;
   }
   public Hashtable getMaterialList(String searchParam) {
      aConnection = JCO.getClient(JCO_POOL);
// Changed to reflect new RFC name
      JCO.Function function = getFunction("Z_RFC_MATERIAL_GETLIST");
/* Note that the new RFC does not require an inbound table
 * so this code has been commented out and can be removed
 *    JCO.ParameterList tabParams = function.getTableParameterList();
 *    JCO.Table materials = tabParams.getTable("MATNRSELECTION");
 *    materials.appendRow();
 *    materials.setRow(0);
 *    materials.setValue("I", "SIGN");
 *    materials.setValue("CP", "OPTION");
 *    materials.setValue(searchParam, "MATNR_LOW");
*/
// This is the new single input parameter
      JCO.ParameterList listParams = function.getImportParameterList();
      listParams.setValue(searchParam, "MATERIAL");
      aConnection.execute(function);
      JCO.releaseClient(aConnection);
      JCO.ParameterList resultParams = function.getExportParameterList();
      JCO.Table materialList =
           function.getTableParameterList().getTable("MATNRLIST");
      Hashtable returnHash = new Hashtable();
      Hashtable rowHash = new Hashtable();
      int i = 0;
```

Appendix

```java
        if (materialList.getNumRows() > 0) {
          do {
            for (JCO.FieldIterator fI = materialList.fields();
                fI.hasMoreElements();)
              {
                JCO.Field tabField = fI.nextField();
                rowHash.put(tabField.getName(),tabField.getString());
            }
                returnHash.put("line" + i, rowHash);
                rowHash = new Hashtable();
                i++;
            }
            while(materialList.nextRow() == true);
        } else {
            System.out.println("Sorry, couldn't find any materials");
        }
        return returnHash;
      }
      public Hashtable checkPassword(String username, String password) {
        aConnection = JCO.getClient(JCO_POOL);
// Be sure to change the name to reflect your chosen BAPI
        JCO.Function function = getFunction("BAPI_XXXXXXX_CHECKPASSWORD");
        JCO.ParameterList listParams = function.getImportParameterList();
// Update the username field based on field name in new BAPI
        listParams.setValue(username, "XXXXXXXXX");
        listParams.setValue(password, "PASSWORD");
        aConnection.execute(function);
        JCO.releaseClient(function);
        JCO.ParameterList resultParams = function.getExportParameterList();
        Hashtable returnHash = new Hashtable();
        returnHash.put("RETURN.TYPE",extractField("RETURN","TYPE",resultParams));
        returnHash.put("RETURN.CODE",extractField("RETURN","CODE",resultParams));
        returnHash.put("RETURN.MESSAGE",
                       extractField("RETURN","MESSAGE",resultParams));
        return returnHash;
      }
      catch (Exception e) {
        System.out.println("failed to retrieve serial file");
        return null;
      }
    }
    public String extractField(String structure,String field,
                                    JCO.ParameterList parameterList) {
        return ((JCO.Structure)parameterList.getValue(structure)).getString(field);
    }
```

```java
    public JCO.Function getFunction(String name) {
       try {
             return
 aRepository.getFunctionTemplate(name.toUpperCase()).getFunction();
       }
       catch (Exception ex) {}
          return null;
       }
 private void createConnectionPool() {
       Properties sapData = new Properties();
       try {
          FileInputStream in = new FileInputStream("sapdata.properties");
          sapData.load(in);
          in.close();
       } catch (Exception ex) {
          ex.printStackTrace();
       }
       JCO.Pool connPool = JCO.getClientPoolManager().getPool(JCO_POOL);
       if (connPool == null) {
          JCO.addClientPool(JCO_POOL,
                            5,
                            sapData);
       }
    }
 private void retrieveRepository() {
    try {
       aConnection = JCO.getClient(JCO_POOL);
       aRepository = new JCO.Repository("SAPRep", aConnection);
       }
       catch (Exception ex) {
          System.out.println("Failed to retrieve SAP repository");
       }
       JCO.releaseClient(aConnection);
    }
 }
```

Notice that the commented lines indicate where the required changes must take place. Update your existing InterfaceCaller with these changes to ensure that you are progressing through the steps outlined in the book. The major modification is in the getMaterialList() method, where you are no longer passing data to the RFC via a table. The material number is now set as a single input field in the import parameters. Likewise, be sure to change the user field name in checkPassword() to reflect the field name required in your chosen check password BAPI.

Appendix

This completes the alternate approach to RFC development in SAP. Although not a requirement for all readers, it does offer some useful insight into enabling access to custom ABAP programs from Java. Hopefully, this will give you a clearer picture regarding the interaction between JCo and SAP, as well as a better understanding of how SAP fields, structures, and tables map to JCo Java objects.

Index

Symbols

! (exclamation point), preceding Java expressions with, 154, 213
" " (double quotes), using with SQL statements, 254
"..." (double quotes), use of, 64, 66
%> scriptlet end tag, example of, 146
*/ (asterisk-slash), meaning of, 63
. (period), use of, 97
// (double-slash), meaning of, 63
/* (slash-asterisk), meaning of, 63
<%...%> scriptlet blocks, using, 147
<%=...%> JSP tags, using, 141
<%@ page...%> JSP tags, using, 141
= (equal) sign, use of, 96, 98
\ (backslash) in Java, escaping characters with, 76, 122
{...} (curly brackets), use of, 62
~ (tilde), appearance in hsql databases, 254

A

ABAP (Advanced Business Application Programming) language, limitations of, 5
ABAP Workbench
  comparing development using MVC pattern to, 177–178
  creating ZJCO_CLIENT application in, 289
abstraction, role in OOP, 25
Action classes
  adding database call to, 265–267
  building for Struts login application, 209–215
  role in Struts model layer, 186–187
  in Struts, 261
<action> tags, using with Struts login application, 217
Actional's Control Broker, Web address for, 14
ActionError class, creating instance of using validate() method, 201–202
ActionErrors class, using with Struts login application, 212–213
ActionForm beans, using with Struts, 196–197
ActionForward instances, using with Struts login application, 213–214
ActionListener interface
  interacting with users by means of, 118–120
  using with MaterialGui class, 116
ActionMappings
  configuring for Struts login application, 230–231
  defining URI paths with, 184–185
ActionServlets
  mapping in Struts, 191–193
  role in Struts Controller, 184, 186
  using with Struts login application, 212
addClientPool() method, specifying parameters sent in, 274
ALTER TABLE statements in SQL, description of, 235–236
append(String text) method of JText Area class, description of, 123
applet component libraries, benefits of, 30
applets, disadvantages of, 20
application libraries in Java, components of, 82
application servers
  configuring for JCo system resources, 168–169
  examining, 134–135
  use of, 32–34
ApplicationResources file
  error message in, 221
  using with Struts login application, 201–203, 205–206, 213, 223, 228
ApplicationResources.properties file, creating for Struts login application, 202
applications, deploying with Java, 27–33
asterisk-slash (*/), meaning of, 63
authenticating with SAP, 148–153
autoexec.bat file, locating, 53

B

backslash (\) in Java, escaping characters with, 76, 122
BAPI (Business Application Programming Interface)
  introduction of, 6
  role in authenticating users with SAP, 148
  using with JCo, 67–69

309

Index

BAPI calls, indicating status of, 155
BAPI metadata interface, structures and fields of, 58–59
BC (Business Connector) tool
    features of, 9–10
    Web address for, 10
BETWEEN clause, using with SQL SELECT queries, 264
bicycle metaphor in OOP, explanation of, 37–40
Bicycle superclass, purpose of, 39–40
binaries, placing in Java PATH statements, 88
black box metaphor, using in OOP, 36–37
buttons, using in GUIs, 114
bytecode, explanation of, 56

C

C API (application programming interface), development of, 13–14
casting objects, explanation of, 159
character display, controlling with JTextArea class, 122–124
checkPassword() method
    adding to InterfaceCaller class, 148–149
    adding to loginResult.jsp, 153–154
CHECKPOINT command, using with hsql databases, 255
class hierarchies in Java, format of, 82
class variables, using in JCo sample application, 79
classes, effect of extending other classes with, 284
CLASSPATH, setting properly in Java applications, 88
client/server architecture, transition to, 3, 134
clustering in Java application server, explanation of, 31
code as black box, using as metaphor in OOP, 36–37
COM (Component Object Model), development of, 14
COM/DCOM bridge, overview of, 14–16
COM objects, use of, 14
comments, formatting with JCo, 63
COMMIT statements in SQL, description of, 235–236
Component Connector, introduction of, 15
conf directory, contents of, 137
configuration files
    internationalizing Java applications by means of, 92–96
    overview of, 92
    using with resource bundles, 96–99
connection pools. *See* JCo connection pools
containsKey(key) method of Hashtable class, description of, 103
contains(value) method of Hashtable class, description of, 103
controller component of MVC pattern, functionality of, 177, 179
controller components of objects, explanation of, 195
cookies, use by ITS, 8
CORBA (Common Object Request Broker Architecture) and Java RFC Server, overview of, 12–14
CREATE statements in SQL, example of, 253
CREATE TABLE statements in SQL
    description of, 235–236
    example of, 248
createConnection() method, adding to JCo sample application, 83–84
CRM (Customer Relationship Management) and Internet sales, overview of, 11
curly brackets ({}), use of, 62
custom Java tags
    creating Image Path, 291–294
    deploying, 294–295
    guidelines for, 290–291
    using in JSP pages, 295–296
customer login JSP, building, 153–156

D

database applications, advisory about high-level traffic in, 261
database classes, executing, 251–253
Database Connector Server JDBC drivers, features of, 239
database connections, advisory about implementation of, 45
database tables. *See also* tables
    adding records to, 248–249
    catching exceptions and closing connection in, 249–252
    creating and deleting, 247–248
    retrieving records from, 249
DatabaseManager class, displaying Connect screen for, 242
databases
    adding command line execution to, 247
    building quickly with hsql (Hypersonic SQL), 253

310

Index

connecting to, 245–247
populating, 244–253
date.jsp file, creating and saving, 140
DCOM Component Connector,
    introduction of, 15
DCOM (Distributed Component Object
    Model), features of, 15
DELETE FROM statements in SQL,
    description of, 235–236
design patterns
    building object systems with, 43–47
    Façade pattern, 46–47
    MVC (Model-View-Controller)
        pattern, 174–181
    power of, 44–45
    Singleton pattern, 45–46
desktop deployment of Java
    overview of, 28
    versus server-side, 29–30
distributed applications
    role in CORBA, 12
    transactions in, 15
DLL files for JCo, copying into system
    directory, 53–54
double quotes (" "), using with SQL
    statements, 254
double quotes ("..."), use of, 64, 66
double-slash (//), meaning of, 63
do...while loops, using with JCo, 74, 108
dressmaker's design pattern,
    explanation of, 44

E

Eclipse, benefits of, 50–51
EDI (Electronic Data Exchange),
    costliness of, 9
elements() method of Hashtable class,
    description of, 103
else conditions, defining in JSP pages,
    146–147
else...if blocks
    role in retrieving records from
        database tables, 249
    using with hsql databases, 258
Enterprise Java platform
    evolution of, 20–21
    flexibility, scalability, and standards-
        based features of, 22–23
    networking a programming
        language, 18–20
enumerators, controlling in Java, 75
equal (=) sign, use of, 96, 98
ERP (Enterprise Resource Planning) and
    SAP, overview of, 2–6
escape characters, implementing in
    Java, 76, 122

exclamation point (!), preceding Java
    expressions with, 154, 213
expressions
    preceding with exclamation point (!),
        154
    writing in Java, 108
ex.printStackTrace() statement in JCo,
    use of, 65

F

Façade pattern, hiding complex object
    interfaces with, 46–47
final variables, defining with JCo, 63–64
finally clauses, using with database
    tables, 250
FirstPerson company, origin of, 19
for loops
    using with JCo, 74–75
    using with material list lookup, 162
    using with rowHash Hashtables, 121
form fields, creating for Struts login
    application, 206
Function Builder, displaying Attributes
    tab in, 282

G

garbage collection in Java, explanation
    of, 26
get() methods, implementing with
    LoginForm beans, 196–199
get(key) method of Hashtable class,
    description of, 103
getMaterialList() method
    adding JCo logic to, 105–112
    example of, 111–112
    implementing in Java classes,
        102–104
getString() method, using with resource
    bundles, 98
GUI applications, components of, 114
GUI components, initializing, 124
GUI windowing components, overview
    of, 114–115
GUIs (graphical user interfaces). *See*
    Java GUI for SAP

H

Half and Half JDBC drivers, features of,
    238
handheld deployment of Java, overview
    of, 28
handRequest() method, using with JCo
    server, 284–285
HashMaps, understanding, 103

Index

Hashtables
  ordering data in, 121
  populating, 107
  populating data in when using GUIs, 120–122
  role in material list lookup, 162
  use of, 103–104
HelloWorld example, compiling for use with JCo, 56
hsql database connectivity, encapsulating, 262–265
hsql database functionality, adding to Struts login application, 262
HSQL Database Manager GUI
  displaying, 242
  table tree structure of, 242
hsql databases
  adding columns to, 255–257
  building from text files, 253–254
  building quickly, 253
  creating plain text files for, 254
  loading from SAP, 255–259
  starting, 252
  updating text file tables in, 255
hsqldb (Hypersonic SQL Database) engine, deploying, 240–244
HTML directives, replacing in Struts login application, 204
HTML forms, retrieving data with, 141–144
HTML scripting tags, integrating Java syntax with, 30
HTML tags, combining in JSP pages, 146
<html:base/> tag, use of, 204
<html:html> tag, format of, 204
HTTP requests, role in Java Servlet Architecture, 182–183
HTTP sessions, purpose of, 156–157
HTTP Web session data, displaying, 144–147
HttpServlet class, implementing, 166
HttpServletRequest object, features of, 182–183
HttpSession class, use of, 159
HttpSession objects
  advisory about, 157
  functionality of, 183
  using with Struts login application, 213–214
Hypersonic SQL (hsqldb) Database engine, deploying, 240–244

I

IDEs (integrated development environments), design criteria for, 50
IDL (Interface Definition Language) interface, role in CORBA, 13
if statements, role in creating database tables, 247–248
if...else blocks
  in materialList.jsp file, 160–161
  using with JCo, 70
  using with JSP pages, 146
IIOP (Internet Interoperability Protocol), role in CORBA, 13
image files, updating materials database with, 259
image lookup and rendering through Web server, diagram of, 260–261
Image Path custom Java tag, creating, 291–294
ImageTag.java file, creating, 293–294
imagetag.tld file, creating for custom Java tag, 294–295
inheritance, expanding objects by means of, 39–40
init() methods of servlets, calling, 167
INSERT statements in SQL
  description of, 235–236
  example of, 242, 249
insert(String text, int pos) method of JText Area class, description of, 123
instances, creating from objects in OOP, 38–39
instantiation in OOP, explanation of, 38
InterfaceCaller.java class
  adding checkPassword() method to, 148–149
  adding getMaterialList() method to, 102–104
  changes made to, 108–111, 149–152
  creating for object-level access, 100–101
  implementing getMaterialDetail() method in, 219–220
  loading into ServletContext, 167
  modifying for use with JCo connection pools, 276–279
internationalization
  of Java applications, 92–96
  of Struts login application, 206
Internet Sales and SAP CRM, overview of, 11
isEmpty() method of Hashtable class, description of, 103
ISO language codes, Web address for, 95
iterators, controlling in Java, 75
ITS (Internet Transaction Server)
  cookies used by, 8
  overview of, 7–9

Index

J

J2EE (Java 2 Platform, Enterprise Edition)
    features of, 21
    versus .NET, 33
    use of HTTP sessions by, 156–157
J2EE SDK, downloading, 166
J2ME (Java 2, Micro Edition), features of, 21
J2SE (Java 2 Platform, Standard Edition), features of, 21
Java application server
    clustering in, 31
    load balancing in, 31
    overview of, 31–33
    transaction monitoring in, 31
Java applications
    deploying over Web, 29–31
    implementing configuration files for, 98
    internationalizing, 92–96
    setting CLASSPATH properly in, 88
Java classes, creating for object-level access, 100–102
Java Collections Framework, Web address for, 103
Java development types
    desktop deployment, 28
    handheld deployment, 28
    server-side deployment, 29
Java executable class, example of, 61
Java GUI for SAP
    building, 115–130
    code for, 128–130
    creating MaterialGui class for, 115–118
    defining look and feel of, 118
    developing, 112–130
    displaying information in using JTextArea, 122–124
    and populating data in Hashtables, 120–122
    using ActionListeners with, 118–120
Java Hashtables, use of, 103–104
Java IDEs (integrated development environments)
    components of, 51–52
    overview of, 50–52
    testing, 54–57
Java language
    application libraries in, 82
    deploying applications with, 27–33
    development of, 19
    escape characters used by, 76
    essentials for SAP, 24–27
    evolution and philosophy behind, 20–21
    fitting into SAP, 21–23
    garbage collection in, 26
    object-oriented basics of, 24–26
    and OOP (object-oriented programming), 24–26
    power of using OOP with, 81
    representing tables in, 75
    writing expressions in, 108
Java Object superclass, role in inheritance, 39
Java objects. *See also* objects in OOP
    calling from within SAP, 279–290
    instantiating on server startup, 165–166
Java programming techniques
    design and development in OOP environments, 26
    exploring key Internet and Web technologies, 27
    integrating databases, 27
Java RFC Server, development of, 13–14
Java Servlet Architecture, role of HTTP requests in, 182–183
Java servlet, example of, 167
Java servlet specification, explanation of, 165
Java session class, location of, 157
Java Swing
    application components, 117
    nesting panels in, 125
    Web address for, 114
Java syntax
    integrating with HTML scripting tags, 30
    using with JCo, 61–62
Java tag directives, formatting, 204
Java tag libraries, customizing, 290–296
Java tags, customizing, 188–189
Java UI variables, initializing, 126
Java variables, defining with JCo, 63–64
javac.exe command line tool, purpose of, 56
Javadoc mechanism, purpose of, 37–38
java.exe command line tool, purpose of, 56
java.sql API, populating databases with, 244–253
java.sql package in JDBC 3.0 API, features of, 239
javax.sql package in JDBC 3.0 API, features of, 240
JCo API, implementing class-server with, 280
JCo classes, using with SAP and MVC pattern, 180
JCo connection pools
    diagram of, 273
    functionality of, 273

313

Index

implementing, 273, 274
overview of, 272–279
JCo (Java Connector)
   adding data to SAP function calls with, 68–79
   authentication in, 273–274
   connecting to SAP by means of, 57–60, 64–65
   creating JCO repository with, 58
   defining Java variables with, 63–64
   developing with, 62–79
   executing call to SAP with, 60
   initializing RFC connection with, 58
   loading, 53–54
   populating metadata structures with, 60
   reading SAP return structure with, 60
   retrieving functions from repository with, 58–59
   retrieving RFC metadata interface with, 66–68
   using basic Java code syntax with, 61–62
JCo libraries
   advisory about, 57
   deploying when authenticating users, 153
JCo logic, adding to getMaterialList() method, 105–112
JCo sample application
   adding data to SAP function calls with, 68–79
   building methods in, 82–88
   cleaning up, 79–88
   compiling, 77
   completing, 77–79
   connecting to SAP, 64–65
   defining variables in, 63–64
   employing variables in, 79–82
   enhanced version of, 86–88
   installing SAP repository for, 66
   retrieving RFC metadata interface with, 66–68
   specifying search parameters in, 77
   using basic Java syntax with, 61–62
JCo server
   building, 283–285
   calling from inside SAP, 288–290
   communication diagram of, 280
   executing, 286–288
   results returned from call to, 290
   testing connection to SAP, 289
JCo system resources
   configuring application server for, 168–169
   optimizing performance with ServletContext class, 164–168
   sharing, 164–171
   using servlet context in JSP pages, 169–171
JCO.Client variables, defining with JCo, 63–64
JCO.Exception instances, throwing, 65
JCO.Function class
   instantiating, 67
   objects in, 71
JCO.ParameterList object, creating instance of, 69, 72
JCO.Repository, retrieving from SAP, 66, 275–276
JCO.Server class, extending, 283
JCP (Java Community Process), purpose of, 23
JDBC API, introduction of, 237
JDBC architecture, diagram of, 237
JDBC connector, example of, 252–253
JDBC drivers, Types 1-4 of, 238–239
JDBC (Java Database Connectivity)
   overview of, 236–237
   SQL statements used with, 234–236
JDBC-ODBC Bridge drivers, features of, 238
JDBC packages, overview of, 239–240
JFC (Java Foundation Classes), purpose of, 113
JFrame class, housing visual components with, 124–130
JLF (Java Look and Feel), example of, 118
JSDK (Java Software Development Kit), downloading and installing, 52
.jsp extension, significance of, 140
JSP pages
   building customer login example, 153–156
   building for Struts login application, 222–227
   combining HTML tags in, 146
   creating for Tomcat sample application, 139–140
   displaying material detail results in, 225–226
   displaying material image in, 267–269
   displaying stored HTTP session data in, 144–147
   features of, 30
   saplogin.jsp, 203
   taking input from users by means of, 143
   using custom Java tags in, 295–296
   using customized Java tags in, 188–189
   using servlet context in, 169–171

Index

JSP tags, using with Tomcat sample application, 140–141
JSRs (Java Specification Requests), purpose of, 23
JSTL (JavaServerPage Standard Tag Library), role in Struts view layer, 187
JTextArea class
  methods of, 123
  using in GUIs, 122–124
JVM (Java Virtual Machine)
  advisory about loading data into, 275
  objects in, 155–156
  optimized deployment of components in, 171
  role in running Java applications, 27–28

K

keys() method of Hashtable class, description of, 103

L

load balancing in Java application server, explanation of, 31
local variables, using in JCo sample application, 79
localhost in URLs
  advisory about, 142
  meaning of, 137
login screens
  displaying session data through, 147
  example of, 144
login view, designing for Struts login application, 203–209
LoginAction.java class, creating for Struts application, 209–211, 214–215
LoginForm beans
  implementing get() and set() methods with, 196–199
  overriding validate() methods with, 199–200
LoginForm class, code for, 200–201
login.jsp file, copying, 142
loginResult.jsp
  example of, 153–154
  modifying, 157–158
  modifying for use with servlet context in JSP pages, 169

M

mainframes, transition to servers, 3–4
Material Detail results screen, displaying, 227
material image, displaying in JSP page, 267–269
material list lookup, adding to Tomcat sample application, 160–163
material list, retrieving from SAP system, 225
Material Search Web page, displaying, 223
MaterialAction.java class, creating for Struts login application, 227–230
MaterialDb.java class, creating for hsql database connectivity, 262–264
MaterialDetailAction.java class
  creating for Struts login application, 229–230
  modifying, 265–266
materialdetail.do, calling with Struts login application, 224–225
materialdetail.Result.jsp, adding tag library declaration to, 295
MaterialForm.java class, creating for Struts login application, 221
MaterialGui class
  creating and using, 115–130
  Java Swing layout used by, 125
MaterialList Java class, example of, 61
materialList table object, example of, 73
MaterialListGui screenshot, displaying, 130
materialList.jsp file
  adding form text field to, 160–161
  creating, 159
materialResult.jsp
  executing call to SAP with, 161–162
  modifying for use with servlet context in JSP pages, 170
materials database, updating with image files, 259
MATERIALS table, creating, 252
MaterialTableAction class
  adding plain text table functionality to, 253–254
  in database connection example, 245–246
  in database table example, 250–251
  executing to create MATERIALS table, 252
  modifying for use with hsql databases, 255
MATNRLIST table, retrieving object representation of, 73
MATNRSELECTION table
  adding data to, 70
  purpose of, 69
member variables, using in JCo sample application, 79–80
method calls, advisory about chaining of, 73

315

Index

methods
   building in JCo sample application, 82–88
   in OOP, 37
Microsoft .NET platform versus J2EE, 33
model component
   of MVC pattern, 174–175
   of objects, 195
model layer in Struts, overview of, 186–187
MTS (Microsoft Transaction Server), introduction of, 15
multilingual resource bundles, example of, 94–95
MVC (Model-View-Controller) pattern
   built-in flexibility of, 177–179
   components of, 174–175
   and SAP, 179–181
MyResources.properties file, role in internationalizing Java applications, 93

N

.NET Passport, Web address for, 33
.NET platform versus J2EE, 33
new(String text, int rows, int cols) method of JTextArea class, description of, 123
null values, returning for JCo connection pools, 274

O

Oak history, Web addresses for, 19
object access, controlling with Singleton pattern, 45–46
object interfaces, hiding with Façade pattern, 46–47
Object Java superclass, role in inheritance, 39
object-level access, providing, 99–112
object methods, using in OOP, 37–38
object systems, building with design patterns, 43–47
objects in application development, MVC components of, 195
objects in OOP. *See also* Java objects
   creating instances from, 38–39
   expanding through inheritance, 39–40
OMG (Object Management Group), Web address for, 12
OODs (object-oriented designs)
   discovering object dependencies in, 42–43
   dividing labor between developers of, 41
   overview of, 40–41
   planning for future of, 41–42
OOP environments, design and development in, 26
OOP (object-oriented programming)
   basics of, 24–26
   power of, 81
   understanding by means of metaphors, 36–40
   using object methods with, 37–38
ORDER BY, using with SQL SELECT queries, 264

P

page tags, using with JSP, 141
panels, nesting in Java Swing, 125, 127
panes, adding to window frames, 128
PATH statements in Java, placing binaries in, 88
pedal function example in OOP, 37
period (.), use of, 97
plain text files, creating for hsql databases, 254
post value, advisory about, 143
printStackTrace() method, importance of, 65
private variable declarations, using in JCo sample application, 81–84
procedural languages
   versus OOP, 25
   resource for, 24
properties files, advisory about, 99
public variable declarations, using in JCo sample application, 81–84
Pure Java JDBC drivers, features of, 239
put(key, value) method of Hashtable class, description of, 103

R

R/3 application, replacement by WebAS, 11–12
R/3 application servers, functionality of, 32
R/3 release, origin of, 3, 5
records, retrieving from database tables, 249
replaceRange(String text, int start, int end) method of JTextArea class, description of, 123
repository, initializing, 66
reset() methods, using with enumerators and iterators in Java, 75
resource bundles
   configuring Java applications with, 96–99

Index

resource bundles, role in internationalizing Java applications, 93–94
resources. *See also* Web sites
 for design patterns, 44
 Java development for Web, 26
 Javadoc formatting and stylistic conventions, 38
 for OOP concepts, 25
 for procedural languages, 24
ResultSet java.sql class, example of, 249
return statements in Java, purpose of, 213
RFC destination, defining when calling JCo server from SAP, 288–289
RFC interface, defining in SAP, 280–283
RFC metadata interface, retrieving with JCo, 66–68
ROLLBACK statements in SQL, description of, 235–236
rowHash Hashtable, initializing, 120
RPC functionality of SAP, limitations of, 6

S

SampleServer.java example, 284–288
SAP and Internet, history of, 7–12
SAP black box, talking to, 4–6
SAP CRM (Customer Relationship Management) system, features of, 11
SAP function calls, adding data to using JCo, 68–79
SAP GUI
 limitation of, 135
 origin of, 3
 as stateful client, 8
SAP login process, MVC diagram of, 180
SAP login screen, displaying, 207
SAP repository, initializing, 66
SAP RPC functionality, limitations of, 6
SAP (Server Application Programming)
 alternative development for, 12–16
 authenticating in, 208
 authenticating users with, 148–153
 building Java GUI for, 115–130
 calling Java objects from within, 279–290
 calling JCo server from, 288–290
 and centralized ERP, 2–6
 connecting to using JCo, 57–60, 64–65
 and CORBA, 12–14
 defining RFC interface in, 280–283
 fitting Java into, 21–23
 Java essentials for, 24–27
 loading hsql databases from, 255–259
 and MVC pattern, 179–181
 results of material search in, 163
 testing JCo server connection to, 289
SAP system, retrieving material list from, 225
SAP user authority, maintaining, 156–160
sapdata.properties text file
 creating and modifying, 96–98
 reusing with JCo connection pools, 274–275
sapjco.jar file, purpose of, 54
saplogin.jsp JSP pages, creating for use with Struts login application, 203, 206–207
saploginResult.jsp, adding link to, 222–223
SapMaterialAction class, implementing, 257
SapTest.java file, executing, 112
screen scraping in ITS, explanation of, 7–9
SELECT statements in SQL
 description of, 235–236
 example of, 242, 249, 264–265
 using AND and OR with, 264
server-side deployment of Java
 versus desktop, 29–30
 overview of, 29
servers, transition from mainframes, 3–4
ServerTest.java file, creating for use with JCo server, 287
servlet context, using in JSP pages, 169–171
servlet specification, explanation of, 165
ServletContext class, optimizing performance with, 164–168
ServletRequest instances, using with JSP pages, 145
session class in Java, location of, 157
session objects, advisory about, 158
set() methods, implementing with LoginForm beans, 196–199
SET TABLE statements
 in SQL, 253–254
 using with hsql databases, 254
setAttribute() method, example of, 158
setFont(Font f) method of JText Area class, description of, 123
setLineWrap(boolean wrap) method of JText Area class, description of, 123
setTabSize(int size) method of JText Area class, description of, 123
Singleton pattern, controlling object access with, 45–46
slash-asterisk (/*), meaning of, 63

317

Index

SQL statements
  using double quotes (" ") with, 254
  using with JDBC, 234–236
SQL (Structured Query Language),
    populating databases with, 244–253
SQLException, example of, 249–250
SRC attribute, example of, 267–268
stateful clients, SAP GUI front ends as, 8
stateless interface, role in ITS, 8
static declaration, using in JCo sample
    code, 85–86
static methods, removal from Java
    classes, 100–101
String instances, initializing in JSP
    pages, 146
String variables
  basing on keys associated with
    values, 98
  defining with JCo, 63–64
Struts application libraries, accessing,
    209–210
struts-config.xml file
  building, 194–195
  configuring screen flow with,
    215–218
  configuring with new action
    mappings, 230–231
Struts Controller, overview of, 183–186
Struts development
  building MaterialForm.java class, 221
  calling material detail BAPI, 219–220
  configuring action mappings,
    230–231
  creating Material Search JSP pages,
    222–227
  developing material action classes
    for, 227–230
Struts framework
  building XML configuration files
    with, 194–195
  configuring, 190–195
  downloading, 189–190
  installing, 189–190
  mapping ActionServlets in, 191–193
  overview of, 181–183
Struts login application
  adding database call to Action class
    in, 265–267
  adding hsql database functionality
    to, 262
  building Action class for, 209–215
  building material search form bean
    for, 220–221
  components of, 195
  configuring, 215–218
  configuring ActionMappings for,
    230–231
  creating form fields for, 206
  creating material search JSP pages
    for, 222–227
  design login view for, 203–209
  developing material action classes
    for, 227–230
  displaying material image in JSP
    pages, 267–269
  implementing form for, 205
  internationalizing, 206
  modeling Web-based forms in,
    196–201
  using ActionForm beans with, 196
  using ApplicationResources file with,
    201–203
Struts model layer, overview of,
    186–187
Struts Submit button, implementing in
    Struts login application, 206
Struts tag libraries
  adding to web.xml file, 193–194
  importing for use with login
    application, 203
Struts view layer, overview of, 187–189
Struts XML configuration file
  ActionMappings for, 184
  diagram of, 184
struts.jar file, accessing, 190
Submit button, HTML version of, 143
subroutines, benefits of, 24–25
Swing
  application components, 117
  nesting panels in, 125
  Web address for, 114
system variables
  advisory about use with JCo, 81
  setting for use with Tomcat, 136
system variables, defining in Windows,
    53

T

tables, representing in Java, 75. *See also*
    database tables
tag directives in Java, formatting, 204
tag handler objects, building, 291–292
TagSupport, extending for Image Path
    custom Java tag, 292
testpage.html Web page, building for
    Tomcat application, 139
text files, building database tables from,
    253–254
TextPad text editor, Web address for, 88
this class name
  example of, 106
  registering objects as action listeners
    to, 127

Index

tilde (~), appearance in hsql databases, 254
.tld extension, meaning of, 203
TLD (Tag Library Descriptor), defining for custom Java tag, 294–295
Tomcat application servers
 installing, 135–138
 shutting down, 138
 testing, 137
 use of, 33
Tomcat sample application
 adding material list lookup to, 160–163
 authenticating users with, 148–153
 building customer login JSP for, 153–156
 building testpage.html Web page for, 139
 creating dynamic JSP with, 139–140
 handling user input from Web pages with, 141–147
 maintaining SAP user authority with, 156–160
 setting up, 138–139
 using JSP tags with, 140–141
transaction monitoring in Java application server, explanation of, 31
transactions in distributed computing, explanation of, 15
try { blocks, formatting in JCo, 65
try...catch blocks, using with database tables, 249–250

U

UIManager, defining look and feel of GUIs with, 118
UML diagrams
 of Façade pattern, 47
 of Singleton object, 46
UML (Universal Modeling Language), use of, 43
UPDATE statements in SQL, description of, 235–236
URIs (Uniform Resource Identifiers), purpose of, 184–185
user input, handling from Web pages, 141–147
users
 authenticating with SAP, 148–153
 interacting with by means of ActionListeners in GUIs, 118–120

V

validate() method
 creating instance of ActionError class with, 201–202
 overriding with LoginForm beans, 199–200
variables
 defining with JCo, 63–64
 using in JCo sample application, 79–82
view component of MVC pattern, functionality of, 176
view components of objects, explanation of, 195
view for login in Struts application, designing, 203–209
view layer in Struts, overview of, 187–189

W

Web applications, developing for SAP. *See* Tomcat sample application
Web-based forms, modeling with Struts, 196–201
Web browser login screen, example of, 144
Web servers, image lookup and rendering through, 260–261
Web sessions, displaying stored HTTP data in, 144–147
Web sites. *See also* resources
 Actional's Control Broker, 14
 application servers, 29
 BC (Business Connector) tool, 10
 COM, CORBA, and Java comparison, 16
 CORBA, 14
 CRM and Internet Sales, 11
 Eclipse, 50
 hsql (Hypersonic SQL), 240
 ISO language codes, 95
 J2EE SDK, 166
 Java Collections Framework, 103
 Java Swing development, 114
 Java syntax, 62
 JDBC drivers, 238
 JFC (Java Foundation Classes), 113
 JSDK, 52
 .NET Passport, 33
 Oak history, 19
 OMG (Object Management Group), 12
 SAP technology offerings, 12
 SAP's Online Services, 53
 SQL Primer, 235
 Struts framework, 189–190
 TextPad text editor, 88
 Tomcat application server binaries, 136
 UML (Universal Modeling Language), 43

webapps\sap directory, creating for use with Tomcat application, 138
WebAS (Web Application Server), features of, 11–12
WebRunner Mosaic clone, development of, 19
web.xml file
    adding Struts tag libraries to, 193–194
    adding to Tomcat application, 138
    adding to Tomcat sample application, 168–169
    modifying for use with Struts, 190–192
WHERE clause, using with hsql databases, 258
window frames, adding panes to, 128
Windows, defining system variables in, 53
windows, using in GUIs, 114

X

XML, adding to imagetag.tld file, 294–295
XML configuration file
    adding to Tomcat application, 138
    mapping to Struts system components, 184
XML configuration files
    building with Struts, 194–195

Z

ZJCO_CLIENT application, creating in ABAP Workbench, 289
ZJCO_STRUCT, creating and defining fields in, 281